Colin J. Smith

# *In fair weather and in foul*

## 30 YEARS OF SCOTTISH PASSENGER SHIPS AND FERRIES

ISBN: 1 871947 56 1

Ferry Publications, P.O. Box 9, Narberth,
Pembrokeshire, SA68 0YT
Tel: (01834) 891460 Fax: (01834) 891463

# Contents

## ACKNOWLEDGEMENTS

The production of this book would not have been possible without the assistance of many industry professionals, maritime organisations and ship watchers across the length and breadth of the country. I am indebted to them all for their support and encouragement.

For assistance with compilation of the text and ensuring accuracy of the facts, I am grateful to Ken Duerden and Robert Donaldson, Caledonian MacBrayne; John Newth, Western Ferries; Scott Colegate, P&O Ferries; Jimmy King, Orkney Ferries; Roy Pedersen, Inverness; Ian Hall, Glasgow; Willie McKay, Stromness; Joe Gray, Lerwick; John Hendy, Staplehurst and the late Alastair McRobb, Glasgow. I am also grateful to Candida Hubbard of Hebridean Island Cruises and Shetland Island Council's Marine Operations Department for assistance. Much of the information was obtained from published sources but additional material on specific ships was supplied by the Mitchell Library, Glasgow, Aberdeen Maritime Museum and Lloyds Register of Shipping, London.

All photographic contributions are gratefully acknowledged and I hope that the contributors, some of whom have not previously had their work published, enjoy the thrill of seeing their pictures on the printed page. Most of the photographs are previously unpublished and unearthing them has been an interesting and challenging task. They have been drawn from many sources, although the majority have been taken either by myself or they reside within my own collection. The substantial contributions of Willie MacKay, Stromness; Roy Pedersen and Alasdair L. Munro, both of Inverness; Terry Primrose, Strathaven; Harold Sinclair, Blanefield; Charles Tait, Kirkwall; Laurence J. Macduff, of Kilmarnock; Brian Maxted, Canterbury; the Don Smith Collection of Keighley, Yorkshire; Robin Boyd, Paisley; Alistair Cormack, Kirkwall; Tommy Watt, Lerwick Museum; Iain Murray, Dundee; and Miles Cowsill of Ferry Publications are gratefully acknowledged. The assistance of Hazel Anderson and Dr. John Shaw of the National Archives of Scotland, formerly the Scottish Record Office, who kindly permitted access to the collection of the late James Aikman Smith (collection reference #GD469), is very much appreciated. I am also indebted to Marilyn Gardner of Haverfordwest and to Mike Brookes and Anne Marie Gibson of Great Scot, Edinburgh for graphics and photographic reproduction. The generous contributions of all of these people have made it possible for the book to provide comprehensive illustrations representing all of the fleets, ranging from north to south and throughout the last thirty plus years.

My sincerest thanks go to Colin Paterson, former Managing Director of Caledonian MacBrayne Ltd, for writing the Foreword. His name stands alongside the greats of the past as an individual who has been deeply involved in shaping the pattern of the operations which we see in our own time. Today, he continues his commitment to the Scottish shipping scene through his involvement, not with modern ferry fleets, but with the restoration of the Loch Lomond paddle steamer *Maid of the Loch*. Most importantly, I am grateful to my wife Mary for her support and encouragement. With fortitude she has endured wild days on the Pentland Firth, autumn gales on Skye, August downpours on the Clyde and much more, in support of my modest efforts.

The days of steam may be largely confined to history, but the modern shipping scene still offers an interesting mix of ships and services, and the story of how today's fleets came about is a fascinating one. However, this book is not intended to be the definitive history of the ferries of Scotland. Other writers are more qualified to address that substantial task. Instead, it seeks to give the casual reader and the enthusiast an overview in text and in photographs, of the main ships which have sailed across the Scottish seascapes in the last thirty years. The book covers a period which witnessed a revolution in the pattern of services and in the types of vessels which were to be found operating the lifeline services to, from and between the islands. Today's fleets are very different from those of thirty years ago but still the importance of the ships remains undiminished as they remain an essential part of life on the coast. Scots have long held an affiliation for their ships and successive generations of steamers have had their aficionados and followers and no doubt the keen eyed enthusiasts will spot errors, as they always do. Whilst much effort has gone into ensuring that factual anomalies are kept to a minimum, apologies are tendered in advance for any which may have passed through the net. Hopefully they will not detract from your enjoyment of. this book.

Colin J Smith   July 1999

# Foreword

I am delighted to have been asked to write the foreword for this excellent book and am particularly pleased to see that the modern era has been covered, especially as I have been closely involved myself for the last 15 years. In 1983 I was honoured to join Caledonian MacBrayne Ltd. and to steer it through a period of substantial development. This was an experience which gave me a deep and lasting admiration for everyone who supports the provision of the Scottish lifeline ferry services, be they professional mariner or lay enthusiast.

Although Caledonian MacBrayne and P&O Scottish Ferries are vitally important modern organisations, the origins of both lie deep within the histories of the island communities which they serve. As they have evolved to meet new demands, a plethora of authors have recorded the ongoing developments in their fleets and in their activities and it is important that the changes which have led us into the modern era should also be recorded. Likewise, the emergence of the smaller companies and the gathering of pace of the maritime preservation movement are an integral part of the story of Scottish shipping and they also deserve their place in history.

The three decades covered encompass an unsurpassed period of change which is so well illustrated in both word and picture. The period witnessed the transition from the end of the steam era to the current roll on - roll off age and readers may be forgiven for speculating on the nature of future developments if the pace of change does not slacken.

I am quite certain that the book will be well received by all who have an interest or involvement with Scotland's ferries and Colin Smith and the publishers, Ferry Publications Limited, are to be congratulated for producing such an accurate, detailed and above all, readable, book.

Colin S. Paterson CBE
Chairman, Loch Lomond Steamship Company
Managing Director,
Caledonian MacBrayne Ltd. 1983 - 1997

*Colin Paterson CBE with the **Maid of the Loch**. (Mitchell & Averell)*

# Introduction

Throughout history, the seas which surround Scotland have been important for communication and often for conflict. The earliest inhabitants of the country undoubtedly journeyed by sea although no written documentation exists of their travels. The first Scots came to the land which ultimately bore their name by crossing the North Channel from Ireland. There followed the Christian pilgrims, including Columba, Adomnan and other Celtic monks, in their frail coracles. Two centuries later, the arrival of the Norsemen was first recorded, making the wild crossing from Norway to Shetland in their longships before taking possession of the islands of the Northern and Western Coasts. The ending of their rule in the 13th Century saw the coming of the Lordship of the Isles and the development of the "birlinn", a galley which was used by the clan Chieftains to ensure that their rule over this great Kingdom of the seas was complete. Eventually, Scottish and subsequently British monarchs sought to rule the waves around these coasts but it was from a West Coast landing spot near Arisaig that Charles Edward Stuart, more colourfully known as Bonnie Prince Charlie, embarked on his fateful Jacobite uprising of 1745. A year later, following the disaster of the Battle of Culloden, the sea was his escape route. There followed the pacification of the Highlands and the tyranny of the Highland Clearances, in the guise of "improvement" of the land. Poverty, humiliation, the persecution of the Gaelic language and mass emigration followed. Paradoxically, over two hundred and fifty years of development of improved sea communications began at the same time.

The steamboat first appeared in 1812 in the shape of Henry Bell's *Comet* and the Victorian era witnessed the coming of mass tourism, inspired by romantic novelists and poets who had influenced the old Queen herself. She was but one influential visitor who travelled widely throughout the Highlands and her writings encouraged others to follow in her footsteps. This period witnessed the laying of the foundations of the network of ferry services which we see today, with several great names coming to the fore - David Hutcheson, David MacBrayne, James Williamson, George Robertson and Arthur Anderson. All had a direct bearing on the modern services which continue to operate around the Scottish coasts at the end of the 20th Century.

In partnership with David Hutcheson, David MacBrayne established a steamship company in 1851 whose successors still carry his name today. 1889 saw the inauguration, by Captain James Williamson, of the Caledonian Steam Packet Company on the Clyde, from whence comes the other half of the name of that successor company - Caledonian MacBrayne. Robertson was a pioneer of steam navigation in the Northern Isles whilst Arthur Anderson was a Shetlander who established the mighty Peninsular and Oriental Steam Navigation Company - the P&O Line - and today it is their blue hulled ferries which serve Anderson's native Shetland, and also its near neighbour of Orkney.

Through two world wars, many of the ships played key roles, often in distant seas, in support of the war effort of the allied forces. Others maintained essential services around their home waters, often threading their way across anchorages thick with the vessels and assorted hardware of wartime. But those dark days passed, giving rise to a new way of life which would create great changes in Scottish society and in the steamer and ferry services themselves. The post war period witnessed the ascendancy of the motor car as the most convenient form of mass transit. Consequently, the shipping services throughout Scottish waters underwent a radical transformation through the decline of the purely passenger, cargo and mail services

*A fine study of the St. Clair as she arrives at Lerwick in June 1995.* (Willie Mackay)

to the development of today's modern drive through vehicular ferry routes. Elderly steamers with long, proud histories and established reputations went to the breakers yards or became pensioned off as floating restaurants, whilst new point to point routes were opened up, in an attempt to catch up with the burgeoning public demand for car ferry services. Eventually a new generation of purpose built ferries swept away the last of the old order and Scotland's shipping services caught up with the late 20th Century.

But within that changing environment, some aspects of the old ways were retained before they were lost forever, whilst the new ships became as essential to the island communities as their illustrious predecessors had been. To soften the dramatic changes, many new ships held on to the names of their predecessors and in many cases, the crews of the former vessels transferred to the new ships, thus ensuring that the long lineage of expert seamanship, indigenous to the coastal waters, was retained and that the links with tradition endured.

This book is a photographic review of the ships of the nineteen seventies, eighties and nineties, beginning with the vessels which were to be found in the various fleets of 1969. That date is not arbitrary but is the year in which the Scottish Transport Group (STG) came into existence and took control of the main shipping services in Clyde and West Highland waters. It is the year in which the wind of change began to blow, stirred by the STG and their new vision of coastal shipping services, and in which the emphasis switched away from focusing on the needs of declining numbers of passengers utilising rail and steamer connections, to addressing the ever increasing number of private motorists wishing to enjoy the convenience of taking their cars with them on island holidays. Islanders themselves were becoming car owners and freight was switching to road transport, at the expense of sea or rail. These factors combined to become the driving force behind the STGs' determination to develop modern ferry routes served by modern ships.

In the Northern Isles, the wind is omnipresent and the wind of change also blew there, a little later perhaps, than on the West Coast, but no less fiercely as radical changes in the early 1970's altered the long standing way of life on the routes of the established North of Scotland, Orkney and Shetland Shipping Company Ltd. The old order was swept away to be replaced by the new and unfamiliar car ferries of P&O, Arthur Anderson's great company. The coming of the North Sea oil industry meant that no longer would the Northern Isles be perceived as remote Atlantic outcrops. Instead, they would become

*A magnificent summer scene across the Sound of Islay towards the Paps of Jura as the **Arran** arrives at Port Askaig whilst in MacBrayne service in 1972.* (Harold Sinclair, Author's Collection)

*As an unintended member of the OISC fleet, the **Varagen** is seen entering Kirkwall Harbour on 15th April 1992 on a sailing from the North Isles.* (Author)

thriving, bustling powerhouses of the Scottish economy, and their increasing transport needs required to be serviced. Within the islands, great strides forward were taken in improving sea communication as the development of inter island car ferry services took place in both Orkney and Shetland, replacing the mail steamer calls at outlying islands by regular, frequent sailings operated by purpose built ferries.

Soon, the new order became the established one. Thirty years on a regular pattern of drive on - drive off vehicular and passenger services has become regarded as the norm. Many communities now benefit from a level of service and passenger convenience which was only dreamed about in bygone years and throughout the islands of the western and northern coasts, the new ferries have contributed significantly to assisting in the difficult task of regenerating the Island economies. They have been essential tools in catalysing the creation of new jobs in new industries, encouraging tourism and in stemming population decline, although the problem still persists, particularly in the Outer Hebrides, the North Isles of Orkney and Argyll. Over the years, thousands of residents and visitors have experienced the pleasures of sailing on the new ships and the modern fleet of today, like its ancestors, even has its own supporters clubs.

On the West Coast, Caledonian MacBrayne has enjoyed many successes since it was established in 1973. It has evolved in response to changing demands for its services and has played an integral role in the ongoing history and life of the West Coast and a vast number of ships dating from as long ago as 1926 have worn its now familiar colours. Caledonian MacBrayne vessels have carried every type of commodity from sheep to royalty and from bicycles to buses and even boats. Through its "Crossings" music festival, its sponsorship of the National Gaelic Mod, participation in the St. Columba 1400th Anniversary celebrations and other activities, Caledonian MacBrayne has played an important role in helping to stimulate the indigenous cultural life of the islands. Its ships have been present at great maritime events such as the visits of the *Queen Elizabeth 2* or the *Norway* to the Clyde, the arrival of HM Yacht *Britannia* to Oban and Arran and at the start of Tall Ships Races. Inevitably, where an organisation is as important to its customers as Caledonian MacBrayne, the company is not always universally adored. Nevertheless, it is still regarded by the Clyde and West Highland communities as an indispensable and irreplaceable cog in the engine room of the West Coast economy.

For P&O Scottish Ferries, the new order has also been firmly established. Their blue hulled ships have become central to the continued success of the economies and cultural life of Orkney and Shetland, building upon the proud heritage of the "North Company" before them and maintaining an unbroken lineage which stretches back over 150 years. Like their West Coast compatriots, P&O Scottish Ferries have become an important part of island life and their activities are tightly woven into the social, cultural and economic tapestry of the Northern Isles.

In parallel with the changes which took place within these long established operations, newcomers have appeared on the scene, offering services which introduced a new concept, namely that of smaller ferries operating on the shortest and most convenient crossing

1969 HOLIDAY SAILINGS TO
**ORKNEY & SHETLAND**

between simple terminals. These ideas owe their origins largely to the expertise of the Norwegians, whose ideas for coastal shipping were adopted by Scottish companies and were instrumental in stirring the wind of change which blasted through the established pattern of services on the Scottish coast. Operated by Western Ferries, Orkney Ferries, Highland Council and Shetland Islands Council, these routes have become well established and are now important tourism links as well as lifeline services and they too, have become an indispensable component of the transport needs of the islanders.

The Scottish ferry scene is constantly evolving and there are a number of fundamental questions which will arise in the near future. High speed ferries have not as yet made an appearance in these waters. Given the nature of the cargoes carried, from cars to large agricultural, commercial and industrial vehicles, and at relatively low traffic volumes, the high speed ferry has not yet been designed which can cater economically for a low frequency, year round type of operation. Likewise, the possible provision of fixed links may affect the future pattern of services, as could the development of a new range of dedicated freight services, capitalising on the apparently increasing demand for freight transhipment. But whatever becomes of the various fleets and their services, the needs of the islands will not diminish. The creation of successful island economies demands the efficient movement of goods and people by sea, meeting the demands of residents and tourists.

In the midst of the modern scene there remain the remnants of the great days of steam. The paddle steamer *Waverley* is renowned world wide whilst the *Maid of the Loch*, following many years of neglect, may now face a brighter future. Once it seemed that their days were over with the public seeming to be mesmerised by the motor car and having apparently discarded such antiquated modes of transport. But against the odds, they have survived, the *Waverley* in active service and the *Maid of the Loch* now undergoing restoration which may see her return to steam in the future. They are tributes to Scottish engineering which survive today because of the commitment of their untiring supporters and a reawakening of public concern for the preservation of Scotland's maritime heritage. Long may they continue to enthral future generations of Scots and visitors alike.

The rugged coasts which make navigation hazardous and communications difficult also make for beautiful scenery and it is the firm belief of anyone who knows these coasts that the one and only way to experience such beauty is to step aboard and to enjoy the view, in fair weather or in foul, from the decks of the ships themselves. If this book encourages at least one visitor to do that, then one of its most important aims will have been achieved. The fleet has been as diverse as the Scottish coastline itself. From the past, old favourites like the *Duchess of Hamilton* are illustrated, whilst we come up to date with the new *Clansman*. The famous are featured - can any ship be more world renowned than the Paddle Steamer *Waverley* - as are the obscure. The ships range from the large, such as the mighty *St. Clair*, to the small, like the tiny *Heather*. From a personal viewpoint, the author and contributors have their own favourites, but those are ours to know and you, the reader, must make up your own mind.

# The Firth of Clyde

*"They watched the engines till the hot air and the odour of oil well-nigh overcame Mrs. Purdie. She moved in the direction of the saloon". J.J. Bell "Wee MacGreegor". First published in the Glasgow Evening News in 1902.*

## FLOREAT CLUTHA

Any child born and brought up in or around the sprawling City of Glasgow is aware of the great shipbuilding heritage of the River Clyde. Even at the end of the 20th Century, the industry, now reduced to a rump of its former glory, is still struggling onwards. But for the city, and for the nearby Burgh of Clydebank in particular, the climax to the nineteen sixties was the launch and completion of the magnificent Cunard Line flagship *Queen Elizabeth 2,* the last of the great liners to be born on the banks of the river which a foreign shipbuilder once called a "trout stream". The sixties witnessed great changes in industrial, technological, transport, social and economic conditions throughout Scotland. They became the full stop at the end of the era of heavy engineering and steam power, witnessing the end of the reliance upon shipbuilding and shipping as major employers. Coupled with this, the sixties also witnessed a gradual decline of the River Clyde as the lifeblood of the West of Scotland economy, whilst the strife ridden seventies saw the virtual decimation of what remained of the shipbuilding industry and the end of Glasgow's role as a major seaport. The motto of the former Clyde Navigation Trust, "Floreat Clutha" - Let the Clyde Flourish - could not have been more inappropriate for the fortunes of the declining river. Indeed the Trust itself, a symbol of Glasgow's Victorian confidence, was replaced by a new Clyde Port Authority in 1966. The eighties and nineties saw attempts to regenerate the banks of the Clyde, through the development of up market housing and leisure facilities, meet with mixed success. Even the hosting of the 1988 Glasgow Garden Festival, with its 4.1 million visitors who breathed new life, colour and hope into the banks of the dying river, promised much but delivered little in terms of creating a long term resurgence in the fortunes of the crumbling quaysides. Recent progress has been more substantive as a host of new developments, including the Scottish Exhibition and Conference Centre, the Braehead retail development and the Glasgow Science Centre, are either underway or have been completed on former industrial sites along the River between Glasgow and Greenock. There is now hope of a brighter future, but the Clyde still has a general air of neglect, one of the few city rivers in Western Europe which has not yet found a new role for itself in the post industrial age. No riverbuses part its waters, no waterfront cafés line its banks and only one excursion ship makes its lonely way along the once busy length of the upper reaches, in search of fellow vessels with which to mingle. Downstream, the scenery remains as magnificent as ever, the mountains of Argyll on the Highland shores of the Firth of Clyde, contrasting with the Lowland side and its former resort towns of Gourock, Largs, Troon and Ayr, now virtual commuter suburbs of Glasgow itself. The sea lochs - Long, Goil, Striven, Riddon and Fyne - still penetrate deep into those mountains, sheltering tiny Highland clachans and historic harbours whilst the islands of Bute, Arran and Cumbrae remain attractive as holiday destinations, even though the thousands of trippers who thronged the waterfronts of Millport, Dunoon and Rothesay in bygone days can now be found promenading on the beaches of Benidorm or lounging in the cafés of Capri. But for river watchers, the daily comings and goings of the steamers and ferries of the Caledonian Steam Packet Company (CSP) and its succes-

*A 1972 view of the **Queen Mary II** as seen from the **Waverley**. She is leaving Rothesay, her bows damaged following a collision with a US Navy tug, the Natick.* (Terry Primrose)

sors continued to offer great interest and debate throughout those decades of change as the river steamer fleets evolved to reflect the changes in society at large.

These changes had started in the late fifties, the last of the heady days of the Clyde Steamers. The immediate post war period witnessed upwardly spiralling costs although passenger numbers remained healthy. However, economy and austerity were the order of the day and much loved steamers like the *Jeanie Deans*, the *Saint Columba* and the *Duchess of Montrose* had gone to the breakers as passenger numbers slumped in the early sixties as a result of new attractions such as the motor car and accessible foreign holidays biting into the excursion traffic. By the late sixties, the CSP fleet was undergoing a painfully slow retrenchment and transition process. Since 1948, and the nationalisation of Britain's railways, the CSP, in several guises, had been the main company involved in the provision of passenger, vehicle and cargo steamer services on the Firth of Clyde and their fleet was a somewhat mixed bag. By 1969, four passenger carrying steamships remained in service. The *Queen Mary II* and *Duchess of Hamilton* were fine steam turbine powered steamers, beautiful mini ocean liners which were built in the heyday of the great transatlantic steamers and which were designed to emulate their sleek lines and comfortable fittings. The more utilitarian but much loved paddle steamers *Caledonia* and *Waverley,* their construction dates separated by the dark years of the Second World War, maintained shorter excursion sailings and railway connection services from Gourock, Craigendoran and Wemyss Bay. The nineteen fifties had seen the internal combustion engine begin to make a substantial impact on the Clyde and diesel, rather than steam, propulsion drove the four small passenger vessels of the "Maid" Class, four car ferries - the *Arran, Bute, Cowal* and the seemingly huge *Glen Sannox* - the Millport passenger ferry *Keppel* and the Holy Loch vessel *Countess of Breadalbane.* The last steamship ever to be built for the CSP was not a Clyde steamer at all. On nearby Loch Lomond, the beautiful but uneconomical paddle steamer *Maid of the Loch* plodded her way to Ardlui, at the head of the loch, every summer day. Amongst all of this activity, the West Highland operators, David MacBrayne Ltd. had a red funnelled representative on the Clyde, in the shape of the *Lochfyne,* which maintained the "Royal Route" passenger and mail service to Tarbert and Ardrishaig.

Although modernisation of the CSP Clyde fleet had begun in the

*In this evocative shot, the **Duchess of Hamilton** is seen arriving at Dunoon, well loaded with day trippers, on a summer evening in July 1967.* (Author's Collection)

1950's, the following decade saw the continuation of a leisurely pattern of service, with the CSP presiding over a slow decline in the number of passengers utilising Clyde steamer services. Owned by British Railways, the CSP strategy was one of cost reduction through withdrawal of passenger ships, closure of longer routes, abandonment of the smaller piers and general retrenchment, aiming to reduce losses, with little real attention being paid to the growing, and more lucrative demand for new car ferry services. Railways were in charge and the emerging popularity of the motor car was largely ignored. This time honoured pattern was soon to be swept away following the approval of the 1968 Transport Act, which led to the coming together of Clyde and West Highland shipping fleets under the auspices of the new Scottish Transport Group. Edinburgh based and road transport focused, rather than being a distant outpost of a railway dominated, London bureaucracy, the new organisation took strategic control of much of Scotland's transport infrastructure in a way which was to prove revolutionary. The CSP was wrested from railway influence and the emphasis moved away, almost overnight, from providing railway connection sailings to catering primarily for car borne traffic. Things began to change even more radically. Within ten years, the scene had

changed beyond recognition and new roll on - roll off passenger and vehicle ferries reigned supreme, whilst the era of steam power was, for all practical purposes, at an end.

The Clyde fleet dragged itself into the seventies. With an average age of almost twenty years, the ferries of the Clyde were not in the first flush of youth and urgent action was required. The Arran car ferry services were the first to be modernised with the introduction, in 1970, of the *Caledonia*, a second hand drive through ferry acquired from Stena Line. Her arrival was accompanied by the opening of the first drive through terminals on the Clyde, at Ardrossan and Brodick. Soon new roll on - roll off ferry terminals were constructed at the other main Clyde Coast terminals at Gourock, Dunoon, Wemyss Bay and Rothesay to service new purpose built stern and side loading car ferries. To underline their commitment to modernisation of the Clyde services, the STG introduced their new drive through ferry, the *Iona*, on the Gourock - Dunoon route in 1970, rather than sending her to the West Highlands as had been originally intended. Existing ships were rapidly converted to provide additional vehicular capacity until new, purpose built ferries appeared on the Clyde and the last excursion steamers soon departed, to be replaced by a modified cruising

*The paddle steamer **Caledonia** poses for the camera as she approaches Dunoon with a good crowd aboard on a fine evening in August 1967.* (Author's Collection)

programme which gave priority to maintaining and developing the essential ferry services. Meanwhile, shorter point to point routes were opened up between Largs and Cumbrae, Kintyre and Arran and across the Kyles of Bute at Colintraive utilising small bow loading ferries. Indirectly, these short ferry crossings replaced the long steamer services to the Kintyre peninsula and to Cumbrae, whilst providing improved access to Bute for motorists. Throughout the late sixties and seventies the old steamers went to their graves in droves and Greenock's East India Harbour became an elephant's graveyard of cast off CSP and MacBrayne tonnage. The establishment of Caledonian MacBrayne in January 1973 blurred still further the distinction between the Clyde and West Highland fleets and Gourock became headquarters for all of the major passenger and car ferries employed within the company. In the mid 1970's, the last steam powered vessels left the Caledonian MacBrayne Clyde fleet and the era of the purely passenger service came to a close on the Clyde, with the ending of the Largs - Millport (Old Pier) route in 1986. In the midst of the STG induced changes, competition arrived on the scene in the shape of Western Ferries who introduced a new car ferry service between the Highland and the Lowland shores of the Firth of Clyde. In a few short years, the scene had changed beyond recognition. The car ferry now reigned supreme.

The 1970's and 1980's saw the arrival on the Clyde of a generation of new vessels with vastly increased vehicular capacity but whose passenger accommodation was a substantial improvement on that of the earlier car ferries. Most of these ships were to become interchangeable amongst the company's main Clyde and West Highland routes. These years brought major changes which saw a tired but once proud steamship fleet become radically transformed into one of Europe's largest and most modern ferry companies. Finally, in the nineties, there appeared the *Caledonian Isles*, the largest ship ever to sail on a regular Clyde service, a fitting tribute to the years of change which saw the old order virtually swept away. The types of vessels in the fleet may have changed dramatically over the years, but their basic purpose has not and the ships of Caledonian MacBrayne remain vital lifeline providers for the Clyde Coast islands in addition to being transports of delight for the thousands of tourists who continue to visit the Firth of Clyde every year. Happily though, something remains of the old order which has not been entirely lost to a new generation of visitors, local travellers and ship lovers, thanks to the preservation of that venerable old favourite, the Paddle Steamer *Waverley*. If fortune favours her, another remnant of older days, the *Maid of the Loch* may also sail again. Because of these ships and because of the dedication of those who have fought to preserve them, the wonderful experience of the paddle steamer, so familiar to readers of "Wee MacGreegor" almost one hundred years ago, is still with us today.

## THE "RAILWAY STEAMERS"

When the Scottish Transport Group was established on 1st January 1969, it took over the steamer services of the Caledonian Steam Packet Company on the Firth of Clyde and inherited a varied but interesting, fleet of ships. The company had been a railway subsidiary since the Caledonian Railway Company had opened Gourock Pier as the base for its steamer fleet in 1889 and the pattern of services continued to reflect a close working relationship between the railway and steamer companies. But this relationship was becoming ever less important as rail borne passenger numbers declined whilst car borne traffic was increasing dramatically. Soon, the Scottish Transport Group's intentions became clear. They revealed a scheme through which it was intended to develop substantially the car ferry services on the Firth of Clyde, in response to rapidly increasing demand. At the expense of the purely passenger services and their dwindling need for railway connections, the focus would now be on

*A murky day sees few passengers daring to go on deck on board the* **Queen Mary**, *en route to Stranraer on 4th September 1975.* (Author)

developing car borne traffic on point to point services utilising new vessels which would replace the existing fleet. Throughout the West Coast, the STG envisaged spending £25 million over 5 years modernising shipping and bus services. Soon, most of the fleet of 1969, whether steam or diesel powered, would be gone forever.

### Duchess of Hamilton

A number of "classic" steamships were inherited by the STG, but sadly for the traditionalists, the imminent arrival of the new generation of ferries led to the rapid demise of most of these old favourites. One such vessel was the magnificent turbine steamer *Duchess of Hamilton* which was built in 1932 for the Caledonian Steam Packet Co. to operate their long distance summer excursion sailings on the Firth of Clyde. A near sister of the *Duchess of Montrose*, built two years earlier, the "Hamilton" was a product of the Harland and Wolff shipyard at Govan, Glasgow, the only Clyde steamer ever to be built there. The *Duchess of Hamilton* represented all that was good about the Clyde fleet in its pre war heyday, when the industrialised Glasgow conurbation relied on the Clyde Steamers to take its multitudes away from the city grime to their natural playground of the Clyde coast resorts. The *Duchess of Hamilton* began her career by being based at Ayr from where she undertook excursions to Ailsa Craig, Campbeltown, Inveraray and to the Arran piers, running in consort with her elder sister, the *Duchess of Montrose*, which was generally based at Gourock. The "Hamilton" played her part in wartime. She was employed as a troop tender at Gourock but also maintained the Stranraer-Larne link

*A morning departure from Gourock for the* **Duchess of Hamilton** *in August 1966 as she leaves for Campbeltown.* (Don Smith Collection)

in the absence of her larger cross-Channel counterparts, many of whom had sailed for distant waters. In post war years, the *Duchess of Hamilton* returned to the Firth of Clyde and remained popular as a summer excursion vessel, visiting distant points such as Inveraray and Campbeltown, and sailing mainly from Gourock, rather than from Ayr. In 1965 she took on the mantle of the *Duchess of Montrose* when that fine vessel was withdrawn at the end of the 1964 season. But the Clyde steamer fleet, faced with mounting losses and upwardly spiralling costs, continued to decline in size and for the *Duchess of Hamilton*, the end came following the 1970 summer season. She made her final sailings in September of that year and on the 28th September 1970, she made her last sailing of all, on her familiar route from Gourock to Campbeltown. In spite of efforts to find an alternative static use, including proposals developed by the Reo Stakis organisation, the vessel was broken up at Troon in 1974 following a period of four years laid up at Greenock, a sad end to a fine ship.

### Queen Mary II

Built in 1933 by Denny of Dumbarton for Williamson Buchanan Steamers' services from Glasgow to the Kyles of Bute and the Clyde Coast resorts, the *Queen Mary* gained the Roman numeral in 1935, becoming *Queen Mary II* for most of her career, following the adoption of her original name for the great transatlantic Cunard liner then under construction at Clydebank and preserved today at Long Beach, California. The original *Queen Mary* entered service on the "all the way" sailings from Glasgow to the Kyles of Bute on 20th May 1933 and, with her fine fittings and spacious capacity for 2086 passengers, she became an immediate success. The wartime years saw her in operation as a troop tender at Gourock and she also undertook general ferry work on the Clyde, maintaining essential links from the railheads. In 1954 the *Queen Mary II* gained a mainmast to comply with new lighting regulations whilst her conversion to oil burning in 1957 saw her twin funnels replaced by a single modern one. These modifications meant that her appearance was now sleek and modern by

*The elegant **Queen Mary II** crosses Gourock Bay in August 1970, her masts shortened to allow her to pass beneath the new Kingston Bridge in Glasgow. (Don Smith Collection)*

comparison to her profile as first built. An ever popular ship, the *Queen Mary II* became familiar to generations of Glaswegians for whom the was synonymous with escape from the toil of the industrial city. She served on her original routes from Glasgow until 7th September 1969, one week before Glasgow's Bridge Wharf steamer terminus was closed, a victim of CSP cutbacks. Following the demise of her main base, the *Queen Mary II* temporarily severed her links with Glasgow, making Gourock her base in subsequent years and also taking up some of the longer distance routes to Campbeltown and Inveraray as an indirect replacement for the *Duchess of Hamilton*. These tasks were undertaken in addition to her own Arran and Kyles of Bute cruises. By 1971, she had become, with the *Waverley*, one of the last two steam driven ships in the CSP Clyde fleet and in 1974, following withdrawal of the paddler, the *Queen Mary II* sailed on alone.

The *Queen Mary II* spent the last five years of her career in the ownership of Caledonian MacBrayne, operating full day excursions

*In earlier times, the **Queen Mary II** steams out of Rothesay in this classic view which dates from 1955. She has twin masts but retains her original two funnels which were replaced in 1957. (Harold Sinclair, Author's Collection)*

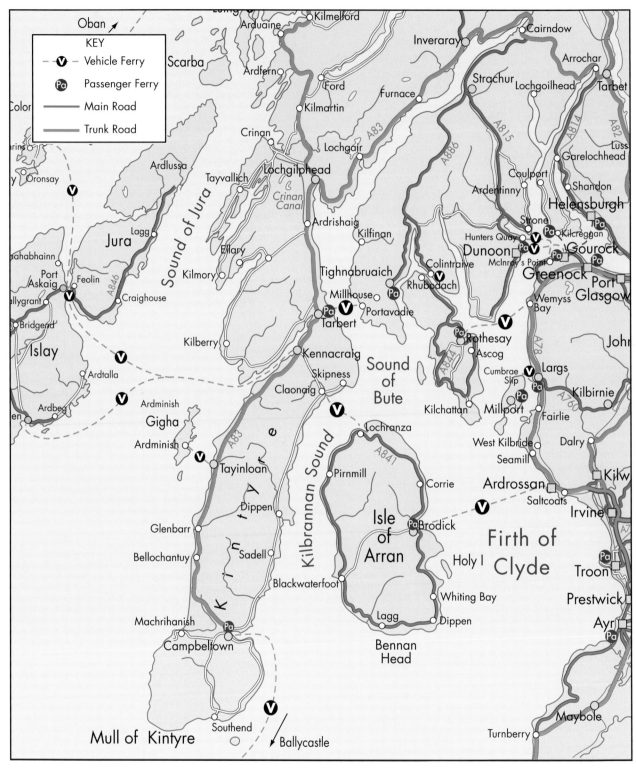

on the Firth of Clyde. A historic event occurred when she regained her original name of *Queen Mary* on 6th May 1976 and reopened her Glasgow sailings from Anderston Quay in direct competition with the *Waverley* which had returned to service under the ownership of the Paddle Steamer Preservation Society. But the dwindling passenger market could support only one steamer and the renamed *Queen Mary* could never compete in popularity with the restored *Waverley* beyond 1975 in spite of being in receipt of substantial local authority subsidy. She made her final sailing for Caledonian MacBrayne on September 12th 1977 following which plans to convert her to a museum ship were unveiled by Glasgow District Council. However, these plans came to nothing and she was sold by the Council to Euroyachts in 1980, and subsequently by them to London owners, Tesright, in

1981. Towed to the Thames in January 1981, the *Queen Mary* lay in Tilbury Docks for several years and was eventually restored to her original twin funnelled condition in 1987, following her sale to Toby Inns Ltd. With her engines removed and substantially altered internally, although still recognisable as the former Clyde favourite, she now serves a different clientele in her role as a floating pub and restaurant on London's Victoria Embankment at the berth formerly occupied by the *Old Caledonia*. Refitted at Chatham in 1997, her restored twin white funnels were repainted yellow once again and she remains open to the public on Victoria Embankment, regularly visited by Glasgow businessmen who find themselves in London and in need of refreshment in familiar surroundings.

*A fine summer day on 3rd August 1977 finds the renamed **Queen Mary** the centre of interest as she leaves Rothesay in her final season.* (Author)

*Caledonia (II)*

The first *Caledonia* had been built in 1889 as one of the first steamers to join James Williamson's new Gourock based fleet. The second was a spacious paddle steamer which was built in 1934 by Denny of Dumbarton, for the Caledonian Steam Packet Company's general ferry and railway connection work. The *Caledonia* and her Fairfield built quasi-sister *Mercury* broke with traditional pre war paddle steamer design in having concealed paddle boxes, two masts and a single funnel. With their large passenger carrying capacity and speed of over 17 knots, they found frequent work on railway connections from Gourock, Greenock and Wemyss Bay but also undertook regular excursion work from those railheads, and other resorts including Ayr and Troon. However, wartime loomed and on Christmas Day 1940, whilst engaged in minesweeping, the *Mercury* struck a mine and sank off Milford Haven, even though the *Caledonia*, renamed *HMS Goatfell* for wartime work, laboured to save her. But her efforts were fruitless and the *Caledonia* sailed on alone. *HMS Goatfell* also saw service as an anti aircraft defence ship, protecting trawler fleets and convoys on the East Coast of England before returning home in 1945 for reconditioning and a return to Clyde service. Following the war, the *Caledonia* continued on similar work to her pre war tasks, with the arrival of the 1954 car ferries allowing her to become the Ayr excursion steamer. In 1965, following the withdrawal of the much loved paddle steamer

*A magnificent view of the paddler **Caledonia** as she rests at Tighnabruaich on an afternoon sailing from Gourock and the Upper Firth piers in August 1969. The scene is largely unchanged today. Only the steamer has gone!* (Harold Sinclair, Author's Collection)

*Jeanie Deans* of 1931, she transferred to the former LNER terminus at Craigendoran where she partnered the *Waverley* on excursion sailings from the North Bank. For five years this arrangement continued but following the 1969 take-over of the Caledonian Steam Packet Co. by the newly formed Scottish Transport Group, the writing was on the wall for two of the four remaining steamers on the Clyde. As a result, the *Caledonia* and the *Duchess of Hamilton* became casualties of economics at the end of the 1969 and 1970 seasons respectively. The *Caledonia* was sold on 11th February 1970 and was sent to the Arnott Young Shipbreakers yard at Dalmuir for scrapping. But she was reprieved from the breakers by Bass Charrington who relocated her to the Thames for use as a floating pub on Victoria Embankment. Renamed the *Old Caledonia*, to allow her historic name to be used on the new car and passenger ferry which entered service on the Ardrossan - Brodick service in 1970, the future seemed secure and there was even talk of a return to active service, raising hopes which were dashed when the vessel suffered a serious fire at her berth on 27th April 1980. Following detailed inspection, the *Old Caledonia* was found to be beyond recovery and she was subsequently broken up at Sittingbourne, Kent.

### Countess of Breadalbane/Countess of Kempock/Countess Fiona

This little ship enjoyed a varied and interesting career on inland lochs and in exposed coastal waters. She was built by Denny of Dumbarton in May 1936 for excursion sailings on Loch Awe where she maintained summer links between Ford, Taychreggan, Portsonachan and Lochawe Pier. She was laid up during World War 2 and resumed sailings in 1948. But in 1952, the CSP required a small vessel to operate a variety of feeder services, particularly the Holy Loch route, on the Clyde. They brought the *Countess of Breadalbane* overland, to Inveraray, on a Pickfords road truck where she was launched into the salt waters of Loch Fyne. Once in service, the *Countess* proved to be a useful little vessel. She became a regular visitor to the Holy Loch piers and she also served Millport whilst visiting quieter piers on a year round basis and deputising for larger steamers at less busy times of the year. The *Countess* also proved popular for charter work, making rare calls at Ormidale and Ardentinny on Clyde River Steamer Club charter sailings.

In November 1971, she was sold to Mr. Walter Roy Ritchie of Gourock who renamed her *Countess of Kempock* and utilised her on his passenger services between Gourock, Kilcreggan and Helensburgh in addition to short cruises on the Upper Firth of Clyde. The *Countess of Kempock* continued in this role for the next seven years before being sold to Offshore Workboats Limited of Oban. Chartered to Staffa Marine between 1979 and 1980, the *Countess of Kempock* linked Ulva Ferry on the Isle of Mull with Iona, a task which saw the onetime

*The Loch Lomond excursion vessel Countess Fiona undergoing renovation at Balloch prior to taking up service on 30th May 1982. (Author)*

*The motor vessel Countess of Kempock is seen arriving at Gourock on 14th July 1978 whilst in the ownership of W.R. Ritchie and operating on services from Gourock to Kilcreggan and Helensburgh. (Author)*

inland vessel visiting the exposed waters of the Sound of Iona. In 1981, she offered a cruise programme based at Oban trading as OWL Cruises.

In 1982 however, the *Countess of Kempock* once again became an inland loch excursion ship. Sold to Alloa Breweries Ltd, she was hoisted out of the Clyde by Glasgow's mighty Stobcross Crane and was taken by low loader to Balloch on Loch Lomond where she was refitted and renamed *Countess Fiona*. In 1982, she took over Loch Lomond excursion sailings from the laid up paddler *Maid of the Loch*, but she continued in this role only until September 25th, 1989. The following year, she succumbed to the financial difficulties of her new owners, Sea Management Corporation of Australia, in spite of substantial investment on the part of her operators, James Fisher & Sons of Barrow in Furness, in renovating her passenger accommodation early in 1989. She has not sailed since and at the time of writing, she remains laid up on the slipway at Balloch whilst her future remains uncertain.

## THE CAR FERRY REVOLUTION

In 1951, the British Transport Commission, the owners of the British Railways Clyde fleet since the nationalisation of Britain's rail network in 1948, announced a £1 million plan to modernise the Clyde Steamer services. The plans envisaged the construction of four small passenger ships which could operate on busy ferry routes, and three general purpose ships which would carry cars, livestock and cargo. Although the passenger vessels were revolutionary only in terms of their diesel propulsion, manoeuvrability, general layout and appearance, the subsequent three vehicle carriers, initially proposed as "general purpose" vessels, were to be the portents of the vehicular ferry revolution which was to come.

In 1953 British Railways placed into service the four small passenger vessels intended for service on the busy railway connection, ferry and commuter routes on the Upper Clyde and on services to the smaller piers. The "Maids" were handy if uninspiring little vessels which were capable of carrying 627 passengers. Although described as being "of pleasing design and trim in appearance", they suffered from a lack of speed and a low carrying capacity which limited their usefulness at peak periods. Their passenger accommodation was rather cramped and spartan by comparison to the larger steamers, with the main passenger lounge resembling a grandiose version of the upper deck of a bus whilst catering facilities were limited and restricted the usefulness of the "Maids" on busier or longer services. Deck space was also limited and from the cramped promenade deck, the view forward was obstructed by life saving equipment. Nevertheless, they were undoubtedly economical, if unspectacular, vessels and although not generally favoured at first by the travelling public, they soon proved their worth in all weathers. With their gross tonnage of 508 and powered by two six cylinder British Polar diesel engines, the "Maids" were designed for a service speed of about 14 knots. Although the promenade deck was well below pier level at low tide, a landing platform above the wheelhouse ensured that they could handle passengers at any state of the tide. They operated throughout the year, mainly on routes from Gourock, Craigendoran, Wemyss Bay and Largs on railway connection work and they also undertook some cruising work and charter sailings, often deputising for larger steamers at quieter times of the year and becoming mainstays of the winter work. Other duties included tendering to North Atlantic passenger liners at the Tail of the Bank whilst from 1969, they handled additional Kilcreggan sailings to carry workers bound for the Royal Naval Armaments Depot at Coulport on Loch Long.

### Maid of Ashton

Launched on 17th February 1953, the first of the four vessels to enter service was the *Maid of Ashton*, which remains the only ship to have been built by Yarrows of Scotstoun for Clyde services. She was associated with the Holy Loch route initially but soon saw other duties as the four ships became interchangeable. In April 1965, she became the first "Maid" to carry the lion rampant emblem on her funnel and April 1967 saw her employed as a Royal Yacht when she carried HRH The Princess Margaret on a short cruise down the River Clyde from Glasgow, which was extended by almost 20 minutes, such was the royal guest's pleasure! The first of the "Maids" to arrive was also the first to leave the fleet and the *Maid of Ashton* was withdrawn from service in 1971, surplus to requirements. On 8th January 1973, she was sold to the Yardarm Club of London where she became the *Hispaniola*. She functioned as a clubhouse and restaurant ship on the Thames Embankment, lying astern of the former Humber paddle steamer *Tattershall Castle*, where she can still be found today.

### Maid of Argyll

Next came the *Maid of Argyll*, launched on 4th March 1953, which initially saw service between Craigendoran and Rothesay and on the Arrochar excursion sailings. In 1964, the CSP indicated that one "Maid" was to be withdrawn from service as a result of the proposed closure of the Holy Loch service. The *Maid of Argyll* was the vessel nominated for withdrawal but public reaction led the CSP to carry on with the service until 1971. In addition to her passenger role in the upper Firth, the *Maid of Argyll* became the Tarbert mail vessel between February and May 1970, following in the footsteps of MacBrayne's *Lochfyne*. The *Maid of Argyll* was the only "Maid" which was to remain on the Clyde as a passenger ship and to don the livery of Caledonian MacBrayne. In this condition she saw just one summer, that of 1973, when she deputised for the *Waverley* on some of her sailings when the steamer was otherwise engaged or suffering from mechanical problems which beset her during that season. Like the *Waverley*, 1973 was the last season for the *Maid of Argyll* in Caledonian MacBrayne service and she soon departed for foreign waters, making her last Clyde sailing on 12th September 1973. She was sold on 1st March 1974 and headed for Greece where she saw further service as the *City of Piraeus* and latterly, as the *City of Corfu* from which island she operated a day cruise programme. However, she suffered substantial fire damage in 1997 following which her future became uncertain. She did not sail in Summer 1998.

### Maid of Skelmorlie

The third of the quartette was the *Maid of Skelmorlie* which was launched on 2nd April 1953, from the A&J Inglis shipyard at Pointhouse, Glasgow, builders of many Clyde paddle steamers over the years. At first she was associated with services form Wemyss Bay but she also undertook a variety of short cruises on the upper Firth of Clyde, whilst sharing other tasks with her sisters. Following the withdrawal of MacBraynes Tarbert and Ardrishaig mail service in September 1969, the *Maid of Skelmorlie* undertook sailings from Gourock to Tarbert, and was fitted with mail lockers for the purpose. She was replaced on the route by the *Maid of Argyll* in February 1970 but on 29th May 1970, thanks to the introduction of the Fairlie - Brodick - Tarbert Loch Fyne car ferry service, the STG closed the service altogether. The *Maid of Skelmorlie* was rendered surplus to the STG requirements at the end of the 1972 season and she was sold in April 1973, following which she sailed for Italy and became the *Ala*. Having been converted to carry several cars and commercial vehicles, she operated in the Bay of Naples between Amalfi, Capri and Sorrento, before moving to the Adriatic in 1997.

### Maid of Cumbrae

The last of the quartette, the *Maid of Cumbrae* was launched at the Ardrossan Dockyard Ltd. on May 13th 1953 and was immediately recognisable from the others by having her name painted in white on the lower black part of the hull. In March 1972, the *Maid of Cumbrae*, having been reprieved from sale to new owners, was hastily converted, by Barclay Curle's Elderslie shipyard, to become a small car ferry capable of carrying 15 cars and was placed on the new, drive on - drive off Gourock - Dunoon service on 27th May 1972 in consort with the *Glen Sannox* and subsequently the *Jupiter*. The car ferry *Maid of Cumbrae* had the honour of becoming the first vessel to wear the new colours of Caledonian MacBrayne when the company was formed in 1973. But the arrival of the *Juno* and *Jupiter* relegated her to become a spare vessel and she left the Caledonian MacBrayne fleet in 1978, being sold to Trieste, firstly as the *Hanseatic*, then being renamed *Noce di Cocco* before joining her former fleetmate *Ala* (ex *Maid of Skelmorlie*), in the Bay of Naples and operating as the *Capri Express*. At first, she cruised between Capri and Positano but more recently, she was running as a car ferry between Naples and Sorrento, in the ownership of Alimar Spa. However, it appears that she has been laid up, out of class, at Naples since 1996. Thus, the four "Maids" left the waters of their birth. Their Firth of Clyde careers were relatively short, unspectacular and marked by steady and generally reliable service in all weathers. The travelling public have rarely regarded any ships with such ambivalence and the withdrawal of the "Maid" vessels was not

*The Maid of Cumbrae shows off her monastral blue hull and red lion rampant emblem on her funnel at Gourock on 17th July 1965. (Aikman Smith Collection)*

universally condemned. Or even noticed. By contrast to the "Maids", the three general purpose car, cargo and livestock carriers envisaged in the British Transport Commission proposals of 1951 revived some far reaching pre-war notions regarding the provision of vehicular ferries on the Firth of Clyde. Ideas for car ferry provision had been advanced in the years preceding World War 2, but it was not until 1954 that the British Transport Commission provided the first vessels which were designed specifically for the carriage of motor vehicles. Prior to 1954, small, but increasing, numbers of cars had been carried on passenger vessels and driven aboard by means of gangplanks placed precariously between steamer and pier at suitable states of the

*In her original condition as a passenger ship, the **Maid of Cumbrae** makes a sweeping arrival at Largs in 1966.* (Terry Primrose)

tide. But the new ships were unique and ushered in a new age, being hailed as the answer to the motorists prayer. With capacity for 34 cars and 600 passengers, their British Polar diesels gave them a service speed of 14 knots and the main passenger accommodation was located on two decks above the car deck and forward of the unique vehicle loading system. This consisted of a large electrically operated hoist located amidships which extended the full width of the ship and could be raised and lowered as required, bringing vehicles from the garage deck to pier level. Ramps were then lowered onto the pier allowing vehicles to drive on and off the ship, at any state of the tide and at virtually any suitable pier. Prior to the completion of roll on - roll off terminals, the hoist loading mechanism became a standard feature of many subsequent vessels up to and including the *Lord of the Isles* of 1989. But at Easter 1994, and the conversion of the Mallaig - Armadale route to drive through operation, the requirement for hoist loading on normal services was dispensed with and the procedure was subsequently used only in emergency or in the event of occasional calls at piers where no linkspan existed.

Nevertheless, when the three 1954 ships entered service, they established the general layout for many future vessels in the Clyde and West Highland fleets. However, their "general purpose" role was seldom utilised and in 1959, space which had been given over to non-containerised cargo carriage was used as additional vehicle capacity, indicating an early response to the already escalating demand for carriage of cars between the Lowland and the Highland shores of the Firth of Clyde. At the time of their construction, it was naively intended that these three vessels, without backup, would service demand on the Dunoon, Rothesay and Brodick routes for many years to come, a lack of foresight which was amply demonstrated within a few months by the delaying of the opening of the Arran car ferry route as the three new vessels were required to service spiralling upward demand on the upper Firth services. By 1955, it was becoming clear that a fourth vessel would be required to serve Arran. The result was the construction, in 1957, of the much larger, but generally similar, *Glen Sannox* to service the Arran traffic.

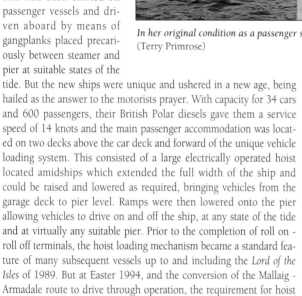

*The former passenger ship **Maid of Cumbrae** is berthed alongside Dunoon Pier in June 1977 as she disembarks cars at the side loading linkspan.* (Author's Collection)

*Maids seen in Italian waters. The Ala (ex **Maid of Skelmorlie**, left) and the Capri Express (ex **Maid of Cumbrae**) are berthed together at Sorrento on 30th July 1993.* (Author)

*The Arran, first of the "ABC" Car ferries, is seen arriving at Dunoon.*(Don Smith Collection)

## Arran

The first of the "ABC" ships to enter service was the *Arran*, the last Clyde vessel to be built by Denny of Dumbarton, although she was fitted out at Troon. On 4$^{th}$ January 1954 she operated the 12.10 sailing from Gourock to Dunoon which was destined to be the first ever Clyde Car ferry service. Symbolically, it was the paddle steamer *Waverley* which she replaced on the route. The *Arran* continued to serve the upper Firth of Clyde routes in consort with her sisters for the next fifteen years, before a new challenge beckoned her. In November 1969 she was chartered to MacBraynes to replace the outdated *Lochiel* on their West Loch Tarbert - Islay route and to operate in competition to the Western Ferries state of the art car ferry, *Sound of Jura*. To assist her further in this role, the *Arran* was sent to Barclay Curle's yard on 31$^{st}$ December 1972, returning to service in April 1973, having been converted to stern loading for the Islay service and calling at Port Ellen only. But the arrival of the new, purpose built *Pioneer* in August 1974 made this exercise a short term one. However,

the *Arran* spent a further four years of active service in the Clyde and Western Isles serving on a variety of routes until she undertook her last sailings in July 1979. She was offered for sale in 1979, becoming a floating night-club in locations as diverse as Dublin and Salford, where she was to be appropriately renamed *Revolution*. However, the name was never registered and the ship was broken up in 1992.

## Cowal

Next on the scene was the *Cowal*, built by the Ailsa Yard at Troon, which entered service on the Wemyss Bay - Rothesay route on the 1$^{st}$ October 1954, bringing car ferry services to the island of Bute. On 6$^{th}$ December 1954, the route was handed over to the third ship which bore the island's name, the *Bute*. The first Clyde ship to be fitted with radar, the *Cowal* worked in consort with her sisters but on 30$^{th}$ May 1970 she opened a new service between Fairlie, Brodick and Tarbert Loch Fyne. This was the STGs replacement for the former MacBrayne "Royal Route" although she did not serve Ardrishaig. However the ser-

*Whilst operating on the short lived Fairlie - Brodick - Tarbert route, the Cowal is seen loading passengers and cargo at Tarbert Loch Fyne.* (Harold Sinclair, Author's Collection)

*It is a typical blustery but bright spring day on the Firth of Clyde as the* Cowal *passes Toward Point, bound for Wemyss Bay, on 19th May 1973.* (Author)

*The Arran was not exactly an object of beauty following her conversion to an end loader. In this shot taken on 14th July 1977, she is seen leaving Largs en route for Millport.* (Author)

vice was short lived, being discontinued on 30th September 1971, pending the opening of the new short link between Lochranza and Claonaig in July of 1972, utilising the first of the Island class vessels, the *Kilbrannan*. With the introduction of the Largs - Cumbrae Slip service, the honour of being the last ship to call at Fairlie fell to the *Cowal* on 11th March 1972. The *Cowal* continued in Clyde service until July 1977, maintaining the Wemyss Bay - Rothesay service where her hoist loading facility was still required, and undertaking charter sailings to the oil rig construction yard at Ardyne Point. In May 1979, she was sold to Greek owners and left the Clyde under tow, being renamed *Med-Star*. Following a difficult tow, during which she broke free in the Bay of Biscay, she arrived in Piraeus where, without ever taking up service, she was laid up and subsequently scrapped.

*Bute*

Like the *Cowal*, this ship was also a product of the Troon shipyard of Ailsa Shipbuilders. She was launched on 28th September 1954 and entered service in December of that year on the Wemyss

Bay - Rothesay service. For the following twenty years she served on the Firth of Clyde, becoming part of the Caledonian MacBrayne fleet in 1973. But further travels awaited her. The *Bute*, having become the first Caledonian MacBrayne ship to call at the McAlpine oil rig yard at Ardyne Point on 1st October 1974, transferred from the Clyde to Mallaig in the Summer of 1975 to operate the seasonal car ferry service to Armadale. But following the transfer of the more modern *Pioneer* to this service on 1st June 1979, the *Bute* became surplus to requirements, and she was sold in 1979 to Thetouris Shipping of Greece, leaving the Clyde in June 1980 for Piraeus to be renamed *Med-Sun*. She was broken up in 1985.

So passed from the scene the three pioneer Clyde car ferries which, revolutionary by the standards of the 1950's, had become largely outdated by the time they left their home waters. Nevertheless, they had developed car and passenger traffic substantially and pointed the way forward for the rapidly changing shipping services on the Firth of Clyde and in the West Highlands. The hoist loading mechanism was to be carried by 12 ships between 1954 and 1989.

*The forlorn looking **Arran** seems to be sailing on a sea of desolation as she awaits her fate at Salford in October 1987.* (Iain R. Murray Collection)

*The hoist loading system introduced by the three 1954 ferries is seen at work on a much later vessel, the **Iona** of 1970.* (Author)

*A spring clean for the **Cowal** as she rests on the blocks in James Lamont's dry dock in Greenock in March 1976.*
(Roy Pedersen)

*The **Glen Sannox**, wearing the CSP monastral blue hull and carrying lion rampant emblems on her funnel, approaches her winter terminal at Fairlie on 17th April 1967. (Aikman Smith Collection)*

### Glen Sannox

In 1957 the newest Caledonian Steam Packet car ferry was regarded as a leviathan of the Clyde fleet. By 1989 she could not meet modern requirements. This was the story of the *Glen Sannox*, a vessel which entered service in the declining years of the era of steam driven passenger ships and left the fleet to be replaced by the largest roll on - roll off vessel then in service. Built with the Caledonian lion rampant emblem carried proudly on her bow, she was also the first ship to carry it on her yellow funnel in 1964. Her career spanned the period of change in West coast shipping services and in many ways, she came to symbolise the joining together of the Clyde and West Highland fleets more than any other vessel. Upon entering service she was regarded as something of an ugly duckling by comparison to the sleek turbine steamers and paddle steamers which were her Clyde consorts in the fifties, but if she had few friends at the outset, the "Great Glen" had become a much loved survivor by the time of her departure.

Built by the Ailsa Shipbuilding Company of Troon in 1957, the *Glen Sannox* was a substantially enlarged and improved version of the *Arran* and her sisters and was capable of carrying 1100 passengers and up to 50 cars on her regular service between Ardrossan and Brodick. With Sulzer engines giving her a trial speed of over 18 knots, she took up the Arran service on 29th June 1957 and immediately became a success, rapidly building up vehicular traffic to the ever popular holiday island. Her arrival brought to an end the cargo sailings operated by the old stager *Kildonan* and allowed a Wemyss Bay - Millport cargo service to be operated by one of the original three ferries, commencing in 1957. In Winter her mainland terminal transferred to Fairlie until 1971 when she became based at Ardrossan all year round, following the closure of Fairlie Pier. As built, she was a larger version of the 1954 ferries and carried a vehicle hoist and a crane for handling cargo. However, her conversion to a stern loader led to the addition of a stern ramp in 1970 and the removal of the crane in 1972. She transferred to the Wemyss Bay - Rothesay route from May 1970, before moving to the Gourock - Dunoon service in

November 1971 where she partnered the converted passenger ferry *Maid of Cumbrae*. For several years, the pair were custodians of the route which had been one of the first to be converted to drive on - drive off operation, the necessary terminals having been opened by the new *Iona* in July 1970.

In 1974, the *Glen Sannox* donned the new Caledonian MacBrayne red and black funnel colours with the red lion rampant mounted on a yellow disk. She illustrated the joining together of Clyde and West Highland fleets by opening the roll on - roll off facilities at Craignure on the Isle of Mull on 29th April 1974. Having maintained the Mull link throughout 1974, the *Glen Sannox* returned to the Clyde in 1975 but became the winter vessel on the Oban - Craignure and Oban - Colonsay routes between November 1977 and December 1988, until the arrival of the new ferry, *Isle of Mull*. On 20th May 1977, the *Glen Sannox* made history in her own right, by becoming the first vessel to use the new roll on - roll off terminal at Wemyss Bay, although side loading was and still is, required at the new terminal at Rothesay.

Re-engined with Wichmann Diesels at Aberdeen in late 1976,

*A sunny day in August 1965 sees the great **Glen Sannox** approaching Ardrossan in her monastral blue livery. (Author's Collection)*

*A period piece at Rothesay Pier in August 1977 as seen from the decks of the **Queen Mary** with the **Cowal** loading for Wemyss Bay and the new ramp under construction.* (Harold Sinclair, Author's Collection)

*On one of many of her charter sailings from Glasgow, the **Glen Sannox** sweeps down the River Clyde past Erskine on 11th June 1988.* (Author)

and with her passenger accommodation upgraded, the *Glen Sannox* found summer employment from May 1978, as the Caledonian MacBrayne Clyde cruising vessel, replacing the *Queen Mary* and competing with the *Waverley* in this role. But her appeal to the cruising market was not great by comparison with the paddle steamer, and her programme of cruises was reduced to a series of "Inter Resort" sailings by 1981 and indeed the cruising programme was withdrawn totally in advance of the 1982 summer, leaving the *Waverley* as the only large Clyde cruising ship. The *Glen Sannox* then found a role as a substantial backup vessel on the Clyde in summer and was often to be found assisting the "streakers" on the main ferry routes whilst undertaking charter work on frequent occasions. Winters continued to see her based at Oban, operating to Craignure and Colonsay.

By 1988, the *Glen Sannox* and her Oban counterpart *Columba*, were reaching the end of their useful lives. Ever increasing passenger and vehicle demand had meant that the imminent arrival of a new vessel at Oban would render them redundant. The redesigning of the Tiree, Coll and Colonsay timetables coupled with the abandonment of the Sacred Isle Cruise and the arrival of the *Isle of Mull* on the Craignure service meant the end for the two veterans. 1989 was the last year in service for the *Glen Sannox* when she ably demonstrated her prowess by undertaking a series of commemorative full day cruises in Clyde and West Highland waters. Having begun life as a utilitarian Clyde car ferry, her last employment of all was as a cruise vessel, on charter to Govan Shipbuilders on 10th June 1989. She left the fleet in August of that year and departed for Greek waters having been renamed *Knooz*. At Perama, she was substantially reconstructed for further service with Arab owners, and went through various name changes, becoming *Nadia*, and *Al Marwah* and she is currently still in service in the Middle East as the *Al Basmalah*.

In her time on the West Coast the *Glen Sannox* carried everything from Aston Martins to Austin A40s and cabin cruisers to coaches.

Many island mothers-to-be had cause to be grateful for a caring crew and more than one West Highlander can call the old ship his or her birthplace. She has been popular with summer trippers, enjoying a bracing sail out on her decks and with winter commuters seeking the warmth of her saloons. Maybe it was for these reasons and for her reliability in all weathers that she is fondly remembered and her place in West Coast affections is therefore assured.

### Keppel

The only 1960's addition to the CSP Clyde fleet appeared in 1967. Until 1966 the Great Cumbrae town of Millport had been served by the diesel electric paddle vessel *Talisman,* dating from 1935 and supported by a "Maid". At first glance, the former Thames ferry *Rose*, built by White's of Southampton in 1961 and one of a trio of identical vessels constructed for the Tilbury - Gravesend service, was hardly the most attractive replacement. Small, relatively slow and with a strange funnel-cum-mast arrangement, the *Rose* was no beauty and her passenger facilities were spartan. Yet, appropriately modified for the route and renamed *Keppel,* she took over the Largs - Millport (Old Pier) service on 12th June 1967 and served the route for many years. She was the first vessel in the Clyde fleet to be powered by Voith Schneider propulsion and with her service speed of around 9

*In her familiar Clyde car ferry role, the **Glen Sannox** leaves Gourock bound for Dunoon on 4th July 1985. (Author)*

*The former **CSP** and MacBrayne veterans, **Glen Sannox** and **Columba** rendezvous at Oban on 4th April 1988, during the penultimate season in service of the Glen Sannox (Author)*

knots, she became a useful and surprisingly popular little ship. The winter service to Millport (Old Pier) ended three years after her arrival so the *Keppel* found herself undertaking various Clyde relief duties. She also operated workers sailings to the Ardyne Point oil rig yard between 1974 and 1977. Following the closure of the summer Largs - Millport (Old Pier) route on 18th June 1986, thanks to the introduction of the *Loch Linnhe* and *Loch Striven* on the Cumbrae Slip car ferry service, the duties of the *Keppel* now included excursion sailings from Gourock to the Kyles of Bute, Loch Long, Carrick Castle and the main resorts whilst in 1988 she was a regular visitor to the Glasgow Garden Festival. Throughout her Clyde career she was a popular vessel for charter sailings and in this capacity she visited attractive corners of the Firth of Clyde such as Portencross, Ormidale, Ardnadam, Strone and

Blairmore, often on charter to enthusiasts organisations such as the Clyde River Steamer Club. However, passenger numbers fell substantially in the early 1990's and in 1992, the *Keppel* was put up for sale. She was sold out of the Caledonian MacBrayne fleet on 20th May 1993. That summer, she made a brief reappearance as a Clyde cruise vessel under the ownership of Inverclyde Marine and bearing the name *Clyde Rose*. Unfortunately, this venture lasted only a few months and, although a timetable was published, the vessel rarely attracted good passenger loadings. Following a period laid up in Cardwell Bay, she was sold to Maltese interests and left the Clyde on 22nd April 1995.

*Passengers enjoy a bright and breezy day on board the **Glen Sannox** as she sails through the Kyles of Bute on 31st August 1987. (Author)*

*The Clyde cruise ship **Keppel** leaves Rothesay on a sunny afternoon bound for Largs on 30th May 1988. (Author)*

*The Caledonian MacBrayne Clyde cruise ship Keppel seen amongst the magnificent scenery of the Kyles of Bute near Glencaladh on 19th August 1986. (Author)*

*Clyde swansong as the **Clyde Rose** (ex **Keppel**) passes close to Gourock Pier on 15th August 1993, a rare view of the ship operating in the colours of Inverclyde Marine. (Author)*

# THE WIND OF CHANGE GATHERS FORCE

*"Clyde cruising…is almost certain to disappear and we shall be left with ferry routes served by car ferries of all shapes and sizes. Perhaps a new generation will obtain great delight in observing and sailing on end loaders."* Iain C. MacArthur, "The Caledonian Steam Packet Company" 1971.

On 1st January 1969, the Scottish Transport Group, the new state transport authority in Scotland, came into existence and assumed control of British Railways interests in the Clyde steamer services of the Caledonian Steam Packet Company. The STG also assumed control of the railway owned piers and on August 1st 1969, they acquired Arran Piers Ltd, taking control of the piers at Brodick and Lochranza. Immediately, plans were developed for work to be undertaken at all of the main terminals in the Firth of Clyde to allow as rapid a changeover as possible to roll on - roll off operation. The STG's wind of change also gripped the West Highlands. Since 1928, 50% of the shares in David MacBrayne had been owned by the railway company and its predecessors, the other half being owned by Coast Lines Ltd. The STG inherited the total shareholding in MacBraynes in July 1969 and the way was cleared for a gradual merging together of the Clyde and West Highland shipping operations. The Edinburgh based STG did not hang about. They set about changing forever the pattern of services on the West Coast of Scotland. An immediate change was apparent in the colour schemes of the Clyde ships as the monastral blue hull, given to all railway owned ships in 1965, was replaced by the more traditional black. The yellow funnels and houseflags retained their red lion rampant emblems, a long established symbol which had first flown at a CSP masthead in 1889.

## Caledonia (III)

One of the first acts of the Scottish Transport Group upon securing control of the major Clyde and West Highland shipping services,

was to introduce roll on - roll off facilities on the Ardrossan - Brodick route and to commission, the former Stena Line car ferry *Stena Baltica* on the route on a year round basis. Built by A/S Langesunds Mek Verksted of Langesund, Norway in 1966, the vessel had operated on a Cross Channel route between Tilbury, Southend and Calais, branded as "The Londoner" service. Following modifications at Scott's Shipbuilding Co. at Greenock, the third CSP ship to be named *Caledonia* entered service, inaugurating the new drive through facilities at Ardrossan and Brodick on 29th May 1970. She was the first drive through car ferry on the Clyde but her introduction was not entirely successful. Although capable of carrying 50 cars, her passenger capacity, at 132 in winter and 650 in summer was barely adequate to service traffic on the route whilst her sailings were frequently disrupted due to bad weather. Powered by twin M.A.N. diesels, her relative lack of speed, at 14 knots in service, did not endear her to the travelling public, even though her turn round time at piers was much shorter than that of the hoist loading *Glen Sannox*. The lack of a suitable alternative mainland terminal to Ardrossan led to the ship diverting to Gourock on many occasions, and she was required to provide additional sailings at peak periods. Notwithstanding this, the *Caledonia,* having cost the STG £1 million in refitting costs and in construction of the new terminals, steadied herself and became a generally reliable unit of the fleet. However, her relatively low passenger capacity led to her replacement on the Arran route in summers from 1976 by the former MacBrayne vessel *Clansman* which had been rebuilt to increase her capacity. As a result, the *Caledonia* found employment as a West Highland vessel, where she became the mainstay of the Oban - Craignure service during the summer months. Deviations from her normal work were rare but on 26th May 1977, she visited the Howard Doris oil rig yard in Loch Kishorn and on 29th October 1983, she visited Tarbert Loch Fyne on a charter sailing. On 29th June 1986, the *Caledonia* made her only visit to the Outer Hebrides when she carried commercial vehicles to Lochboisdale.

Winter months saw her back on the Arran service until the introduction of the *Isle of Arran* in 1984 allowed her to continue operating out of Oban in summer whilst becoming a spare vessel in winter

*The wind of change is in full force as the new Arran ferry* **Caledonia** *arrives at Ardrossan on 1st August 1970, whilst the* **Queen Mary II** *waits for trade.* (Aikman Smith Collection)

*The **Caledonia** was one of several Clyde vessels to move into the West Highlands. Here, she is seen leaving Oban Bay en route to Craignure on 5th August 1986. (Author)*

months. During the period between 1984 and 1987, she was relieved at Oban in winter by the *Glen Sannox*, the ship she had herself replaced at Brodick. This pattern continued until the entry into service of the new *Isle of Mull*, which rendered the *Caledonia* surplus to requirements. She was sold in December 1987 to Mr. J. Docherty of Broughty Ferry with a view to operating her as a restaurant ship in Dundee.

The *Caledonia* sailed to Dundee on 4th January 1988 where she was laid up in the city's Victoria Dock. But the restaurant proposals came to nothing and the ship departed for Italy where she saw further service in Italian waters as the *Heidi*. She continues to sail between Naples, Pozzuoli and Ischia in the ownership of Linee Lauro although her lack of speed was proving to be something of a disadvantage on this busy route. Plus ça change!

*In the somewhat sunnier Italian climate, the **Heidi**, formerly the **Caledonia**, is moored in the harbour at Ischia on 12th October 1992. (Ian Hall)*

HM2-011

Recent developments in high speed ferry technology have had major impact on ferry services worldwide. However, the history of such craft in Scottish coastal waters has been one of little success. The mid 1960's had seen an abortive attempt to establish hovercraft services on the Clyde using Westland SRN6 craft but the venture was short lived. The next attempt was in 1970, when the STG acquired a Hovermarine HM-2 hovercraft which was capable of carrying 62 passengers at a cruising speed of 35 knots. Enthused, the CSP placed her into service on passenger services from Gourock. However, largely due to technical reasons, the experiment was not a great success and the vessel was sold to American interests after only two seasons. Neither the STG nor Caledonian MacBrayne have revisited the idea of fast ferries since, although Western Ferries Ltd. met with limited success with their catamaran *Highland Seabird* in the late 1970s.

## BACK DOORS TO BUTE AND CUMBRAE

On 23rd December 1969 the Caledonian Steam Packet Company acquired the Bute Ferry Company and took over the operation of their car ferry service between Colintraive and Rhubodach. The name Colintraive means "the narrows at the swimming place" and is where Highland drovers encouraged their cattle to swim to the mainland on their way to market. Located in the beautiful Kyles of Bute, the magnificent straits separating the island of Bute from the Cowal peninsula, this 5 minute crossing had been established as the "back door" into the island in July 1950, by the Marquis of Bute himself . The service was operated by a converted landing craft, the *Eilean Dhu*, a ferry of plywood construction, the *Eilean Buidhe* and the turntable ferry *Dhuirinish*. With the improvement of roads on the Cowal peninsula, traffic on the route was beginning to increase substantially and the STG immediately set about developing the service further. Two displaced bow loading ferries from the CSP Skye ferry service, the *Portree* and the *Broadford*, came south to operate the Colintraive - Rhubodach service.

### Portree (II)

The *Portree* had been built by James Lamont & Co. of Port Glasgow in 1965 and was initially a side loader. But for the Kyles of Bute crossing, she returned to her builders to be converted to bow loading and at 65 gross tons, with capacity for 10 cars, she took up service in May 1970 on the Colintraive - Rhubodach service.

### Broadford (II)

A near sister ship of the *Portree*, the *Broadford* was also built at Lamont's Port Glasgow shipyard and she arrived on the Skye Ferry crossing in 1967. Upon the arrival of the new *Lochalsh* and *Kyleakin*, the *Broadford* followed her sister through conversion to bow loading and into service on the former Bute Ferry Company's Colintraive - Rhubodach service across the Kyles of Bute which she took up in June 1971. Both the *Portree* and the *Broadford* were sold out of the Caledonian MacBrayne fleet to a Mr. Hooper of Sandbank, on 4th November 1987, following the introduction of the *Loch Riddon* in the previous year.

The introduction of these small ferries on the Colintraive - Rhubodach service was to lead to substantial traffic growth on the crossing, which required the provision of ever larger ferries on this, the most scenic and shortest crossing onto Bute. These drovers of centuries ago certainly knew a thing or two. By contrast, the first Car ferry services to Great Cumbrae and its "capital" of Millport had been provided from the mainland terminals of Largs, Wemyss Bay or Fairlie to Millport (Old Pier) by the 1954 hoist loading ferries. But in March 1972, a shorter and more frequent vehicle ferry service was inaugurated by the car ferry *Coruisk*, utilising purpose built slipways at Largs and at "Tattie Pier" on the north end of Cumbrae, which was reconstructed and eloquently renamed Cumbrae Slip. With regular bus connections linking Cumbrae Slip to Millport, the establishment of the car ferry service soon led to the scaling down of the Old Pier service. It became a passenger only service, operated solely by the *Keppel*, on a summer only basis until the service ceased totally in 1986.

### Coruisk

This vessel, the predecessor of the "Small Island" Class vessels, was built in 1969 by the Ailsa shipyard of Troon for service on the CSP Kyleakin - Kyle of Lochalsh Skye Ferry crossing but she did not operate on that route for long. Having been converted to bow loading in September 1971, she inaugurated the new point to point Largs - Cumbrae Slip car ferry service on 11th March 1972. With a speed of 9 knots and capacity for only 6 cars, she was soon joined by other vessels, forming a potent armada of small Largs based ferries and initiating traffic growth on the Cumbrae Slip crossing which has continued ever since. The *Coruisk* remained a member of the Caledonian MacBrayne fleet, spending most of her time at Largs, until 1986 when she was sold to Euroyachts of Glasgow.

### Largs

Built in 1960 as the *Kyleakin* by Ailsa Shipbuilding of Troon, this was the last turntable ferry in a long line which had included others such as the *Portree* of 1951 and the *Broadford* of 1953. She served on the Kyle of Lochalsh - Kyleakin service for the CSP from 1960 until superseded by a larger ferry of the same name in 1970 and was converted to bow loading at Troon, becoming the *Largs* in 1972. She transferred to the Largs - Cumbrae Slip route on the Clyde, taking up service in July 1972 in consort with the *Coruisk*. She left the Caledonian MacBrayne fleet in 1983 and departed from the Clyde on board a cargo ship, bound for South Yemen, in 1987.

The *Coruisk* was the forerunner of the "Island" class of ferries

*The **Portree**, dressed overall, prepares to leave Colintraive on a sunny day in the early eighties.* (Iain R. Murray)

which were to become important members of the fleet. Most of them served Cumbrae at some time, although they were largely passing through on their way to other parts of the STG empire, or undertaking relief duties. The *Coruisk* and the *Largs* were followed at Largs by the purpose built *Isle of Cumbrae* in 1977 and in 1986, four new ferries, the first of the "Loch" class vessels, which began to replace the earlier "Island" class vessels.

By the end of 1972, much progress had been made on changing the Clyde fleet and its services forever. Growth in vehicular traffic had continued unabated throughout the 1960s although less spectacularly than the STG might have hoped for, whilst passenger figures continued to give cause for concern. In spite of substantial investment in drive on - drive off ferry services in the preceding few years, Clyde traffic continued to perform poorly and 1972 saw a further reduction of 7% in passenger traffic although vehicle traffic increased marginally. Meanwhile, the pace of change did not slacken. The Gourock - Dunoon route had been upgraded to roll on - roll off operation in 1970, with the construction of new terminals permitting stern loading at Gourock and side loading at Dunoon, where ships used the new ramp which had been built into the pier. In 1972, the passenger vessel *Maid of Cumbrae* was converted to become a car ferry capable of carrying 15 cars and together with the modifications to the *Glen Sannox*, these improvements allowed the introduction of a two ship service on the Gourock - Dunoon route. Meanwhile the *Cowal* continued to operate on the Wemyss Bay - Rothesay service which remained as a much slower hoist loading operation until 1978. Major and far reaching changes were to continue and 1973 saw the wind of change become a gale which blew throughout the Clyde and West Highlands as the two fleets were moulded into a new and powerful force under the name of Caledonian MacBrayne.

*Looking as powerful as she can, the **Largs** thunders away from the slipway at Largs in July 1975.* (Roy Pedersen)

*The former Dutch ferry **Sound of Sleat** approaches McInroy's Point on 17th July 1997. (Author)*

*The second **Sound of Sanda** departing from McInroy's Point on 16th July 1997. (Author)*

*The double ended ferry* **Isle of Cumbrae** *loads for Cumbrae Slip as the* **Arran** *approaches Largs Pier on 14th July 1977. (Author)*

*Later years see the* **Isle of Cumbrae** *awaiting departure from Rhubodach on 4th July 1998. (Author)*

## WESTERN FERRIES ON THE CLYDE

In the late nineteen sixties, a private concern, Western Ferries Ltd., had led the way in demonstrating that low cost drive on - drive off ferry services, based on the Norwegian approach, could be operated in the West Highlands. In 1972, proposals to acquire Western Ferries had been put forward by the STG but their £2.25 million bid was usurped at the eleventh hour by the Dornoch Shipping Company, a bid which had the backing of Sir William Lithgow and other major private investors. The operating company became known as Western Ferries (Argyll) Ltd.

Keen to demonstrate the Norwegian principle on the Firth of Clyde, the company took the battle between the state owned STG and its own private sector backers to the very heart of Caledonian MacBrayne territory by establishing a vehicle ferry service across the Firth of Clyde, operating between purpose built terminals near Gourock and at the former steamer pier at Hunter's Quay on the Cowal Coast.

*Sound of Scarba, Sound of Shuna, Sound of Sanda (I),*

In June 1973 Western Ferries opened their Clyde car ferry service linking a new purpose built roll on - roll off terminal at McInroy's Point, three miles west of Caledonian MacBrayne's headquarters at Gourock Pier with Hunter's Quay, about 2 miles north of Dunoon Pier on the Cowal shore. Their intention was to service the route with drive through vessels operating on a point to point basis, substantially shortening the crossing time across the Firth of Clyde and thereby providing a more frequent service.

Initially, two double ended drive through vessels were placed in service, the *Ölandssund IV* (built in 1962) and *Ölandssund III*, (built in 1960) both having been purchased from Sweden where they had been employed on services between Revsudden and the island of Öland. The two vessels were renamed *Sound of Shuna* and *Sound of Scarba* respectively. On 3rd June 1973, the *Sound of Shuna* was the first vessel to take up service, being followed by her sister, *Sound of Scarba* on 14th July 1973. The "Shuna" was capable of carrying 27 cars whilst

*The Western Ferries double ended ferry* **Sound of Shuna** *is seen arriving at Hunter's Quay in July 1975. (Author's Collection)*

the "Scarba" had capacity for 22 cars and they combined to give a half hourly service on the "Clyde - Argyll Ferry", as the route quickly became known.

They were joined in August 1974 by the former Southern Railway and Sealink ferry *Lymington* which had operated on the Lymington - Yarmouth service and had been displaced by the arrival of new tonnage. Renamed *Sound of Sanda*, she was capable of carrying 17 cars. She was built in 1938 by Denny of Dumbarton and was thus the oldest and smallest of the trio. These three vessels provided substantial opposition to the longer Caledonian MacBrayne Gourock - Dunoon service whilst the "Shuna" also saw employment on freight runs to Portavadie in connection with the construction of the oil rig yard and she occasionally served Ardyne Point in a similar capacity. Although the Clyde - Argyll Ferry was to become a great success, it would be some years before the achievements of the three original vessels led to further developments at McInroy's Point.

*Sound of Seil, Sound of Sleat, Sound of Scalpay and Sound of Sanda (II)*

Western Ferries' operations on the Firth of Clyde underwent a management buyout in April 1985 to become Western Ferries (Clyde) Ltd. Growing traffic meant that new tonnage was required and another redundant Isle of Wight ferry, the *Freshwater*, built by Ailsa of Troon in 1959, came to the Clyde. Renamed the *Sound of Seil*, she entered service on 18th June 1986, rendering the *Sound of Sanda* surplus and available for charter work. In this capacity, the "Sanda" undertook sailings to the naval establishments at Coulport and Faslane but the arrival of yet another vessel in October 1988 meant that the "Sanda" became completely redundant at the end of 1989. She was sold in 1994 and was reduced to a hulk on Loch Etive during 1996. The new arrival had been built in 1961 at Hardinxveld in The Netherlands and was capable of carrying about 30 cars. This vessel

was the former Dutch ferry *De Hoorn* which had been employed between Maasluis and Rozenburg, on the New Waterway and she became a Clyde ferry on 12th October 1988, having been renamed *Sound of Sleat*. The fleet strength continued to increase and a further vessel was added on 7th July 1995 when the *Sound of Scalpay*, the former Amsterdam City Council ferry *Gemeentepont 23*, took up service in the Western Ferries fleet. Built in 1961 at Arnhem, this vessel can carry 34 cars and 220 passengers. Her arrival allowed the *Sound of Seil* to be laid up as a spare vessel prior to being sold out of the Western Ferries fleet in April 1996. She was towed from the Clyde in July 1996 to be demolished at Garston a year later.

In 1996, Western Ferries returned to The Netherlands and acquired *Gemeentepont 24*, which had operated for Amsterdam City Council from Centraal Station across the River Ijs. As a sister ship of the *Sound of Scalpay* she was ideal for the McInroy's Point - Hunter's Quay route and became the second *Sound of Sanda* four days before her entry into service on 5th August 1996. Of the original pair, the *Sound of Shuna* is now utilised only at peak periods and spends most of her time on standby at Kilmun whilst the *Sound of Scarba* has been laid up since the arrival of the second *Sound of Sanda*.

In addition to their normal duties, the Western Ferries vessels have been employed on some unusual duties since 1985. Evening cruises were operated to Carrick Castle and other Clyde beauty spots whilst regular charters to the US Navy were undertaken in connection with the servicing of the mother ship of the Polaris Submarine Base which was formerly moored in Holy Loch. In addition, one of the vessels is generally on hand to provide spectator facilities for the visits of the *Queen Elizabeth 2* or other well known cruise liners which are fast becoming regular events on the Clyde. On a day to day basis, Western Ferries have steadily built up their traffic on the route and are now the main carrier on the Gourock - Cowal services, claiming to carry 70% of all traffic bound for the Cowal peninsula.

*The Highland Seabird powers away from the North Pier at Oban on a grey day, 16th July 1980. (Author)*

## Highland Seabird

In 1976, the innovative Western Ferries took delivery of a type of craft more familiar in Norwegian waters than on Scotland's west coast. The *Highland Seabird* was a twin hulled passenger catamaran of aluminium construction, built by Westermœn Hydrofoils A/S of Mandal, Norway. Capable of cruising at 27 knots and carrying 160 passengers, the *Highland Seabird* took up a programme of excursion sailings to a variety of Clyde destinations for which task she was based at Rothesay. However, plans to operate her into the centre of Glasgow foundered at an early stage due to the tidal range on the river and to the potential for damage to the ship from the floating debris which is generally to be found on the upper reaches of the River Clyde. Nevertheless she managed to set a new Glasgow - Dunoon record journey time of 42 minutes and 38 seconds, prior to entering service.

Clearly, her speed was impressive and it was possible for her to reach several of the more remote ports of the Clyde within a single day. However, expensive fares and high operating overheads made her uneconomical, although she was popular with the travelling public. Western Ferries moved her to the West Highlands for the 1977 Summer season, where she offered day excursions from Oban and Fort William to far flung destinations such as Crinan, Iona and Loch Leven. In September 1977, Western Ferries purchased the "Seabird" outright from her builders whilst 1978 saw her extending her Oban excursion programme to include the Irish ports of Portrush and Moville. Between October 1977 and May 1978, she was chartered to Howard Doris Ltd and was based at Stromeferry to carry construction workers to the oil platform yard at Loch Kishorn. She carried 17,500 passengers during the summer of 1977 and her Oban sailings continued until 1980, but with the Portrush and Moville calls abandoned. In spite of her continued popularity, and having undertaken unique sailings to St. Kilda and Castlebay, her excursions became unprofitable due to increasing fuel costs and she was withdrawn at the end of that summer.

In March 1980, a trial period of service in the Solent led to Sealink placing orders for their two catamarans, *Our Lady Patricia* and *Our Lady Pamela* which entered service in 1986. In July 1981 proposals were devised by Government to withdraw the subsidised Caledonian MacBrayne vehicle ferry service and for Western Ferries' McInroy's Point service to become the sole vehicle link with Dunoon. A fast passenger service was to be provided from Gourock by the *Highland Seabird*. But the proposals were abandoned due largely to strong public criticism and concerns over the suitability of the *Highland Seabird* to operate in all weathers. Although Caledonian MacBrayne continued to operate their vehicle ferry service, they paid the penalty of a reduction in their subsidy to cover passenger fares only and restriction to an hourly frequency on their Gourock - Dunoon route. Early in 1982, the *Highland Seabird* sailed for the River Mersey, on charter to Merseyside Passenger Transport Authority in order to evaluate the potential for use of this type of craft on Mersey Ferry services. She repeated the exercise in the Thames during June and July 1982, paving the way for establishment of the short lived Thames Line riverbus service. Following a spell back on the Mersey late in the year, she was laid up on the Clyde until October 1984 when she spent some time on charter to the CIE at Galway, returning to the Clyde in December of that year. The *Highland Seabird* remained in the Western Ferries fleet until March 1985 when she was sold to Emeraude Ferries for their Channel Islands services as the *Trident 2*. She was sold out of that company's fleet in 1991 and operated for a local authority on the West Coast of France as the *Cap Suroit*. In 1997 she was renamed *Dumont D'Urville*.

*Western Ferries red hulled catamaran **Highland Seabird** is seen approaching Dunoon in June 1976* (Author's Collection)

# The West Highlands

*"We were becalmed exactly in the middle of the channel which separates Lewis from the mainland and the evening being remarkably fine and clear we could see distinctly the Isle of Skye, the Shant Isles (sic), the Lewis, and all that range of mountains in Ross-shire and Sutherland stretching from Torridon to Cape Wrath". James Hogg, the Ettrick Shepherd, on the Lewis ferry in 1803*

## "MACBRAYNE'S FOR THE HIGHLANDS"

So ran a well known advertising slogan, reflecting the dominant role of MacBrayne's in the transport network of the West Highlands throughout the early part of the 20th Century. In addition to their steamer services, the company operated local coach and road haulage services throughout the Highlands and Islands and between the area and the major cities. Although the services existed primarily to serve the needs of the islanders, the ships were also providers of pleasure for tourists and their reliability and punctuality continue to affect the very way of life throughout this wild and beautiful maritime region. The ongoing development and improvement of the shipping services is at the core of the economic and cultural resurgence which is now underway in the Highlands and Islands and the very survival of many communities has been, and remains, dependant upon the lifeline ferry services. Life in the Highlands and Islands has always been difficult. For centuries, the people of the region faced adversity through invasion, famine, conflict, depopulation and the despoliation of their land, in spite of the beauty of the landscape in which they lived. It is only in the last fifty years that the Highlands have been regarded by national government as anything other than "The Highland Problem" as it was formerly perceived from afar. Indeed, it is the Highlanders themselves who have done most to assert their rights to fair treatment at the hand of landowners, bureaucrats and politicians, generally in spite of rather than because of, the efforts of Government. And so it is no surprise to the visitor to find that this resilience in the face of adversity continues to drive the economic and cultural life of the Highlands today. In the 1960's, the establishment of the Highlands & Islands Development Board offered new hope that life might improve and that the sentiments of one Iona resident who famously begged Caledonian MacBrayne to take the island "out of the age of the coracle", would be achieved in all aspects of Highland life. Although the need to balance the pace of development with a unique environment and culture must be taken into account to ensure that appropriate policies are implemented, there is little doubt that the pace of change in the improvement of shipping services has done much in helping to address the economic and social problems which still challenge the area today.

Following the failure of the 1745 Jacobite Rising and the subsequent ravaging of the Gaelic culture, the task of reinventing the Highlands fell to authors such as the romantic novelist Sir Walter Scott. Through his writings, regarded nowadays as either the works of the finest Scottish author or dismissed as the scribbling of a kailyard Lowlander, Scott made the wider public aware of the beauties of the Highlands and created a more positive, if somewhat romanticised, view of Highland life. Other writers such as James Hogg, Dorothy Wordsworth, Dr. Samuel Johnson and Queen Victoria added to the growing public clamour for all things Highland and, even though poverty, despair and mass emigration were widespread, the impact of these writers remains strong today. For the modern visitor, the Highlands and Islands, now striving to become an economically diverse and culturally dynamic region, continue to offer

*Old and new meet at Kennacraig as a restored AEC Reliance MacBrayne bus waits by the **Isle of Arran** on 15th June 1996.* (Laurence J. MacDuff)

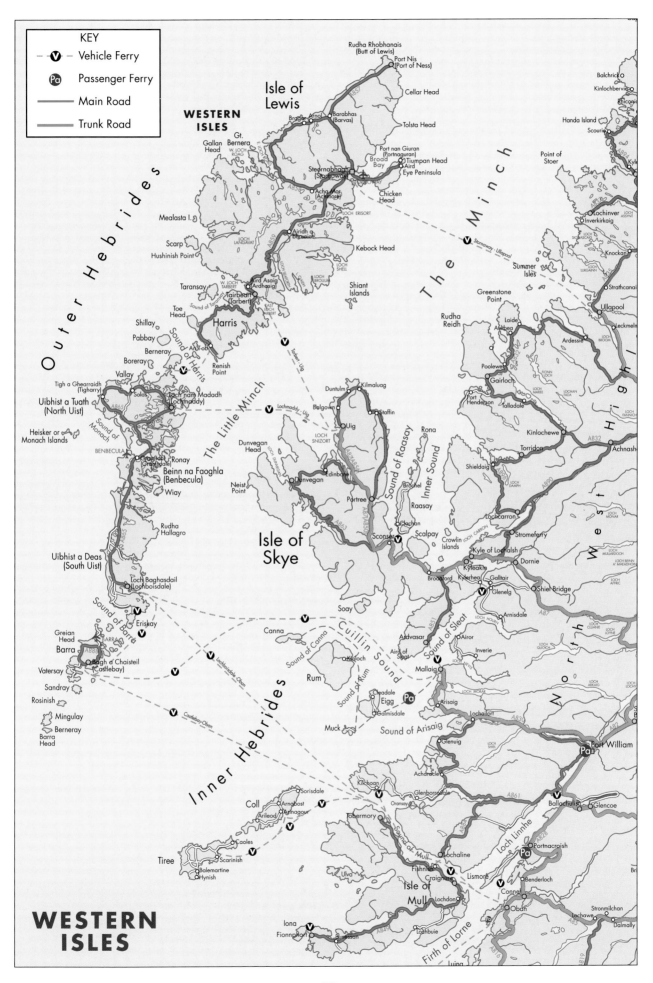

one of the most scenically attractive areas in Europe. The area has an intangible magic and a sharp spring day on the deck of the Stornoway ferry as she glides out of Loch Broom, below the mountains of Wester Ross is an experience that cannot be equalled, and because of their appeal, the Highlands and Islands, and the ships which have served them, have enthusiasts all over the world.

The earliest steamer services originated, as on the Clyde and everywhere else in Europe, with the *Comet* of 1812, which first appeared on the Glasgow - Crinan Canal - Fort William route, in 1819. She was wrecked on Craignish Point on 13th December 1820, but steamboats had arrived to stay, although the services developed through the early years of the 19th Century in a somewhat *ad hoc* manner with several companies operating on particular routes. Companies such as the Castle Steam Packet Co. and Messrs. G & J Burns operated the main steam packet services but it was David Hutcheson and David MacBrayne who inherited Burns' West Highland trade and established the forerunner of today's major ferry company, Caledonian MacBrayne.

The long history of Caledonian MacBrayne in the West Highland context began in 1851 when David and Alexander Hutcheson formed their company David Hutcheson & Co. with their partner David MacBrayne and began steamer services on the west coast. In 1876 David Hutcheson retired and MacBrayne continued for a further two years in partnership with Alexander Hutcheson. Between 1879 and 1902, MacBrayne operated the company in his own name but David MacBrayne Ltd. was not established until 1907 when, upon the old man's death, control of the company passed to his sons. MacBrayne had laid the foundations of the modern era. MacBraynes also operated on the Clyde - custodians of the Ardrishaig mail service which rejoiced in the title "The Royal Route" on account of a passage made by Queen Victoria in 1847, upon which she commented most favourably. The First World War saw the inevitable disruption to MacBrayne services whilst 1927 saw disaster as the company lost three fine steamers, the *Grenadier, Chevalier* and *Sheila*, in unhappy circumstances. 1928 witnessed the acquisition of 50% of the company's business by the London, Midland & Scottish Railway Company. The LMS also operated Clyde steamer services and their involvement in MacBraynes was a portent of the formation of Caledonian MacBrayne, still almost fifty years into the future. The 1930s saw the introduction of several fine new vessels which took over the main passenger and cargo services and maintained these services throughout the difficult years of World War 2 and beyond. These vessels, mainly diesel powered passenger and mail ships, together with the magnificent former Clyde turbine steamers *King George V* and *Saint Columba* became the mainstay of MacBrayne services for many years. The *Saint Columba* did not last beyond 1958 whilst the "George" and the other ships in the MacBrayne fleet were inherited by the Scottish Transport Group. On 1st January 1969, the shareholding of British Railways, acquired from the LMS in 1948 upon railway nationalisation, was acquired by the STG, to be followed by the shares of Coast Lines in July 1969. Thus, both the CSP and David MacBrayne became wholly owned nationalised organisations. This paved the way for the two fleets to work ever more closely together and the corporate cement was provided on 1st January 1973 when the CSP, renamed Caledonian MacBrayne, took over control of most of the MacBrayne shipping operations in the West Highlands.

As on the Clyde, great changes were soon to be afoot in West Highland waters. As vehicular traffic increased, the requirement for purpose built ferries had become ever more apparent, leading to the entry into service of the first true West Highland car ferries - the *Clansman, Columba* and *Hebrides* - in 1964. These fine vessels opened up new point to point car ferry routes which permitted easier access to and from many communities, some of which had previously been almost inaccessible by motor vehicle. However, the

*A deck view on board the **King George V** in the Firth of Clyde on 19th May 1973.* (Author)

process of modernisation stalled somewhat in the mid sixties, although there was no shortage of good ideas for new routes and vessels. Further ship construction was fuelled by the appearance on the Islay scene of Western Ferries Ltd. who placed two revolutionary vessels, the *Sound of Islay*, followed by the *Sound of Jura* on a new roll on - roll off route from their Argyll terminal at Kennacraig to Port Askaig on Islay. Spurred into action, the Scottish Transport Group responded and it was a combination of patronage, politics and the construction of new purpose built ferries which eventually saw off the Western Ferries competition. But the legacy of Western Ferries was a positive one, as they had provided the impetus which the STG needed to revolutionise shipping services throughout the West Highlands. Following the establishment of Caledonian MacBrayne, the West Highlands saw the ongoing introduction of new vessels throughout the seventies, eighties and nineties. As on the Clyde, long distance sailings were replaced by new, shorter, point to point services where service provision was more frequent than ever before. In parallel with the improvement of facilities for the carriage of motor vehicles, the last twenty years has also witnessed a vast improvement in passenger facilities and indeed, the *Isle of Mull* which became the regular Colonsay vessel in 1988, has sufficient capacity to carry all of the population and motor vehicles of that island and still leave room for more.

The ultimate development was the introduction of the *Isle of Lewis* in 1995, the largest and fastest vessel ever to serve in the West Highlands, contrasting sharply with the little *Sheila* which had been the regular Stornoway vessel seventy years before. The transformation of West Highland shipping services was complete. But the introduction of new vessels continues, with the *Clansman* recently delivered, whilst new ships, destined to serve a number of West Highland routes, are currently on the stocks. Through this investment programme, Caledonian MacBrayne are seeking to ensure that the residents of the islands now enjoy a far superior service than they have ever experienced. Granted, some of the romance of steam engines, teak decks and silver service dining room fare may be gone forever, but today's modern fleet is essential in safeguarding the fragile communities which are a feature of this wild and beautiful part of the world. And the sense of community, the ship borne use of the Gaelic language and the personalities of the crews themselves are as real today as they ever were. The period between the late sixties and the nineties was an era which witnessed the almost inevitable linkage with the Clyde fleet and the development of a fleet of ships which compares favourably with any similar operation anywhere in the world. What would the Ettrick Shepherd have made of it all?

## THE OLD STAGERS

As they had done on the Firth of Clyde, the Scottish Transport Group inherited a varied and interesting, if ageing, fleet of ships when it took over the operations of David MacBrayne Ltd. in the West Highlands. The company fleet included the veteran former Clyde turbine steamer *King George V*, which contrasted sharply with the modern, five year old car ferries, *Hebrides, Clansman* and *Columba*, which represented the epitome of car ferry design. Between these extremes, there existed a collection of 1930's and post war passenger, cargo and mail vessels, operating long routes with high costs, year round operation and low frequencies of service. Whilst many of these vessels were undoubtedly fine ships, the economics of such an operation were questionable. In addition, increasing public demand for the convenience of improved vehicular transport allied to the improvement of roads on the mainland and on the islands themselves meant that the old ships were rapidly becoming weak links in the communications network of the Highlands and Islands. As on the Firth of Clyde, the STG were determined to press rapidly onward with a modernisation programme and within a few years of their control being established, the West Highland shipping scene had changed beyond recognition.

In tandem with the development of a more modern fleet, there arose the need to construct new, purpose built terminals to service the developing point to point roll on - roll off ferry services. As a result, the last thirty years have seen many long established piers and harbours lose their direct steamer services whilst new terminals have been constructed, some of them seemingly in the middle of nowhere, to service car borne demand, whilst shortening the sea journey to the main islands. Piers such as Portree, Salen, Kyle of Lochalsh, Lochaline (West Pier) and most recently, Tobermory (Mishnish Pier) have all witnessed their last regular steamer calls whilst new terminals such as Sconser, Fishnish, Craignure, Uig and Kennacraig have all been developed, even though some lie several miles from the nearest substantial towns.

### King George V

This ever popular turbine steamer was built by Denny of Dumbarton in 1926 for the Clyde fleet of Turbine Steamers Ltd and undertook their long distance excursion sailings from Greenock (Princes Pier) to Inveraray and Campbeltown. She joined their fleet on 8th September 1926 and in Summer 1927 settled into her regular roster. A handsome ship, the *King George V* introduced new features to the Clyde fleet - an enclosed promenade deck and the fitting of large panoramic windows, features which would become standard in many subsequent passenger vessels. But her most novel feature was her machinery. Originally fitted with a unique high pressure Parsons steam turbine and Yarrow boiler system, the *King George V* achieved 20.78 knots on trials. However, problems with her machinery were frequent and the experimental boilers were replaced in February 1935 by a new Scotch boiler which operated at a lower steam pressure of 200 psi, whilst modifications were made to her turbines. In September 1935, the *King George V* and her Turbine Steamers fleetmate, the *Queen Alexandra* of 1912, were transferred to the fleet of David MacBrayne Ltd., the "Queen" becoming the three funnelled *Saint Columba*. Both she and the *King George V* adopted the red and black funnel colours of MacBraynes and the "George" was transferred to Oban from where she was to operate the company's popular summer excursion programme for most of the next 39 seasons. This sterling service was broken only by a break for wartime service during which period the *King George V* made five crossings to assist in the evacuation of the British Expeditionary Force from Dunkirk in June 1940. Her heroics over, she was subsequently based on the Clyde as a troop tender and in 1941 she carried Winston Churchill out to the battleship which would convey him to his historic "Atlantic Charter" meeting with President Roosevelt. Upon return to peacetime service, the *King George V* proudly took up her role as flagship of the MacBrayne fleet and undertook a variety of day excursions from Oban and Fort William including the "Sacred Isle" cruise to Iona and Staffa and sailings on

*The Veteran Monarch **King George V** seen approaching Gourock
(Harold Sinclair. Author's Collection)*

*In her penultimate season, the **King George V** is berthed at Inveraray with Duniquoich in the background on 19th May 1973.* (Author)

*Deck crew await the order to "Let Go" as the **King George V** prepares to depart from Tobermory on a sunny day in 1966.* (Terry Primrose)

the "Six Lochs Cruise" although these ceased in 1971, with additional Iona sailings being undertaken instead. Frequently, the *King George V* returned to the Clyde in spring and autumn to undertake charter work.

In this capacity she visited such diverse destinations as Bangor in Northern Ireland, on 16th May 1970, and her old haunts of Inveraray and the Arran coast. However, following creation of Caledonian MacBrayne in 1973, the future was never certain for the veteran turbine and 1974 was to be her last season in service. Her last sailing was to Loch Sunart and Tobermory on 15th September 1974 and although no announcement had been made by her owners, it was widely suspected that she had steamed out of Oban for the last time. In December 1974, Caledonian MacBrayne formally announced that she had been retired from service, her Oban cruise programme being modified to a series of "mini cruises" which were operated by the 1964 car ferry *Columba*. The *King George V* was sold in 1975 to Cardiff owners, Nationwide Transport Ltd and moved to South Wales where she lay in dry dock for several years. In 1981 she was sold to Bass Charrington for use as a replacement for the burnt

out former Clyde paddler *Old Caledonia* on the Thames. But on 26th August 1981, fire also claimed the *King George V* whilst she was undergoing conversion for her new role and she was finally broken up on the Cardiff foreshore in 1984, a sad end for a distinguished and historic vessel. She was the oldest ship ever to wear the Caledonian MacBrayne colours.

When the Scottish Transport Group took control of the David MacBrayne fleet in 1969, several ships remained in service which had been built as long ago as the 1930s, At that time, the company had been investing heavily in new vessels, thanks to the stake taken by Coast Lines Ltd in 1928 and the securing of new mail contracts. They were mainly diesel powered passenger and cargo vessels which had come to serve the West Highlands well in all weathers. But these fine ships were now somewhat elderly and were struggling to keep pace with new demands, especially for carriage of cars and commercial vehicles. Even with the introduction of the 1964 car ferries, the average age of the ships in the MacBrayne fleet remained at about twenty two years. Given the changes in car ownership patterns, the movement of freight to road transport and the STGs strategy of mov-

*Nearing the end of her long and prestigious career, the **King George V** is seen passing Dunollie as she leaves Oban in September 1974.* (Aikman Smith Collection)

ing towards point to point car ferry services, changes were urgently required and these ageing vessels required to be replaced. The result was that many of these fine old vessels were withdrawn within the space of only a few years as the former MacBrayne empire was catapulted into the age of the car ferry.

### Lochfyne

The 1960's found the *Lochfyne* still operating on the MacBrayne "Royal Route" passenger and mail sailing from Greenock to Tarbert and Ardrishaig, following in the great traditions of the paddle steamer *Columba* (1878) and the turbine steamer *Saint Columba* of 1912. But the *Lochfyne* had been built in 1931 by Denny of Dumbarton as a replacement for the paddle steamer *Fusilier* and she entered service on 8th June 1931, not on the Royal Route, but operating excursion sailings from Oban, visiting Fort William, Staffa and Iona. Her diesel electric machinery was revolutionary for her time, with a combination of Paxman diesel engines driving generators to supply power to electric motors which were linked to her propellers. This arrangement gave the *Lochfyne* a top speed of 16.5 knots although the machinery also created substantial vibration which was apparent on the passenger decks. Another unexpected by-product was a series of major breakdowns which plagued the *Lochfyne* throughout her early career, the most spectacular being on 25th July 1939 when her starboard engine exploded at Oban and brought her pre-war career to a premature end.

During World War 2, the *Lochfyne* operated on the Ardrishaig mail service, sailing from Wemyss Bay rather than from the Upper Firth piers, thanks to the anti submarine boom which stretched across the estuary between the Cloch Light and the Gantock Rocks throughout the Second World War. In post war years, the *Lochfyne*

returned to Oban and she underwent an engine transplant in March 1953 when the Paxman machinery was replaced by British Polar diesels which saw her safely through most of her remaining days. She again took up regular service on the Clyde on 22nd May 1959, operating in place of the *Saint Columba*. For most of the next ten years, the *Lochfyne* maintained the Tarbert and Ardrishaig mail service, although in October 1965 a fire in the port engine led to a seven month absence to effect repairs. The *Lochfyne* undertook her final sailing to Ardrishaig on 13th September 1969 and her last sailing of all took place on 30th September 1969 to Tarbert Loch Fyne, which was also the last ever sailing of a MacBrayne vessel on the Royal Route. The Tarbert service passed into the hands of the Caledonian Steam Packet Co. whose *Maid of Argyll* and *Maid of Skelmorlie* took over the service until the route finally closed on 29th May 1970. Meanwhile, the *Lochfyne,* having been sold in January 1970 to Northern Slipway Ltd. of Dublin, was used at Faslane as a floating generator and accommodation ship for nearly three years before being sold to Scottish & Newcastle Breweries in 1972. Hopes arose of a second career as a floating restaurant, renamed *Old Lochfyne*, but this was not to be and she eventually succumbed to the breakers torch in April 1974 at Arnott Young Shipbreakers, at Dalmuir. With her passing in 1969, the departure of the red funnel from the Clyde was lamented. However, it would not be absent for long.

### Lochnevis

Like the *Lochfyne*, the *Lochnevis* was a product of the Denny Shipyard of Dumbarton and she was, in many respects, a smaller and slower version of the *Lochfyne*, being capable of only 15 knots. Built in 1934, she also possessed diesel electric propulsion, although

*The Royal Route veteran Lochfyne leaves Rothesay in August 1967 on MacBraynes' Ardrishaig mail service.* (Harold Sinclair, Author's Collection)

*A busy scene at Rothesay in 1965 as the Lochfyne departs for Ardrishaig whilst the Duchess of Hamilton arrives from Gourock and the car ferry Bute loads for Wemyss Bay.* (Terry Primrose)

*The Lochfyne approaches Dunoon on an evening inbound run from Ardrishaig and Tarbert Loch Fyne.* (Harold Sinclair, Author's Collection)

she carried only a single funnel. By contrast to the *Lochfyne*, whose machinery generated much noise and vibration, the problem was largely eliminated on the *Lochnevis* due to the mounting of the machinery on sprung engine bed plates. In 1957, she was re-engined with Mirrlees National diesels which improved her speed slightly with no adverse effects on the relative absence of vibration. Launched on 15th May 1934, the *Lochnevis* took up service on the Mallaig - Kyle of Lochalsh - Portree mail service. She also operated cruises from Mallaig to Loch Scavaig and from Portree to Gairloch and Loch Torridon, to the heart of some of the most magnificent scenery in the Highlands. In early 1940, the *Lochnevis* saw service on the Ardrishaig mail run, but having been requisitioned for war service in December 1940, she operated as a minelayer under the name *HMS Lochnevis*. She returned to MacBrayne service in June 1944 and served Ardrishaig until November 1945. A good sea boat, she was well suited for all year round work on the Mallaig - Kyle of Lochalsh - Portree - Raasay mail service but with a reduction in traffic on this route, 1959 saw her transferred to Oban from where she maintained the Sound of Mull service to piers such as Salen, Lochaline and Tobermory. In addition, the *Lochnevis* operated the excursion programme vacated by the *Lochfyne* when that ship transferred to the Clyde in place of the *Saint Columba*. But the *Lochnevis* also saw Clyde service, when she annually relieved the *Lochfyne* on the Royal Route in winter. The *Lochnevis* also became an Islay mail steamer at peak periods in 1965 and 1966 where she assisted the *Lochiel* as the latter attempted to provide some sort of car ferry service to Islay. However, with the introduction of the *Columba* in 1964, on the new car ferry route between Oban and Craignure, passenger traffic for the *Lochnevis*, now the secondary Oban excursion vessel, dwindled and she became an early casualty of STG rationalisation. She made the last of her Six Lochs cruises on 25th September 1969, her last sailings of all being for livestock shipments in early October 1969. She was sold to Firma A.C. Slooten of Holland and left the Clyde on 23rd March 1970, arriving at Ijmuiden under her own power on 27th March 1970. She was eventually broken up in 1974.

### Lochiel

-

Built in 1939 by Denny of Dumbarton for MacBrayne's Islay mail service, the fourth ship to be named *Lochiel* spent part of her first season based at Oban before completion of an extension of the pier at West Loch Tarbert allowed her to take up service as the Islay mailboat. She succeeded the little paddle steamer *Pioneer* on the Islay services, replacing a famous name which would return in future years on a very different type of ship. Unlike on board the *Lochfyne* and *Lochnevis*, the engines of the *Lochiel* were of the direct coupled diesel variety, with no electrical transmission, but she could achieve a top speed of only 14 knots although she seldom broke twelve in normal service. She served both Port Ellen and Port Askaig, in addition to calling at Craighouse (Jura) and ferrying passengers and cargo ashore at the north end of Gigha, whilst on Port Askaig sailings, by using red boats as tenders. Alternatively, her Port Ellen services included a call at Gigha's island pier. In wartime, she saw her share of work as the Portree mail steamer and she also saw service on the Clyde, relieving the *Lochfyne* and *Lochnevis* in their respective roles. Post war, she returned to Islay and from 1949, the *Lochiel* also served Colonsay, extending her Port Askaig sailings. Misfortune struck her on October 8th 1960, when the *Lochiel* struck rocks and sunk at the mouth of West Loch Tarbert. Subsequently raised by the salvage vessel *Plantagenet*, she was out of service until the following March, being replaced by the *Lochearn*, which operated from Oban in her absence.

The *Lochiel* was responsible for providing MacBrayne's first, and somewhat rudimentary car ferry service to Islay, a task which required the support of the *Lochnevis* at peak periods. MacBrayne's

lack of a suitable car ferry for Islay was a weakness which was cruelly exposed by the arrival of Western Ferries' *Sound of Islay*. In January 1970, the *Lochiel* was replaced on the Islay service by the former CSP Clyde car ferry *Arran*, in a bid to provide greater car carrying capacity on the MacBrayne route, in competition to the direct threat posed by Western Ferries. The *Lochiel* was of little further use to the STG and was sold out of the MacBrayne fleet on 23rd March 1970.

By this time, the *Lochiel* was in dire need of a major engine overhaul and was fortunate in seeing further employment linking the Lancashire town of Fleetwood with Douglas, Isle of Man, as the *Norwest Laird*. However she was unsuitable for the service and provided competition to the Isle of Man Steam Packet Co. for only a short time during of the summer of 1970. She was laid up at Glasson Dock and was sold in 1974 to Courage Breweries for further use as a floating restaurant and bar at Bristol where she was renamed *Old Lochiel*. She fulfilled this role until 1994 and was sold for scrapping in November 1995 being broken up at Bristol in December of that year.

### Loch Seaforth

The largest of the older MacBrayne vessels acquired by the STG was the handsome passenger and mail ship *Loch Seaforth*. MacBraynes introduced this impressive ship into service on 6th December 1947, having ordered her from the yard of Denny of Dumbarton, to fulfil the 1938 Government mail contract. The regular beat of the *Loch Seaforth* was the overnight Stornoway mailboat service to Mallaig via Kyle of Lochalsh on which route she honoured the Sabbatarian tradition of the Western Isles by departing from Stornoway at fifteen minutes past midnight every Monday morning, to avoid breaking the Sabbath. In addition, she operated an infrequent crossing from Mallaig to Armadale between 1959 and 1963, for the carriage of cars.

She was acquired by the STG in 1969 but remained in the ownership of David MacBrayne Ltd, now an STG subsidiary company, who continued to operate the former MacBrayne cargo vessels together with the passenger/cargo ships, including both the *Claymore* and *Loch Seaforth*. On 22nd October 1971 she suffered a minor mishap, running aground on Longay Island in the Sound of Raasay, whilst outward bound from Kyle of Lochalsh. Although the *Loch Seaforth* was undamaged, this was but a foretaste of the disaster which was to befall her. Having taken up the services to Barra, South

*Early morning at Mallaig on 5th June 1964 as a trio of MacBrayne steamers await departure, the **Loch Seaforth** with the **Loch Arkaig** berthed alongside and the **Clansman** across the end of the pier.*
(Alasdair L. Munro)

*MacBrayne's for the Highlands is summed up in this view of the Lochnevis waiting to embark passengers and cargo at Port Ellen on 6th July 1969.* (Aikman Smith Collection)

*MacBrayne memories are rekindled in this fine view taken on a summer day in June 1969 with the **Lochiel** arriving at Port Askaig.* (Aikman Smith Collection)

*The first hints of Autumn gold touch the Highlands as the **Loch Seaforth** makes her way towards Kyle of Lochalsh whilst Glenelg - Kylerhea ferry passes astern of her on 17th September 1968.* (Alasdair L. Munro)

Uist, Coll and Tiree, she excelled herself on 22nd March 1973 when, inbound to Tiree from Lochboisdale and with the Chairman of the Scottish Transport Group and the General Manager of Caledonian MacBrayne aboard, she ran aground on the Cleit Rock in the Sound of Gunna, between Coll and Tiree. Passengers and crew abandoned the ship but the vessel was later re-boarded and successfully towed into Scarinish by the Clyde tug *Cruiser*. But she sank at the pier and posed an obstacle to navigation until salvaged on 14th May 1973 by the Dutch crane *Magnus III*. The ship was moved to nearby Gott Bay for temporary repairs and inspection. She was towed to Troon where the subsequent survey deemed her to be unworthy of reconstruction and she was scrapped by the end of June 1973, leaving the Tiree service in the hands of the *Claymore* which had been hastily reactivated at Greenock to cover for the lost ship. The loss of the *Loch Seaforth* is the only occasion on which an

STG or Caledonian MacBrayne ship has been written off whilst on passenger service.

### Lochnell

Built in 1941 as the hospital launch *Galen*, this 25 passenger vessel started her MacBrayne career on the Oban - Lismore service on 30th June 1947 and remained there for seventeen years. She became the regular vessel on the passenger service between Kyle of Lochalsh, Kylerhea and Toscaig from 1965 to 1968. She moved south and took up service between Tobermory and Mingary in May 1968, in succession to another small vessel, the *Lochbuie*, which was scrapped in that month. Sold out of the MacBrayne fleet in 1981 to Dumbarton owners, Strathclyde Cruisers, the *Lochnell* was subsequently used for *ad hoc* charters and a limited public cruise programme on the River Clyde. She subsequently passed to various owners and is no longer listed.

### Claymore (II)

As a requirement of the 1952 mail contract, MacBraynes placed a fine new ship into service on the Inner Isles mail service. Built by Denny's of Dumbarton in 1955, the second *Claymore* was the last purely passenger vessel to be built for David MacBrayne Ltd, and was also the last West Highland ship to be built by the famous Dumbarton shipyard. With a gross tonnage of 1024, the *Claymore* was capable of carrying 500 passengers with overnight accommodation for 56 people and she also carried freight which was loaded by derrick into her spacious hold. She was a fine vessel, although at 12.5 knots in service, she was a less than speedy ship. Nevertheless, she became a popular vessel on the Inner Isles mail services from Oban to Tobermory, Coll, Tiree, Castlebay and Lochboisdale, until her eventual withdrawal in 1976. Her internal fittings were of an extremely high standard and she was to be the last two class vessel in the MacBrayne fleet. Unlike most of her former MacBrayne fleetmates, she did not wear the colours of Caledonian MacBrayne Ltd. Instead, the *Claymore* remained, in 1973, in the ownership of David MacBrayne Ltd. and her fleetmates became the cargo vessels *Loch*

*The heaving line is ashore and final berthing manoeuvres are underway as the **Loch Seaforth** arrives at Stornoway on 16th June 1964.* (Aikman Smith Collection)

*The **Claymore** arrives at the Mishnish Pier on 23rd July 1970. Note the cars on the foredeck awaiting disembarkation by derrick.* (Aikman Smith Collection)

*Carron* and *Lochdunvegan* and the doomed Stornoway mail ship *Loch Seaforth,* which she replaced upon her stranding at Tiree. Although she was built a year after the first car ferries appeared on the Clyde, and hence well into the car ferry era, the *Claymore* had no provision for carriage of vehicles on a dedicated car deck. Instead, she used her derrick to hoist her 11 cars and 100 tons of cargo aboard in the time honoured fashion. In 1955, it was to be many years before the Outer Isles, Coll and Tiree received a dedicated car ferry service.

Between 1974 and 1976, the *Claymore* was used less frequently and spent much of her time laid up at Greenock. At the end of October 1975, having lain at Greenock for over a year, she began her final, brief period of service on the West Coast. Her last sailing was on 7th November 1975 from Colonsay to Oban following which she was declared redundant and was sold to Greek owners, Cycladic Cruises, in early 1976. The *Claymore* left for Greek waters on 28th April 1976, renamed the *City of Andros*. Subsequently renamed *City of Hydra* and substantially rebuilt, the Denny veteran was last known to be laid up at Piraeus. She is still fondly remembered on the West Coast, in many ways regarded as the last of the old fashioned MacBrayne passenger and mail boats and no ship seemed to sum up the phrase "MacBrayne's for the Highlands" quite as well as the *Claymore* did.

### Loch Toscaig

The converted fishing vessel *Irene Julia* was acquired by MacBrayne's in 1955 to operate between Toscaig and Kyle of Lochalsh, allowing the Stornoway mail vessel to abandon her ferry calls at nearby Applecross. From 1964 to 1971 the *Loch Toscaig* ran between Oban and Lismore. She was sold out of the STG fleet in November 1975 and sunk at her moorings at Gourock on 29th December 1978, finally being broken up on the beach there in September 1986.

### Loch Eynort

A ten year career in the MacBrayne fleet was in store for the former Irish pilot boat *Valonia* which became the *Loch Eynort* in 1961 and operated with passengers, cargo and mail on her regular service

between Portree, Raasay and Kyle of Lochalsh. However, she also appeared on a number of other passenger only routes and even operated on the Mallaig - Armadale route for a short time in 1970. She was laid up in the Gareloch in November 1970 before being sold to Brixham owners in 1971 who renamed her *Skellig*.

### Loch Arkaig

The predecessor to the *Lochmor* on the Small Isles services from Mallaig and the regular vessel on the Portree - Raasay - Kyle - Mallaig mail run until 1975, the *Loch Arkaig* had been built in 1942 by John Bolson of Poole as a wooden inshore minesweeper. She was refitted for her Western Isles role by James Lamont & Co. at Greenock and Timbacraft of Shandon and she was renamed *Loch Arkaig* on 14th April 1960 at Rosneath following which she took up the Portree service. She also fulfilled a role as an excursion ship,

*A gentle departure from Achnacroish on Lismore for the **Loch Eynort** on 17th October 1969.* (Aikman Smith Collection)

*The Loch Arkaig seems to be making a bid for freedom at Kyle of Lochalsh on 10th September 1968.* (Aikman Smith Collection)

operating from Portree to Raasay and from Mallaig to Loch Scavaig, with its magnificent view of the Cuillin of Skye. In 1965, following a season on the Small Isles service to Eigg, Rum and Canna, the Portree and Small Isles rosters were combined and it fell to the *Loch Arkaig* to handle these services, her duties now including calls at Muck. On 17th March 1975, the *Loch Arkaig* made her last calls on the Portree mail service which was abandoned due to the opening the next day of the more convenient Raasay car ferry service. But from 1977, the *Loch Arkaig* reintroduced calls at the Skye "capital" once per week, and introduced cruises from Kyle of Lochalsh to Loch Duich, and Eilean Donan Castle in addition to her Small Isles sailings. Throughout her career, she remained in the ownership of David MacBrayne Ltd, in the company of the *Loch Seaforth* and the *Claymore*. She sank in Mallaig Harbour on 28th March 1979 but was recovered and was sold to Spain, where her end came when she again sank in October 1985, whilst undergoing trials at Cadiz. For the three months between her sinking at Mallaig and the arrival of

the new *Lochmor*, services to the Small Isles were shared by the "Small Island" class ferry *Coll*, the *Arran* and the privately owned *Etive Shearwater*.

## MACBRAYNE'S RED BOATS

Where inadequate piers existed for berthing of large vessels, MacBrayne's had, for many years, maintained a fleet of small motor boats some of which sported red hulls. They inevitably became known as "red boats" and were provided for the purpose of tendering as the steamer hove to off the ferry slipway. It was commonplace for freight to be transferred to and from the red boat by the steamer's derrick whilst a ferry door was provided in the side of her hull where the red boat came alongside to transfer passengers. Gradually, the practice disappeared as improved piers were constructed, or road access to these small communities was improved, dispensing

*The motor boat **Applecross** operated between Tobermory and Mingary. She is seen arriving at Tobermory in May 1984 .(Harold Sinclair, Author's Collection)*

with the need for the steamer call. Elsewhere, the "Small Island" class vessels allowed the introduction of dedicated car ferry services to many of the isolated communities where tendering had formerly been employed. Several red boats were inherited by the STG and by the time of the establishment of Caledonian MacBrayne, the red boats *Iona, Ulva, Eigg, Tiger* and *Craignure* were still required to tender to passenger vessels, but generally only at Iona or at one of the Small Isles. In May 1975, the *Staffa* and the *Kildonan* were bought from Largs and Fort William owners respectively, the former to replace the *Tiger*, whilst the latter took up service at Eigg. By and large, these vessels became surplus to requirements as the general upgrading of routes and piers continued at pace.

However, even in the late nineties, the procedure is still essential at the Small Isles of Muck, Rum and Eigg, where no piers exist. The locally owned ferry boat *Wave* tenders at Muck, whilst the *Rhouma* continues to do the job at Rum. At Eigg, the *Ulva* is the last former MacBrayne "red boat" employed directly by Caledonian MacBrayne on such duties, tendering to the *Lochmor* as she goes about her business. Another boat, the *Dart Princess* was advertised for sale in 1995 and left the fleet in September 1996. The days of tendering are numbered, as the introduction of a new purpose built Small Isles ferry will soon consign the last red boats to the history books.

### Applecross

A number of red boats operated services to small communities. In 1964 MacBrayne's placed the launch *Highlander* on the Toscaig - Kyle of Lochalsh service under the name *Applecross*. She also operated cruises and undertook the mail service to Kylerhea, but her time on this route was short as she transferred to the Tobermory - Mingary passenger service in 1965. Soon, she joined the Iona flotilla and was sold to a Fionnphort owner in 1969. However, she was acquired once again by Caledonian MacBrayne for the Iona service in 1973 and from 1981, she again saw service at Tobermory. However, the arrival of the "Small Island" class vessels on the Mingary route in 1986 led to the *Applecross* being sold for further private use to Mr. Alisdair Gibson of Lochbuie, Isle of Mull.

### Lochshiel and Lochailort

These two red hulled launches provided passenger services between Glenfinnan and Acharacle on Loch Shiel, famous in history as the loch by whose shores Prince Charles Edward Stuart raised his Jacobite standard at the beginning of the 1745 Rebellion. The *Lochshiel* appeared in October 1953 and the *Lochailort* in June 1954. However, in June 1962 the *Lochshiel* was transferred to the Iona ferry fleet and the *Lochailort* sailed alone on Loch Shiel until the construction of the Lochailort to Kinlochmoidart road rendered her surplus to requirements. Tragedy overtook the *Lochshiel* on 28th April 1970 when she was sunk by an unknown vessel near Toward Point in the Clyde, whilst on her way to the Gareloch for overhaul. The *Lochailort*, having transferred to the Kyle of Lochalsh - Toscaig service in 1968, was found to be in poor condition and was scrapped by burning at Kyle of Lochalsh in 1969.

## MACBRAYNE CARGO SERVICES

For many years, MacBrayne's and their predecessors had operated cargo services to the Western Isles. These routes had been modernised during the post World War 2 era through the introduction

*The use of red boats or other small craft as tenders remained widespread in the sixties. In this view, a ferry has come out to meet the **Lochiel** off the north end of Gigha in 1967. (Harold Sinclair, Author's Collection)*

of purpose built cargo ships or the acquisition of appropriate second hand tonnage. Even by this time, road haulage was becoming the dominant mode of freight transport for many of the Highland communities which had hitherto been served by MacBrayne's cargo services. These services had operated from Glasgow to the principal ports in the Western Isles but their routes also took them to more remote ports such as Bruichladdich, Elgol, Aultbea, Gairloch, Lochinver, Leverburgh, Rodel, Stockinish and many other small island and mainland communities.

Traffic on the services declined as mainland roads improved and roll on - roll off passenger and vehicular ferries were gradually introduced. All the more surprising then, that in response to the requirements of the 1949 and 1952 mail contracts, MacBraynes constructed or acquired several cargo vessels, whilst at the same time, opening up some new road transport services with no apparent thought being given to provision of vehicular ferries. Several of these ships remained in operation in 1969 and were taken under the overall control of the STG, although their heavily subsidised operations continued to function under the aegis of David MacBrayne Ltd and the ships did not adopt the new Caledonian MacBrayne livery in 1973. However their days were numbered as most cargo transport was rapidly transferring to the road services operated by MacBrayne Haulage Ltd. or by private companies, utilising the rapidly developing ferry services of Caledonian MacBrayne themselves. MacBrayne's cargo services finally succumbed to these factors in 1976 and the *Loch Carron,* by this time the sole remaining cargo ship, operated the last cargo sailing in October that year. With the ending of her services, there disappeared a long established pattern of cargo sailings on the West Coast. With the passing of the cargo fleet, many "outsize" loads which could not be handled by the ferries were now handled by the ships of the Glenlight company, whose coasters, the successors of the "Clyde Puffers" became a familiar sight until their own demise in late 1994 following loss of Government subsidy. In 1969, however, several cargo vessels remained in service in the MacBrayne fleet.

### Lochdunvegan

In 1950, MacBraynes acquired the cargo vessel *Ornen* from Dutch owners and placed her on the Glasgow - Stornoway service, naming her *Lochdunvegan*. As built, her hull had been strengthened to allow her to withstand ice, and in 1951 she was fitted with refrigeration facilities for the carriage of fresh fish. She also carried four passengers on her somewhat leisurely rosters. But with the continued decline of cargo traffic, the *Lochdunvegan* was sold in 1973 to Greek owners and was renamed *Fanis*.

### Lochbroom

The longest serving MacBrayne cargo ship inherited by the STG was a standard "C" type coaster, the *Empire Maysong*, which was built by Scott & Sons of Bowling in 1946. She was purchased by MacBraynes in 1947 for service between Glasgow and Stornoway. But the *Lochbroom* saw little service for the STG and like the *Loch Ard*, she was sold to Greek owners and left for Piraeus on 14th August 1971, renamed *Fokomar*. She ran aground on Andros in September 1974.

### Loch Carron

The *Loch Carron* entered service on the Glasgow - Outer Islands cargo service in 1951 and was a modern cargo ship with a large hold forward of her superstructure and twin derricks capable of handling a maximum load of about seven tons. She could also carry 148 cattle and four passengers. She operated in consort with her

The MacBrayne cargo vessel **Loch Carron** unloads cargo on a still morning at Stornoway on 6th February 1975. (Alasdair L. Munro)

quasi sister *Loch Ard* from 1955 but the gradual transfer of freight from sea to road led to the slimming down of the fleet and the *Loch Carron* operated the last cargo service from Glasgow to Stornoway on 26th October 1976 returning to Glasgow on 7th November. She was subsequently sold in January 1977 to Cypriot owners and was delivered to them in May that year, becoming the *Georgis K* although she is believed to be still in service under the name *Ranada* and is registered in Honduras. Her departure brought to an end the long history of direct cargo sailings to the Western Isles from Glasgow.

### Loch Ard

A later version of the *Loch Carron*, this ship was built to meet the terms of the 1952 mail contract and she operated initially on the fortnightly cargo service to the Outer Isles from Glasgow. Her derricks could handle up to ten tons of cargo, a facility which would be required in support of the road and engineering works which were planned for the islands during the years following her introduction. She could also carry 130 cattle and a variety of deck cargo and had accommodation for four passengers. Although she entered service on the Outer Isles cargo service, 1964 saw her transfer to the Glasgow - Islay cargo run. But her time as an STG ship was short, the introduction of the *Arran* on the Islay car ferry route making her redundant. Between March and June 1970 she was chartered for service between Glasgow and Dublin and was eventually sold to Greek owners. She sailed for Piraeus on 27th April 1971, named *Holborn*. She was subsequently sold to Spanish operators as the *Candiera* and she sank in the Mediterranean on 7th May 1984 although she appears to have been salvaged and scrapped at Bilbao in 1985.

The cargo ship *Lochdunvegan* has arrived at Stornoway whilst the Iona lies at the other side of the pier on 8th June 1973. (Alasdair L. Munro)

# NEW CAR FERRIES FOR THE WEST HIGHLANDS

In 1964, three large, identical and very attractive sister ships were introduced by David MacBrayne Ltd. As a result of the passing of the Highlands and Islands Shipping Services Act in 1960, these impressive ships had been ordered by the Secretary of State for Scotland within an overall programme of developments which was intended to open up new vehicle ferry routes to the Western Isles and thus create social and economic benefits for these declining communities. This Act heralded the beginning of the car ferry revolution in the West Highlands as it made provision, not only for the construction of the three ships, but also for the upgrading of the associated terminal facilities at locations such as Uig, Tarbert, Lochaline and the construction of a new pier at Craignure, which would become the main gateway point for the island of Mull.

The three ships were built by Hall Russell & Co. of Aberdeen in 1964. At 2104 tons, they were the largest ships ever to enter MacBrayne service until that time. Powered by Crossley diesel engines, giving a service speed of 14 knots, they were each provided with a large vehicle hoist situated forward of the passenger accommodation which was provided on several decks. Like the Clyde car ferries of 1954, the hoist allowed the handling of cars at any suitable pier at all states of the tide. The new ships could carry 600 passengers and they boasted plenty of open deck space, together with overnight accommodation for 51 people. Coupled with the capacity to carry 50 cars on their watertight car decks, their facilities for vehicles and passengers were far superior to those of the 1954 Clyde car ferries and were even an improvement upon those of the *Glen Sannox*. Initially, they opened up three car ferry routes between Oban and Craignure (Mull), also serving Lochaline on a twice daily basis, Mallaig and Armadale (Skye) and between Uig (Skye), Tarbert (Harris) and Lochmaddy (North Uist). These new routes allowed the replacement of the elderly *Lochearn* and *Lochmor* and the withdrawal of cargo services to islands such as Iona, Scalpay and Eriskay where visits by the cargo steamer were replaced indirectly by road haulage services. During and after World War 2, causeways had been built linking North and South Uist and Benbecula, which allowed much of the traffic for these islands to utilise the new Uig - Tarbert - Lochmaddy ferry, allowing more convenient access to the mainland for islanders. The new ships also allowed coach tours to be operated to the islands on a much more frequent basis than had previously been the case. The potential economic benefit of the new ships was therefore substantial and they changed the pattern of communication in the islands. All three of the new ships bore the names of famous MacBrayne vessels of the past, names which, for some years after the passing of the 1964 ships from the fleet, were allowed to lapse into history but which may now be making a welcome come-back

Being owned by the Secretary of State for Scotland, the three new ships were registered at Leith, although they were operated on his behalf by MacBraynes. A more mysterious side of their design was the potential for military use. Built at the height of the Cold War, they were suitable for use as evacuation vessels, being capable of self containment in the event of the need to operate in conditions of nuclear fallout although the necessary equipment was later removed. The ships remained in the ownership of the Secretary of State until January 1973 when they passed to Caledonian MacBrayne and became registered at Glasgow, in common with all other fleet members.

## Hebrides

The *Hebrides* was the first ship of the 1964 trio to enter service, reviving a name previously bestowed upon the veteran McCallum steamer of 1898. She was the first purpose built car ferry ever to operate on the West Highland routes of David MacBrayne Ltd. and,

*The Hebrides rests at one of her regular ports of call, namely Tarbert on the Isle of Harris.* (Roy Pedersen)

*In her first year in service, the car ferry **Clansman** is seen departing from Mallaig for Armadale on Skye in June 1964. (Author's Collection)*

like her sisters, she passed into Caledonian MacBrayne ownership in 1973. Launched at Aberdeen on 20th November 1963 the *Hebrides* introduced vehicular ferry services to the Outer Isles on 15th April 1964, and on the same day the long established Outer Isles mail service from Kyle of Lochalsh, serving North Uist, South Uist, Harris and the Small Isles, ceased. The new *Hebrides* saw regular service on the Uig - Tarbert - Lochmaddy route on which she spent the majority of her career. However she frequently undertook relief sailings and from 1973, and the merging of Clyde and West Highland fleets, she saw occasional Clyde service on the Ardrossan - Brodick route. In 1981, she also saw service on the "Sacred Isle" cruise from Oban for a time, due to the absence of the *Columba*, but otherwise, Uig was her home port until she was replaced in 1985. Latterly her hoist loading mechanism had proved to be too slow for the rapidly developing vehicular traffic on the route and inevitably, her replacement was a drive through ship, the *Hebridean Isles*. Following her sale out of the Caledonian MacBrayne fleet, the *Hebrides* spent several summers operating between Torbay and the Channel Islands as the *Devoniun*, sporting a blue funnel and eventually a blue hull but oth-

erwise remaining largely unaltered, before being sold to Falcon Marine of Monrovia in 1994. Renamed *Illyria,* she commenced sailings in the Adriatic, between Bari in Italy and the Albanian port of Durres, during 1994. She remains in their ownership, now operating out of Kingston, on the island of St. Vincent in the Grenadines.

### Clansman (IV)

The *Clansman,* launched on 16th January 1964, was the second vessel of the 1964 trio to enter service and she inaugurated the Mallaig - Armadale car ferry service on 5th June 1964, replacing the *Lochmor* of 1930. The latter ship transferred to Oban to assist the *Lochearn* on the new Oban - Craignure service until the arrival on the scene of the third ferry, the *Columba*. The winter work of the *Clansman* consisted of relief sailings on the Stornoway mail service and on the Uig Triangle and Craignure services in place of her sisters. Uniquely, the *Clansman* visited the Thames in January 1969 when she served as a floating exhibition centre at Tower Pier as the centrepiece of the "Highland Fling" exhibition, attracting 40,000 visitors over a ten day period. In 1970 she sailed South again, but only as far as the Clyde and illustrated the growing linkages between Clyde and West Highland fleets when she donned the yellow funnel of the CSP Company and saw service on their Gourock - Dunoon Clyde service between 5th January and 29th May of that year, whilst the CSP awaited the arrival of the new ship then under construction at Troon, the *Iona*.

Alone amongst the three

*The old stager **Hebrides** backs away from the pier at Uig near the end of her West Highland career on 20th August 1984. (Author)*

*Following her conversion to become a drive through ferry, the same Clansman is seen on approach to Ardrossan on her regular crossing from Brodick.* (Roy Pedersen)

*The third ship of the trio, Columba makes a tight turn in Oban Bay on 4th April 1988.* (Author)

*In her new guise as a cruise ship, the **Hebridean Princess** (ex **Columba**) cuts a dash as she passes the Maiden Isle whilst outbound from Oban.* (Hebridean Princess Cruises Ltd.)

sisters, the *Clansman* underwent a major nine month modification programme between October 1972 and June 1973 to become a drive through vessel. The intention was that she would take over the newly opened Ullapool - Stornoway crossing but when she took up service on 29th June 1973 it was to be for only one year. With the arrival of the larger *Suilven* at Ullapool in August 1974, the *Clansman* found other employment. She appeared on the Oban - Craignure run between September 1974 and 28th October 1975, linkspan facilities having opened at the Mull terminal on 29th September 1974. Although her rebuild had left her under-powered, she had built up the traffic substantially in her short time at both Ullapool and Oban and the next phase of her career took her to another rapidly developing route. From 26th April 1976 she was employed mainly on the Ardrossan - Brodick service during the summer months, which she served faithfully until 1984, replacing the *Caledonia* and providing greater capacity on the route. She became familiar as the year round Arran boat, as consort to the *Caledonia* but winter months also saw her undertake relief work on the Lewis crossing. During several winters, the *Clansman* also saw service in more distant waters when she replaced the *St. Ola* on the Scrabster - Stromness route during the overhaul periods of the P&O ship.

But even the *Clansman* became unsuitable for the Arran route and with the introduction of the *Isle of Arran* in 1984, the *Clansman* was laid up. Her last day as a Caledonian MacBrayne ship was 17th March 1984 during which she suffered an engine breakdown and was replaced by the *Caledonia*. Sold for further service on 14th August 1984 to Torbay Seaways, she eventually found employment as a pilgrim ship in the Gulf of Aqaba, being re-named *Al-Hussein* and subsequently the *Al-Rasheed*, under which name she is still registered at Jeddah. The historic name *Clansman*, first bestowed upon a MacBrayne ship in 1855, was not to reappear for another fourteen years.

### Columba/Hebridean Princess

The third, and probably the best known, of the 1964 sisters bore a famous name, previously bestowed upon the renowned Royal Mail paddle steamer which sailed on MacBrayne's Royal Route from Glasgow and Greenock to Ardrishaig between 1878 and 1935. However, the new *Columba* spent almost her entire career as a West Highland car ferry and, like her sisters, she was built as a hoist loader. Initially employed on the new Oban - Craignure - Lochaline car ferry service, where she replaced the passenger ship *Lochearn* of 1930, the *Columba* took up service on 30th July 1964, signalling the completion of the overall package of developments envisaged under the Highlands and Islands Shipping Services Act. Generally regarded as the most important vessel in the MacBrayne fleet when built, the *Columba* made Oban her base but she also relieved for her sisters during overhaul periods. In this capacity, she saw service on the Stornoway mail service and subsequently, on the Ullapool - Stornoway route, replacing the *Iona* for a short time in 1973. During the summers of 1973 and 1974 the *Columba* was based at Mallaig from where she operated to Armadale and, in 1973 only, she undertook the overnight run to Barra and Lochboisdale. She returned to Oban upon the withdrawal of the *King George V* in 1974 and with effect from 1975 her duties included the Colonsay, Tiree and Coll services, which she combined with the Iona and Staffa "Sacred Isle" excursion, in a programme marketed as "Mini Cruises from Oban". Due to the introduction, in 1973, of the "back door" route to Mull between Fishnish and the new slipway at Lochaline, calls at Lochaline West Pier were no longer included in the Craignure roster but they continued to be undertaken as part of the Coll and Tiree sailings and the *Columba* also called at Tobermory when bound for these islands. In addition to her regular work, the *Columba* visited St. Kilda on two occasions, in May 1979 and again in May 1980,

*The Columba makes her only call at Tarbert Loch Fyne on 2nd April 1988 whilst on a special sailing.* (Author)

and she acted as a Royal Yacht, when she carried HRH The Prince of Wales from Stromeferry to the naming of the oil platform *Maureen* at the Howard Doris oil rig yard at Loch Kishorn on 12th May 1983. Having undertaken many special sailings during her career, the *Columba* continued on her regular duties until 1988, making her last "Sacred Isle" sailing on 22nd September of that year. On 1st October, bad weather meant the cancellation of her final sailing to Tiree, much to the disappointment of her supporters who had gathered to mark the event. Thus the 1964 veteran, having become an extremely popular ship, was sold out of the Caledonian MacBrayne fleet without public ceremony or acknowledgement of her final day in service.

But the story of the *Columba* did not end there. Happily, she took up a second West Highland career in 1989 having been converted for luxury cruising by a Skipton based concern, Hebridean Island Cruises Ltd. They identified the potential for the development of luxury cruising in Scottish waters which the former ferry now offered, carrying 49 passengers in her home waters as the *Hebridean Princess*. Based at Oban during the summer season she continues to offer passengers, or guests, a choice of 7 to 14 night cruises in the atmosphere of a country house hotel at sea and she has become the holder of the coveted Berlitz Five Star award for cruise ships. Her main itineraries find her visiting ports throughout the Western Isles, although she spends her winters laid up at Great Yarmouth. The ship has been substantially rebuilt over recent years and she has been internally transformed with the provision of luxury staterooms and magnificent public areas. She retains, perhaps more than ever, her "classic" traditional appearance as her hoist has been removed and the deck plating now allows a graceful sheer from bow to superstructure. Her black hull has been repainted dark blue and she carries a gold bead reminiscent of a royal yacht. The *Hebridean Princess* commenced her second career in 1989 and she introduced a demanding schedule which, from 1996 onwards, also included destinations much further afield such as Ireland, Orkney, Shetland and the Norwegian Fjords in addition to her Western Isles cruises. In April 1998 she was sold to the Greenock based Altnamara Shipping for £4 million although this did not affect her management or cruise itineraries. In her luxury cruise ship role, the former Craignure ferry is still a very welcome sight in her home waters.

### Scalpay (I)

Following the withdrawal of the Outer Isles mail steamer in April 1964 and the focusing of the Harris services on the car ferry service to Uig, services to Scalpay were entrusted to the first MacBrayne turntable ferry boat, the *Scalpay*, in 1965. Built for the Ballachulish Ferry Company by Noble's of Fraserburgh in 1957 as the *Maid of Glencoe*, she operated from a jetty at Kyles Scalpay and was replaced in 1971 being sold to Timbacraft of Shandon.

*Scalpay (II)*

Entering service in 1957, the *Scalpay* was originally the CSP's Skye Ferry *Lochalsh* and was built by Ailsa of Troon with capacity to carry six cars. She was a turntable ferry and was joined three years later by a sister ship, the *Kyleakin*. In 1971, upon arrival of the newest ship to bear the name *Lochalsh*, she was transferred to the MacBrayne fleet and wasrenamed *Scalpay*, being transferred to the Scalpay - Kyles Scalpay route. She was replaced on the service by the *Kilbrannan* in 1977 and was sold in 1979 to the Ardmaleish Boat Building Company of Rothesay who employed her as a barge in support of harbour works at Ardrossan and Ayr. The Scalpay - Kyles Scalpay route continued to be operated by one of the "Island" class ships until 16th December 1997 when the completion of the Scalpay Bridge meant that the service ceased to operate. The final crossing was made by the *Rhum*.

# THE WIND OF CHANGE BEGINS TO BLOW

In the mid 1960's, a division of labour which had prevailed for over a century was coming to its end. Most of the West Highland sea borne traffic was carried by the ships of MacBrayne's fleet of passenger and cargo ships and new car ferries. But most bulk cargoes bound for the islands were carried by the still sizeable fleet of small coasters or "puffers" which found their way into the jetties, quays, beaches and inlets of the west coast, where they could deliver their cargoes close to their customers' front door. Owned by two main companies, Hay, Hamilton Ltd. and Ross & Marshall, which merged in 1968 to form Glenlight Shipping Ltd, the puffer had evolved from a simple steam driven scow into a versatile motor coaster. However, in 1966, this time honoured, and rather cosy, division of traffic was rudely shattered when a small and seemingly insignificant vessel arrived on the scene. Resembling a landing craft, the *Isle of Gigha* may have been tiny in size but her impact was to be substantial in determining the future course of events. Part of the reason for the STG's rapid move towards establishment of roll on - roll off ferry services during the seventies was the dramatic demonstration by the *Isle of Gigha*, and then by her larger consorts the *Sound of Islay* and the *Sound of Jura* under the ownership of Western Ferries Ltd, established in July 1967, that the Norwegian model of basic terminals and unsophisticated ships offered more frequent and cheaper shipping services than those of MacBrayne's.

Following the construction of the 1964 car ferries, MacBrayne's proposed to serve Islay and Colonsay with another new purpose built ferry which would operate from a terminal at Redhouse on West Loch Tarbert. Meanwhile, local interests on Jura and Islay pressed for provision of an overland route which envisaged using Jura as a stepping stone. It took some time for the various options to be considered and prevarication ensued long enough to allow Western Ferries to move. A new ship, the *Sound of Islay*, was introduced on a roll on - roll off service between purpose built terminals at Kennacraig and at Port Askaig on Islay. Soon, passenger, freight and vehicular traffic warranted construction of a larger ship, the *Sound of Jura*. In November 1968, MacBrayne's finally ordered their own new ship but in the continued absence of the new pier at Redhouse, the *Iona* was introduced, not on Islay services, but on the Clyde. In an effort to respond to the arrival of Western Ferries, the STG drafted in the former Clyde ferry *Arran* on 19th January 1970, to compete with the new private sector operation, replacing the obsolete *Lochiel* which had failed miserably to compete with the newcomers. In November 1971, the Government announced that the STG's subsidy for operating the Islay services was to be withdrawn and given to Western Ferries and in response, the STG pro-

posed to withdraw their Islay services entirely, with effect from 31st March 1972. Faced with stiff competition from Western Ferries, and with the STG claiming that traffic levels were capable of supporting only one operator, moves were made to merge the two operations. But Western Ferries were bought by new owners who kept the company in existence as an independent operation which continued to take the fight to the STG.

Unwilling to lose the services of the state owned company, islanders hedged their bets and claimed that the *Sound of Jura* was not entirely suitable for operating the service alone. The outcome was that the *Arran* underwent substantial modifications between 30th December 1972 and 19th April 1973 to allow her to operate a new drive - on service between West Loch Tarbert and Port Ellen in competition to the *Sound of Jura*. Traffic was gradually clawed back and the STG played their master card with the introduction of the new *Pioneer* in 1974. Meanwhile, Western Ferries continued to operate their small but innovative fleet of Islay ferries and moved into the Clyde in 1973 by opening a new service from purpose built terminals between McInroy's Point and Hunter's Quay. The die was cast, the pace of change accelerated and soon the remaining elements of the old order would be swept away throughout the Highlands. But it would be the state backed Caledonian MacBrayne, rather than Western Ferries, which ushered in the new era. Their strength eventually saw off their upstart competitor, economics dictating that there was indeed, only enough room for one operator on the Islay services, and Western Ferries ended their interest in Islay in September 1981.

*Sound of Gigha*

In 1966 a new company, Eilean Sea Services, built a small landing craft type of vessel and named her *Isle of Gigha*. Employed mainly on transporting lorries and construction traffic on a charter basis, she could operate from simple slipways and beaches and demonstrated that roll on - roll off operations represented the future direction for ferry services on the West Coast. The *Isle of Gigha* capsized on 11th November 1966 but reappeared the following year on a variety of routes. She was purchased in 1969 by Western Ferries Ltd who renamed her *Sound of Gigha* and placed her on the five minute crossing between Port Askaig (Islay) and Feolin (Jura) across the Sound of Jura, where she commenced operations on 1st March 1969. She remained on the route until 15th July 1998 when the service passed into the control of Argyll and Bute Council who placed a new vessel, the *Eilean Dhiura*, on the crossing. Following the last sailing of the *Sound of Gigha*, she was sold to Irish owners based at Waterford.

*Western Ferries Sound of Gigha departs from Port Askaig on her short crossing to Feolin on Jura on 27th May 1996. (Author)*

*The red revolutionary **Sound of Islay** shares the pier at Campbeltown with the **Queen Mary II** as she loads for Red Bay, County Antrim on 5th June 1971.* (Robin B. Boyd)

### Sound of Islay

Two further innovative ships represented the future for West Highland shipping services. Western Ferries Ltd. was established by a group of businessmen, with a view to building on the potential which the *Isle of Gigha* represented. Built at Port Glasgow in 1968, their first ship, the *Sound of Islay,* pioneered Western Ferries' service between their new terminals at Kennacraig, in West Loch Tarbert and at Port Askaig on Islay.

The *Sound of Islay* was a unique vessel in West Coast terms. Her design owed more to Norwegian ship design, having relatively spartan accommodation for only 93 passengers and an open car deck for 20 vehicles and was able to operate from simple terminals on point to point routes. But by comparison to MacBrayne's elderly *Lochiel,* her main competitor, she was a vision of the future. With her owners now generating increasing levels of vehicular traffic, she quickly became a victim of her own success and was replaced in 1969 by the larger *Sound of Jura*, following which the *Sound of Islay* operated as a relief vessel at Islay. However, in 1970 she opened a new service between Campbeltown and Red Bay, in Northern Ireland, a service for which the vessel was not entirely suitable. The link was reduced to summer only operation in 1971 but even with this modification, the service was abandoned altogether in late 1973. The *Sound of Islay* then found charter work including a period undertaking the Portree and Small Isles mail services in October 1972 on charter to MacBraynes, her main competitor, before introducing a regular freight service on the Clyde, between McInroy's Point and the oil rig construction yard at Ardyne Point. She continued in this capacity until 1976 when she once again became the regular ship on the Islay route, replacing the *Sound of Jura* which had been sold due to falling traffic figures, following the introduction of a new and powerful competitor in the shape of Caledonian MacBrayne's *Pioneer*. But traffic continued to decline and the *Sound of Islay* operated only until 30th September 1981 when she handled the company's last ever crossing from Kennacraig to Islay. She was sold to Canadian interests, terminating Western Ferries connections between Islay and the mainland. Not a handsome ship, her legacy remains in the general layout of many subsequent, and better looking, Caledonian MacBrayne vessels and in the general move towards introduction of roll on - roll off services on a wider scale throughout the West Coast.

### Sound of Jura

The success of the *Sound of Islay* quickly led to the provision of a larger and faster vessel. The *Sound of Jura*, Western Ferries second new ship, was built in Norway by Hatlo Verksted A/S of Ulsteinvik and entered service on 1st August 1969, having visited Shetland and Orkney *en route* from Norway. Unlike the *Sound of Islay*, she had a bow visor and was therefore the first true drive through ferry in West Coast waters. She was provided with a greater car carrying capacity of 35 cars and offered improved passenger accommodation for 200, whilst her speed of 14 knots reduced the passage time to Islay to just two hours. The *Sound of Jura* consolidated Western Ferries' presence on the company's dedicated route to Port Askaig, and in 1970 she also initiated calls at Gigha. Western Ferries domination of the Islay routes was complete, whilst MacBrayne's mounting losses, accrued in spite of utilising the former Clyde car ferry *Arran* in place of the *Lochiel* and the cargo ship *Loch Ard,* led in 1972, to the threat of withdrawal of the STG services from West Loch Tarbert. This threat did not become reality but with the *Arran* converted to end loading at the end of that year, traffic began to flow in the STG's direction once again. The *Arran* was superseded on the Caledonian MacBrayne route by the new *Pioneer* and she began to challenge seriously the domination which Western Ferries had enjoyed. For the *Sound of Jura* the strong competition led to a reduction in Western Ferries' traffic and the ship was sold to Mexican Government interests in 1976 where she

*Western Ferries innovative ferry **Sound of Jura** awaits departure from Port Askaig on 19th April 1971.* (Robin B. Boyd)

*Wearing the yellow funnel of the CSP, the MacBrayne ferry **Iona** approaches Gourock whilst on charter operations on the Dunoon service in August 1970.* (Don Smith Collection)

was renamed *Quintana Roo*. Her replacement was her predecessor the *Sound of Islay*. The inevitable outcome was that Caledonian MacBrayne took over the former Western Ferries' terminal at Kennacraig and commenced operations from there in June 1978. In 1979, the larger *Iona* became the regular Caledonian MacBrayne vessel and Western Ferries were now seriously threatened by ships which offered the same convenience of service, but coupled it with superior capacity and passenger facilities. Although operating only to Port Ellen at first, sailings to Port Askaig were resumed in October 1979, utilising the *Iona*. The *Sound of Islay* continued to provide ever weakening opposition to Caledonian MacBrayne until her last crossing took place on 30th September 1981. The Western Ferries era at Kennacraig had ended.

## Iona

Ordered by MacBrayne's on 10th December 1968, it had been intended to operate the fourth dedicated West Highland car ferry on the Port Askaig and Colonsay routes and the introduction of the *Iona* was to be linked to the construction of the new pier at Redhouse, in response to MacBrayne's 1965 proposals for provision of a car ferry for Islay. But the political problems associated with the Islay services meant that the *Iona* took up service as a Firth of Clyde ferry. In some ways reminiscent of a larger *Sound of Jura*, she was a truly unique ship, being the first roll on - roll off vessel with drive through capability to be constructed by a Scottish shipyard for service on the Scottish West Coast. Between her introduction in 1970 and her

*As the regular ferry on the seasonal Mallaig - Armadale crossing, the **Iona** is seen leaving the Skye terminal on 4th June 1992.* (Author)

withdrawal at the end of October 1997 she had opened more new terminals and sailed on more routes than any other vessel in the Caledonian MacBrayne fleet. Indeed her history is synonymous with the conversion and upgrading of routes to drive through operation.

Her story begins at the Ailsa Shipyard at Troon in 1970, having been the last vessel ordered specifically by David MacBrayne Ltd, but the first to be completed by the Scottish Transport Group. With the construction of new drive through facilities delayed on the Islay routes and an urgent requirement for a vessel such as the *Iona* on the Upper Clyde, she entered service on 29th May 1970 wearing the yellow and black funnel colours of the Caledonian Steam Packet Company and not the red and black of her owners. Duly chartered to their STG partners, MacBrayne's *Iona* began her career on the Gourock - Dunoon route and on 26th July 1971, she opened the new linkspan terminals at these piers. Thus began a long process of developing, improving and integrating Clyde and West Highland ships and services under the auspices of a single fleet and the *Iona* was the harbinger of change. Eventually, the *Iona* moved north and on 4th April 1972, she made her first sailing to Islay, but from Oban rather than from the West Loch. But her time at Oban was short. On 1st May 1972, she began a two year spell as the regular vessel on the Mallaig - Kyle of Lochalsh - Stornoway service, prior to opening the new Ullapool - Stornoway roll on - roll off crossing on 26th March 1973. She built up traffic on this major new route in advance of the arrival of the converted *Clansman* and subsequently the *Suilven* in August 1974. On 15th October 1973 the *Iona* witnessed another first as she opened the Oban linkspan, and drive through facilities on the Oban - Castlebay - Lochboisdale station, although hoist loading was still required at Castlebay. In 1975, she lost her small dummy funnel as her exhaust uptakes were heightened and painted in the colours of Caledonian MacBrayne. The arrival of the new *Claymore* at Oban saw the *Iona* finally taking up the Islay services on 15th February 1979, but sailing from the former Western Ferries terminal at Kennacraig to where company services had transferred on 26th June 1978. Initially, the *Iona* sailed only to Port Ellen but, with effect from 24th October 1979, she also sailed to Port Askaig, reopening the Caledonian MacBrayne service which had lain dormant since 1972. Following a ten year attachment to Islay, the *Iona* was replaced at Kennacraig in May 1989 by the *Claymore* which had herself, been relieved at Oban by the new *Lord of the Isles*. The *Iona* became the regular ship on the summer only Mallaig - Armadale service where she opened the drive through facilities on 1st April 1994. Her employment on the seasonal Skye route also meant that she became available to undertake various winter duties.

A much travelled ship, the *Iona* has also been seen on relief duties at Brodick, Uig and Craignure and has undertaken charter

*Captain John Smith takes the* Iona, *bound for Stornoway, away from Kyle of Lochalsh for the last time on 24th March 1973.* (Alasdair L. Munro)

sailings to places as diverse as Tighnabruaich, Canna and Tarbert Loch Fyne and is the only vessel to have bow loaded at Wemyss Bay. She was generally a great success and wherever she operated, she developed traffic substantially. Her tenure on the Armadale route witnessed a 94% increase in car traffic and a 78% increase in passenger figures.

The introduction of the new *Clansman* in 1998 saw the *Lord of the Isles* taking over as the Mallaig - Armadale vessel with effect from July 1998. Surplus to requirements, the veteran *Iona* was sold in August 1997 and she made her last sailing from Armadale to Mallaig on the 25th of October 1997 following which she sailed to Orkney. She arrived at St. Margaret's Hope on 26th October 1997 and passed into the ownership of Pentland Ferries who renamed her *Pentalina B* with the intention of operating her on a passenger and car ferry service from Gill's Bay to Burwick or St. Margaret's Hope. Meanwhile on the West coast, Caledonian MacBrayne had run into problems when the *Isle of Lewis* suffered a major breakdown in April 1998. Without a backup vessel, the company resorted to chartering the *Pentalina B* and she again saw West Highland service on the Oban - Craignure run, between 28th April and 14th May 1998, sharing the route with the *Pioneer*. She returned to Orkney at the end of the charter and she has remained at St. Margaret's Hope since then.

By the end of 1972, some progress had been made by the STG in the West Highlands, although the Islay question was still the dominant issue. West Highland traffic growth had been healthier in 1972 than on the Clyde, with a 20% increase in vehicles and a 10% increase in passenger traffic although cargo business continued to decline. Nevertheless, 1973 dawned with the knowledge that the one time MacBrayne stronghold would now be ruled from Gourock and that the merging together of the West Highland fleet with that of the Clyde was about to become reality.

*Following repairs at Greenock, the* Iona *leaves the East India Harbour on 27th February 1987.* (Author)

# Unification

*"On a summer evening, when there is almost no night in northern latitudes, the sail across the Minch is an adventure into fairyland. It is also a voyage into history". James Shaw Grant, "Discovering Lewis & Harris", 1987.*

## NEW SHIPS FOR OLD

On January 1st 1973, the Firth of Clyde fleet of the Caledonian Steam Packet Co. Ltd. and the ships of the West Highland fleet of David MacBrayne Ltd. came under joint control with the company headquarters located at Gourock. The CSP was renamed Caledonian MacBrayne Ltd. and took over all passenger and vehicle services on the Clyde and in the West Highlands, except for eight vessels which continued to be owned by MacBraynes, now an STG subsidiary, and which received direct government subsidy for their services. All of the surviving former CSP Clyde vessels and all of the new fleets' West Highland ships donned the new corporate, and compromise, colour scheme of red and black funnels (MacBrayne) with a red lion mounted on a yellow background disc (CSP). All vessels were given black hulls and duck egg blue deck fittings. A new company house-flag was adopted, reflecting those of both of the former companies by having the Caledonian red lion rampant on a yellow ground superimposed as a disc on the familiar MacBrayne red and white double saltire on a dark blue ground. But this houseflag lasted for only a few years, the Lord Lyon, with whom the ultimate authority in Scottish heraldic matters rests, ruling that it clashed with the arms of the Wemyss family. A new pennant, based on the new company funnel colours, was unfurled on 2nd June 1980 and the now famil-iar colour scheme was completed by the addition of the company name to the ship's hulls with effect from 1984. Thus came into being a company which has now become a household name.

The establishment of Caledonian MacBrayne had an immediate impact upon the shipping services in the West Highlands. Virtually all of the passenger steamers and car ferries which were former MacBrayne vessels came under the direct control of the new organi-sation's Gourock headquarters and adopted the joint funnel and hull colour scheme whilst flying the new houseflag. Government inten-tions had been that the car and passenger ferry fleet should operate without direct Government subsidy whilst the remaining marginal routes continued to receive direct Scottish Office support. To this end, only the *Loch Seaforth*, *Claymore*, the two remaining cargo ves-sels, *Loch Carron* and *Lochdunvegan* and the small vessels *Loch Arkaig, Lochnell, Loch Toscaig* and *Scalpay* remained within the rump of the David MacBrayne fleet, although its vessels were managed by Caledonian MacBrayne. David MacBrayne Ltd. continued shoulder-ing the heavy loss making cargo services and ceased trading in 1980, although it remains registered as a dormant company. But it soon became apparent that provision of an unsubsidised service, even on the supposedly less marginal routes, could not be maintained and April 16th 1975 saw the reintroduction of subsidy for certain Caledonian MacBrayne lifeline services. On land, the dismember-ment of the old MacBrayne empire was rapidly implemented. The establishment of the STG, in 1969, had seen MacBraynes' buses transferred to Highland Omnibuses Ltd whilst 1973 saw MacBraynes road services being taken over by a new company, MacBrayne Haulage Ltd. Within months, the *Loch Seaforth*, following her grounding, was gone and the *Claymore* became the last of the old mail steamers. Within two years, two major new passenger and vehicle carrying vessels had been built for the West Highland ser-

vices whilst the conversion of other ships and the introduction of new routes meant that rapid progress was made in developing new drive through services. One of the new vessels, the *Pioneer*, was to be a significant factor in driving Western Ferries out of the scene whilst the other, the *Suilven*, would be the Company's largest vessel for many years to come. Overall, the scene was set for the cre-ation of what was to become the largest fleet on the British mer-chant shipping register, and one which would carry the mantle of the proud old fleets of the past into the future.

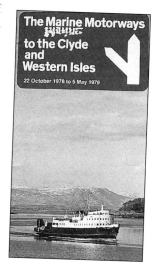

On the Firth of Clyde, the ships of the former CSP fleet appeared in the new livery throughout 1973 and 1974 at the same time as the new colours were being applied to the company's West Highland vessels. But on the Clyde, the first new ships to carry the colours were about to arrive. Their design reflected the dawn of the new era and indeed they would be the first major new vessels built specifically for the Clyde since the *Glen Sannox*, seventeen years pre-viously. The introduction of the *Arran, Bute* and *Cowal* had heralded an important change in the type of vessel which was to become prevalent on the West Coast. Their arrival indicated the imminent demise of the Clyde passenger steamer and its replacement by pur-pose built vehicular ferries of a type which would change forever the pattern of services on the West Coast.

Proposals had been under development for a number of years to provide further large vehicular ferries to serve the main Upper Clyde routes. When these vessels finally appeared on the Firth of Clyde, they were unlike anything ever seen before. Caledonian MacBrayne, in one of its early actions, broke new ground when they placed the new *Jupiter* and *Juno* into service on the Gourock - Dunoon route. Two large stern and side loading ferries, they would service the flag-ship route, providing a half hourly service at peak periods and utilis-ing the new terminals at the two piers. Their Voith Schneider propulsion system would allow them to negotiate piers in a way never before seen on the Clyde whilst their quick turn round capa-bility meant that loading and unloading could be accomplished much more quickly than by the older hoist loading method. Still in service, both are of approximately 850 gross tons and with a top speed of almost sixteen knots ahead and thirteen astern, they are also capable of proceeding at three knots sideways. Highly effective and reliable, and responsible for generating substantial upswings in traffic figures, they were joined three years later by the third ship of the type, the *Saturn*.

### Jupiter

The new ferries revived famous Clyde names which had been given to paddle steamers dating from as far back as the 1850's, the most recent being the *Jupiter* and *Juno* of 1937. The new *Jupiter* was introduced on the Dunoon route on 19th March 1974, followed by the almost identical *Juno* later in the year. Although the *Jupiter*

*Winter sunshine illuminates the* **Juno** *as she departs from Wemyss Bay on December 27th 1993.* (Author)

lacked the flying bridge carried by the *Juno*, she was fitted with one during her first overhaul in February 1975, making the two ships indistinguishable. Built by James Lamont & Co. of Port Glasgow, the *Jupiter* was capable of carrying 40 cars and up to 680 passengers and with Mirrlees Blackstone engines driving Voith-Schneider propulsion units, her manoeuvrability and turn around speed soon eclipsed the efforts of her predecessors and brought new standards of reliability to the route. In addition to operating on the Dunoon service she also undertook sailings to Kilcreggan on charter to the RNAD and to the McAlpine oil platform yard at Ardyne Point. In her first few years she also handled weekly gas tanker runs to Rothesay, sharing the roster with her sister. With the arrival of the *Saturn* and associated conversion of the Wemyss Bay - Rothesay service to roll on - roll off operation in 1978 the *Jupiter* also operated from Wemyss Bay. Politics intervened in 1981 when the Government

reviewed operations on the Dunoon service and appeared keen to provide subsidy to the rival operator Western Ferries Ltd, which would allow them to purchase a new vessel and to operate a passenger only service between Gourock and Dunoon utilising the catamaran *Highland Seabird*. These changes did not materialise but the possible withdrawal of the Caledonian MacBrayne service was of great concern to Cowal residents especially when a Monopolies and Mergers Commission report in 1983, suggested that all subsidies on the Cowal services should be ended, raising fears that the premature end of the *Jupiter* was nigh. Although subsidy arrangements were modified, these fears came to nothing and the *Jupiter* continued to sail.

Apart from providing her usual services, the *Jupiter* has undertaken sailings to more unusual destinations such as Blairmore, Loch Striven, Loch Goil and to the US Navy Holy Loch Base. In addition,

*By contrast, a summer day sees the* **Saturn** *manoeuvre into the car ferry berth at Rothesay on 13th August 1995.* (Author)

*The **Jupiter** leaves Gourock on a bright September morning on 11th September 1992. (Author)*

the *Jupiter* is permitted to visit Brodick and has sailed to the Arran "capital" on several occasions. She also handles her share of the summer excursion programme on the Clyde, visiting the Kyles of Bute and Tarbert Loch Fyne when engaged on these sailings.

### Juno

The second of the twins entered service on 2<sup>nd</sup> December 1974 and differed from the *Jupiter* by possessing a flying bridge which she carried from her first day. Like the *Jupiter*, she was built by James Lamont & Co. of Port Glasgow and was fitted with the Mirrlees Blackstone / Voith Schneider propulsion system. She worked hand in hand with her sister on the main Dunoon route and on the Kilcreggan RNAD services whilst also taking her share of the Rothesay gas tanker services. From 1977 she also saw occasional ser-

vice on the Wemyss Bay - Rothesay route in partnership with her sister and with the new *Saturn*. Nowadays, the *Juno* is interchangeable with her two consorts and in addition to her normal service runs, she has also visited a variety of locations on charter, such as Helensburgh, Loch Striven and Loch Goil and also shares the excursion sailings during the summer months.

As built, both the *Jupiter* and *Juno* carried "Gourock - Dunoon Ferry" titles on their hulls although these titles had been replaced by the company name by 1985. Their passenger accommodation was a great improvement on that of the 1954 car ferries, with passengers carried on three decks forward of their open vehicle decks. The ships carry large bipedal mainmasts which rise from their twin funnels which are set athwartships. Unlike the 1954 ships they have no hoists, fixed side and stern ramps being used in conjunction with the side loading terminals at the piers they serve.

*The **Jupiter** is seen as she approaches Gourock against a darkening sky on 31st August 1987. (Author)*

*Well loaded with vehicles, the **Juno** leaves Rothesay on 3rd August 1997.* (Author)

### Saturn

In response to continued growth in car borne traffic on the Wemyss Bay - Rothesay route, the *Cowal* was replaced by a third purpose built stern and side loading ferry, which accompanied construction of stern and side loading terminals at these piers respectively. On 2nd February 1978 the *Saturn*, built by the Ailsa shipyard at Troon, entered service. A new name in the Roman deity nomenclature style adopted by the former Glasgow and South Western Railway Company for their steamers of the 1890's, the *Saturn* was dedicated at first to the Wemyss Bay - Rothesay route. But from 1986 the three "streakers", as they became known, were interchangeable with all three serving on the Dunoon and Rothesay services whilst also undertaking the RNAD passenger runs from Gourock to Kilcreggan. Like her sisters, the *Saturn* has also been employed on Summer excursion sailings to destinations such as Tarbert Loch Fyne, Tighnabruaich and Millport. In addition, she visited Ardrishaig, on charter to the Clyde River Steamer Club on 29th

April 1978, soon after entering service. But like her elder sisters, her normal sphere of operation is confined to the more sheltered waters of the Upper Firth of Clyde and it was to her that the honour of re-opening the rebuilt Millport Old Pier fell on 4th April 1992, following its closure to larger vessels since 1990. In addition, the *Saturn* has visited Helensburgh and, like the *Jupiter*, she has been upriver to Glasgow, whilst 1st September 1990 saw her make the long journey, on charter, from Gourock to Inveraray. Her general layout is similar to the1974 vessels but she carries a tripod mainmast and does not possess a flying bridge, whilst passenger access to the forward end of the upper deck is permitted, by contrast to the *Jupiter* and *Juno*.

But time has begun to catch up on the "streakers" as they are affectionately known. With the rival Western Ferries service between McInroy's Point and Hunter's Quay now swallowing up to 70% of the Cowal traffic, consideration is being given to the options which are available for the replacement of the three ships. In 1997, Caledonian MacBrayne made a loss of £600,000 on the Dunoon service, with much of the blame placed on the inadequacies of the side loading arrangements at Dunoon. In its centenary year of 1998, Dunoon Pier suffered substantial damage at the hands of the winter weather and various options are now under consideration for the future of the Gourock - Dunoon service. Nevertheless, the *Jupiter*, *Juno* and *Saturn*, having been the mainstays of the Upper Clyde services for many years, have provided sterling service and effective replacements will be difficult to find.

The arrival of the trio of new vessels rendered the pioneer Clyde car ferries *Arran, Bute* and *Cowal* redundant and allowed the *Glen Sannox* to become the Caledonian MacBrayne Clyde Cruise vessel in the late seventies and early eighties, whilst operating in support of the three "streakers" at peak periods such as on Cowal Games Saturday in August of every year.

Meanwhile on the Islay routes, Caledonian MacBrayne had begun a state sponsored fightback against the ships of Western Ferries. With the converted *Arran* competing well to win back customers who had been attracted by the new ships of the private sector concern, the establishment of Caledonian MacBrayne allowed the STG to play their strongest, and most decisive, card in 1974.

*The **Saturn** creates a stir as she punches into the same Force 8 gale which wrecked the tanker **Braer** on the Shetland Islands on 5th January 1993.* (Author)

*Pioneer*

The *Pioneer* was the first large ferry to be built specifically for the West Highland services of Caledonian MacBrayne. Built at a cost of £1 million she could carry 30 cars and was fitted with Mirrlees Blackstone diesel engines, achieving 15.8 knots on trials. Although the *Pioneer* began life as a West Highland ship she has found herself a niche in recent years sailing on the Clyde in support of the three "streaker" vessels and has also been chosen to undertake various public and private charter sailings. Built in 1974 by the Robb Caledon shipyard at Leith, her design indicated that she was intended for the Islay services from West Loch Tarbert to Port Ellen and she entered service on this route, also serving Gigha, on 14th August 1974, in direct competition to Western Ferries' *Sound of Jura*. For handling cargo at Gigha, the *Pioneer* was fitted with two hydraulic cranes, each with a lifting capacity of 3.5 tons. The *Pioneer* continued the trend started by the *Arran* by attracting back much of the traffic which had been lost to Western Ferries, to the extent that the *Sound of Jura* was sold in 1976, Kennacraig became the mainland Caledonian MacBrayne terminal in June 1978 and the calls at Gigha were abandoned when the *Bruernish* began a dedicated service to that island in February 1979. All of this led to the ending of Western Ferries Islay services in September 1981 and the departure of the *Sound of Islay*. Credit for this success lies largely with the *Pioneer*, whose reward was to have her cranes removed and to be given a vehicle hoist by her builders, in early 1979. She was transferred to the Mallaig - Armadale route from 1st June 1979, in place of the *Bute,* being followed at Kennacraig by the *Iona*. In addition to her regular summer job at Mallaig, the *Pioneer* saw winter service on a

variety of company routes and has visited most of the piers and harbours on the West Coast. To increase her vehicle capacity to 32, the hoist was removed in July 1989, and the *Pioneer* made the Clyde her Summer home, being replaced at Mallaig by the *Iona*. She assisted the "streaker" ships on peak period ferry work and excursions although she continued to relieve in West Highland waters when required, generally being a spare vessel, particularly in Winter. But since April 25th 1994, she again found a regular niche, being employed on the two ship Rothesay service and providing a new Rothesay - Brodick link three times per week in summer until 1998 whilst on 29th September 1995, she made the last RNAD sailing to Kilcreggan. She has also visited some interesting places during her career, such as Fort William, Iona and Campbeltown whilst on 3rd June 1993 she visited Douglas, Isle of Man on a relief charter sailing from Gourock in support of the TT Races. She also paid a unique call to remote Douglas Pier in Loch Goil on 9th October 1989, whilst conveying HRH The Princess Royal.

The *Pioneer* remains a useful member of the Caledonian MacBrayne fleet although her role now consists mainly of Clyde and West Highland relief sailings throughout the year and Clyde ferry work in summer months. She has done it all.

*Suilven*

1974 saw the introduction into service of the largest vessel ever to take up service on the West Coast until that time. The new giant was the *Suilven,* bought by the STG whilst under construction at the Moss Rosenborg Vaerft A/S yard in Norway and she was appropriately modified to meet UK Department of Trade and Industry regu-

*With her hoist added, the **Pioneer** saw service on the Sound of Sleat crossing where she is seen underway on 13th August 1982. (Author)*

*The **Pioneer** turns to berth at Kennacraig on a murky day in October 1985 whilst serving on the Islay routes.*
(Author)

*Now a regular ferry on upper Firth of Clyde services, the **Pioneer** is seen approaching Wemyss Bay on 1st September 1994. (Author)*

lations. Named after the well known mountain in Sutherland, the *Suilven* was one of a pair of vessels, the other being completed as the *Bastø V* for service in Norwegian waters. Launched on 19th April 1974, the new Caledonian MacBrayne ship was capable of carrying 120 cars and 408 passengers and her Wichmann engines drove her at a speed of 15.8 knots. She towered over the other vessels in the fleet when she visited Gourock for the first time upon her delivery voyage on 19th August 1974. It was not long before she was displacing the converted drive through ferry *Clansman* and settling into the route which she was to make her own for over twenty years, namely the Ullapool - Stornoway crossing. In summer sun and in winter storms the *Suilven* became a vessel much loved and sometimes loathed by the Lewis community which she served. Apart from the period of her visits to the Clyde for her annual overhaul, the *Suilven* rarely left her native waters except for a short period between 9th and 15th October 1989 when she operated between Oban and Craignure, relieving the *Isle of Mull*. Otherwise, she was dedicated to the Lewis route and remained so until her replacement by the new *Isle of Lewis*, making her last crossing to Stornoway on 29th July 1995. Passing the new ship in the Minch *en route*, it was a new experience for the *Suilven*, the ship which had dwarfed all of the others, to be dwarfed herself, by Caledonian MacBrayne's new baby. Following her sale out of the Caledonian MacBrayne fleet, the *Suilven* was prepared at Troon for an epic journey to New Zealand via the Panama Canal during which she found herself embroiled in anti - nuclear demonstrations at Muroroa Atoll. She arrived at Wellington on 13th October 1995 and subsequently took up employment on services across the Cook Strait from Wellington to Picton, where, complete with blue funnel, she retains her original name and is operated by the Straits Shipping Company.

*The **Suilven** turns in Stornoway harbour prior to departing for her crossing of the Minch to Ullapool on 14th April 1993.* (Author)

## "SMALL ISLAND" CLASS CAR FERRIES

These bow loading car ferries resembled small landing craft and became a familiar sight all over the West Coast and further afield as they opened up new short routes, firstly in the Firth of Clyde and then in West Highland waters. More properly known as the Burnett - Corless class, they were put into service over a four year period between 1972 and 1976 and all were built by the shipyard of James Lamont & Son, Port Glasgow. Fitted with Bergius Kelvin diesel engines, driving them at 8 knots, all of the ships were capable of car-

*Once the largest vessel in the Caledonian MacBrayne fleet, the Norwegian built **Suilven** is seen arriving at Ullapool on 12th April 1993.* (Author)

rying 50 passengers, accommodated in a rather claustrophobic deck shelter situated aft of the open car deck, and up to six cars.

In many ways they represented the first tangible signs of the coming of Caledonian MacBrayne. Their design and construction was supervised by Caledonian MacBrayne Services, set up in February 1972 to co-ordinate the merger of the two companies and the new ships were registered in their ownership, although initially, the *Kilbrannan* carried CSP colours whilst the *Morvern* carried MacBrayne's red funnel. Intended to carry the names of Hebridean islands - *Bernera, Eriskay, Vatersay, Soay, Raasay* and *Staffa* - they gained the designation "Small Island Class" ferries even though only one of the names was available. In January 1973, Caledonian MacBrayne Ltd. became a reality and inherited all of the ships of the two fleets, including the first of what became known simply as the "Island Class" ships.

Based on the general layout of the *Coruisk*, the first ship to enter service was the *Kilbrannan*, followed by the second vessel *Morvern*, both of which could carry only 5 cars compared to the 6 car capacity of all subsequent vessels. New point to point short car ferry routes were opened up and developed by the Island class vessels between 1972 and 1994, including Lochranza - Claonaig, Oban - Lismore, Fionnphort - Iona, Fishnish - Lochaline, Tobermory - Kilchoan, Raasay - Sconser and Tarbert - Portavadie. Having closed for the 1996/97 winter, the last named is once again a year round service which also provides a link between Lochranza and Tarbert. Although certain vessels became associated with particular routes, these ferries were highly interchangeable and appeared on many services over the course of their careers.

### Kilbrannan

The *Kilbrannan* was the first ship of the class to enter service when she opened the Lochranza - Claonaig service on 8th July 1972. She saw service on the route for her first four years following which she became the regular vessel on the Scalpay - Kyles Scalpay route between 1977 and 1990. In 1990 she became spare but saw service on charter on the Burtonport - Aranmore service in County Donegal in summer 1991, becoming the first Caledonian MacBrayne vessel to operate outside of Scotland. The *Kilbrannan* was sold to Aranmore Island Ferry Services in 1992 and is now operating between Burtonport and Leabgarrow (Aran Mor) in County Donegal, Eire as the *Arainn Mhor*.

### Morvern

The second ferry of the class entered service in April 1973 at

The first "Small Island" class ferry, the **Kilbrannan**, is seen arriving at Largs soon after entering service in 1972. (Author's Collection)

*The **Raasay** makes a sweeping arrival at Sconser on 4th June 1992.* (Author)

Largs and sported full MacBrayne livery. She inaugurated the Fishnish - Lochaline service on 1st May 1973, replacing calls at Lochaline Pier by the Oban - Craignure ferry. In 1974 and 1975 she served Lismore and between 1976 and 1979 she spent time serving the oil rig yards at Portavadie and Ardyne Point. On 29th May 1979 she opened the Iona - Fionnphort car ferry service, but carrying residents vehicles only. From 1992 and the arrival of the *Loch Buie* at Iona, she became a spare vessel and also assisted at Eriskay and Berneray. In 1995 she followed the *Kilbrannan* to Ireland, for service between Burtonport and Aran Mor where she continues to operate in consort with her sister ship.

### Bruernish

When the *Bruernish* arrived in May 1973, she became the regular vessel on the Fishnish - Lochaline service, but for her next few years in service, she was something of a nomad. She served the Kishorn oil rig yard on charter until 1979 when she took up the Gigha service from Kennacraig, subsequently introducing the Tayinloan - Gigha service on 14th November 1980. Upon the transfer of the *Loch Ranza* to Gigha in 1992 the *Bruernish* again became spare and found herself undertaking a variety of tasks on charter which took her to exotic places in the Sound of Mull such as Calve Island, Rhubha na Gal Lighthouse and Ardlussa. She performed a sailing on 29th May 1995 to Ardveenish, with Western Isles Council officials on board, to evaluate potential for an Eriskay - Barra service in conjunction with a causeway to South Uist. On 16th December 1996 she became the Ballycastle - Rathlin ferry, becoming the first Caledonian MacBrayne vessel to carry cars to the island, before being relieved on 22nd April 1997 by the regular vessel *Canna*. Displaced once again, the *Bruernish* spent the summer of 1998 on the Oban - Lismore service and is now spare.

### Rhum

The *Rhum* appeared as the regular vessel on the Lochranza - Claonaig route in June 1973 and remained so until the arrival of the *Loch Ranza* in 1987. She became a spare vessel until 7th July 1994 when she opened the most recent new Clyde route between Tarbert Loch Fyne and Portavadie. After three seasons on Loch Fyne, she transferred to Scalpay and served the island until the opening of the Scalpay Bridge on 16th December 1997. On 18th January 1998, she and the *Coll* were laid up at Campbeltown, having been rendered redundant and both were sold on 14th April 1998 to Mr. Cornelius Bonner for Irish service.

*The Morvern, well loaded with tourists, is seen crossing the Sound of Iona on 3rd April 1988.* (Author)

### Coll

Taking up service in November 1973, the *Coll* first became associated with the Fishnish - Lochaline route but in 1977 she went on charter to Howard Doris to serve their Loch Kishorn oil rig construction yard. Between 1978 and 1986 she was used for general duties but on 12th May 1986 she took up the reprieved Tobermory - Kilchoan service, initially carrying passengers only, but conveying cars from 29th April 1991. Further service followed at Lismore from 1996 but the *Coll* was placed on the sale list and she was laid up at Campbeltown on 2nd February 1998, alongside the *Rhum*. Like her the *Coll* was sold to Mr. Cornelius Bonner on 14th April 1998 for Irish services.

### Eigg

The first duty of the *Eigg* when she took up service in February 1975 was to operate on the Portree - Raasay service in advance of the opening of the new terminal at Sconser. But the *Eigg* became associated with the Oban - Lismore service for most of her career. However, she saw a change of scene when she took over the Tobermory - Kilchoan summer service in 1996. Being the only Island class vessel with a Class IIA Certificate, she took up the arduous task of operating a limited car ferry service between Mallaig and Armadale in early 1998 when lack of spare ships and a major breakdown of the *Isle of Lewis* combined to create difficulties in finding suitable ships for the West Highland routes. Her summer employment in 1998 was on the Tobermory - Kilchoan service.

### Canna

Entering the fleet in January 1976, the *Canna* opened the long awaited Raasay - Sconser service on 16th April 1976, before moving to the Fishnish - Lochaline service which she made her own for ten years. In 1986 the *Isle of Cumbrae* appeared at Fishnish and relegated her to become a spare vessel, during which time she found a variety of tasks including relieving the *Eynhallow* in Orcadian waters. Between 1990 and 1997, the *Canna* became the regular vessel on the Scalpay - Kyles Scalpay service, relieving the *Kilbrannan*, before moving into Irish waters and becoming the dedicated ship on the new Caledonian MacBrayne link between Ballycastle and Rathlin on 22nd April 1997.

### Raasay

The eighth and final Small Island class vessel entered service on the Largs - Cumbrae Slip service on 30th April 1976 before moving north to take up the Raasay - Sconser service on 9th July of that year. The *Raasay* demonstrated the reliability of the "Island" ships as she never missed a full days sailing on the route as a result of either bad weather or mechanical failure. She spent virtually all of her career on this route but was replaced by the *Loch Striven* on 28th July 1997. The *Raasay* became spare vessel but she was mainly associated with the Tobermory - Kilchoan service in summer 1998 and became the Lismore ferry in 1999..

In addition to operating on their regular services, the "Island" class ships have appeared on charter work at some unusual destinations, including Bunessan, Girvan, Inverliever, Glensanda Quarry,

*The **Coll** is dwarfed by the **Lord of the Isles** as she backs away from the slipway at Oban, bound for Lismore, on 24th September 1997.*(Author)

and at the islands of Gunna, Fladda, Kerrera, Wee Cumbrae, Inchmarnock, Ailsa Craig, Calve Island, the Treshnish Isles and Eilean Shona, none of which figure in normal Caledonian MacBrayne schedules. All of the ships could pass through the Crinan Canal, a facility which made them capable of transferring easily between the Clyde and West Highland waters when weather conditions made the long journey round the Mull of Kintyre difficult for larger vessels. However, recent years saw them confined mainly to the West Highlands, thanks to the arrival of the first batch of "Loch" class ships on the Clyde in 1986

As a result of the introduction into service of the newer "Loch" class vessels and the reactivation of the *Loch Fyne* and the *Loch Dunvegan*, the bow loaders are now disappearing from the scene. Their success is illustrated by the fact that several routes, which may not otherwise exist, have developed rapidly. An example is the Tobermory - Kilchoan service. In 1983 this route was considered for closure but, instead, the introduction of an "Island" class vessel on the passenger service in 1986 and subsequent conversion to car ferry operation by the *Coll* in April 1991, has seen dramatic traffic growth. For 1994 and 1995, a year round service was provided although this experience indicated that traffic does not yet warrant a year round service, although a winter passenger service is provided by a local operator. The *Kilbrannan* and the *Morvern* departed from the fleet in the early nineties and from late 1997, Caledonian MacBrayne began to retire the remaining vessels. However, the class helped the Caledonian MacBrayne empire to expand beyond Scotland in 1997 when, on contract to the Northern Ireland Department of the Environment, the company entered the Irish

scene in their own right and placed the *Bruernish*, followed by the *Canna* into service between Ballycastle and Rathlin Island.

The introduction of the "Island" class ships into service allowed the completion of the STGs programme of point to point vehicle ferry services and meant the end of the longer coastwise services and of the MacBrayne cargo ships. Within a few short years, the pattern of services had been changed beyond recognition and the scene was now set for consolidation and further development of the services in response to increasing traffic levels, which were now showing growth in almost every year of operation.

*In its first year of operation, the Tarbert - Portavadie service was operated by the **Rhum** which is seen arriving at Tarbert on 3rd September 1995.* (Author)

# DOUBLE ENDERS AND DRIVE THROUGHS

The arrival of new ships of various shapes and sizes was relentless. Throughout the seventies and eighties a large number of vessels arrived in response to the need to provide new car ferry services and to service increasing demand on those services where the first car ferries had been introduced only ten or twenty years earlier.

### Isle of Cumbrae

With increasing demand for car ferry provision on the Largs - Cumbrae Slip service, generated by the success of the *Coruisk*, the *Largs* and the various ships of the Island class, a dedicated ferry was required. Built by the Ailsa Shipyard of Troon in 1977, the *Isle of Cumbrae* could carry 18 cars and 160 passengers and was a double ended vessel modelled largely on the two Skye ferries *Lochalsh* and *Kyleakin*. Her name was chosen by Millport schoolchildren and she entered service on 1st April 1977, serving almost continuously on the Cumbrae route until 1986. Displaced by the new "Loch" class vessels, *Loch Linnhe* and *Loch Striven*, she moved to the Fishnish - Lochaline route, taking up her new service on 4th August 1986. Her wheelhouse was painted in Caledonian MacBrayne livery during February 1987, similar to those of the new "Loch" class ferries. Although her main employment now saw her on the Sound of Mull crossing, the *Isle of Cumbrae* also saw service elsewhere in relief and has proven herself to be a useful vessel on a variety of tasks. However, thanks to the arrival of the *Loch Alainn* eleven years later, she retraced her steps to the Clyde where she took up service on July 26th 1997 on the Colintraive - Rhubodach crossing in the Kyles of Bute. Her stay was intended to be short, but plans to replace her

with the former Skye ferry *Loch Dunvegan* became protracted and the *Isle of Cumbrae* was still operating in the Kyles of Bute in Summer 1998. However, in 1999 the larger *Loch Dunvegan* took over the service from the *Isle of Cumbrae* which transferred to the Tarbert - Portavadie crossing.

### Claymore (III)

Launched on 31st August 1978, the third ship to bear the name *Claymore* was one of the last ships to be built by the long established Henry Robb shipyard at Leith. The last of all was Wightlinks' Portsmouth - Fishbourne ferry *St. Helen* which was launched on September 15th 1983. With her Mirrlees Blackstone engines giving her a speed of 15 knots, the *Claymore* was essentially an enlarged version of the *Pioneer* which had been built by the same yard five years earlier. But the newer ship was built with service to the Outer Hebrides in mind and as such, she was a substantial vessel of 1631 tons which was capable of carrying 47 cars and 500 passengers, with overnight accommodation for 32. Being fitted with a stern ramp, as well as a large vehicle hoist, the *Claymore* has turned out to be a versatile ship. She entered service on 3rd January 1979 and made the Oban - Castlebay - Lochboisdale service her own for ten years whilst in winter months she also served Coll and Tiree. Following the arrival of the new *Lord of the Isles* in 1989, the *Claymore* had her passenger accommodation upgraded and became the regular Islay ferry on 16th June 1989, being based at Kennacraig and replacing the *Iona*. Four years later, the *Claymore* was herself replaced by the *Isle of Arran* on the Islay station on 26th August 1993 and she became something of a nomad, finding employment on winter reliefs on the Clyde as well as in West Highland waters, and indeed she became a useful vessel for charter work on the Clyde during summer months. But between May 1994 and August 1996, the

*The much travelled* **Claymore** *is seen in earlier times arriving at Oban from the Outer Isles on 18th June 1988.* (Author)

*Wearing the colours of the Argyll & Antrim Steam Packet Company, the* **Claymore** *makes a fine sight as she sails up Campbeltown Loch on 21st September 1997, on arrival from Ballycastle.* (Laurence J. MacDuff)

*The robust Small Isles vessel* **Lochmor** *makes an early start from Mallaig on 11th August 1986.* (Author)

*Claymore* broke new ground by operating the joint Caledonian MacBrayne / Isle of Man Steam Packet service between Ardrossan and Douglas. This weekend link ran for several weeks throughout the summers of 1994 to 1996 but failed to attract substantial passenger numbers and the last return sailing was made on 11th August 1996. On 5th and 6th September 1995, the *Claymore* undertook special sailings from Llandudno in connection with the Morecambe Bay gas industry, becoming the first Caledonian MacBrayne vessel to visit Wales. Between 2nd and 6th July 1996 she became the first large Caledonian MacBrayne vessel to visit the Irish Republic. She acted as tender to the US Navy's aircraft carrier *U.S.S. John F. Kennedy* which had anchored off Dun Laoghaire whilst on a courtesy visit to the Irish capital, being too large to enter Dublin Harbour. The same year also saw the *Claymore* visit Heysham on 2nd and 9th June to undertake charter sailings for the Isle of Man Steam Packet Co. in connection with the TT Races.

But in late 1996, a new career beckoned for the much travelled *Claymore*. Caledonian MacBrayne, having been unsuccessful in their bid to operate the proposed Campbeltown - Ballycastle ferry service, were instructed by Michael Forsyth MP, Secretary of State for Scotland, to sell the *Claymore* to Sea Containers Ltd. and this company broke new ground the following summer by reviving the ancient sea link between Argyll and Ireland. On 1st July 1997, the *Claymore* opened the route between Ballycastle and Campbeltown on behalf of a SeaCon subsidiary, the Argyll & Antrim Steam Packet Company. For the task, the *Claymore* was repainted in that company's colour scheme and was given a £250,000 upgrading of her passenger accommodation. New terminals were built at Campbeltown and Ballycastle at a total cost of £8.5 million. However, the North Channel service remains a seasonal operation and the *Claymore* continues to operate as a relief vessel for Caledonian MacBrayne over the winter months, mainly on the Kennacraig - Islay routes. On 15th June 1998 the *Claymore* returned to the Irish link for her second season, although she again saw service for Caledonian MacBrayne during the following winter. She continues to operate the Ballycastle service in summer months.

### Lochmor

Built by the Ailsa Shipbuilding Company of Troon in 1979, the second *Lochmor* is a small and attractive passenger vessel capable of carrying 130 passengers and several tons of freight which is swung on board by means of a hydraulic crane situated aft on the vessels'

main deck. With a length of 102 feet and a gross tonnage of 189, her Volvo engines drive her at 10 knots in service. Uniquely in the fleet, the *Lochmor* does not normally carry cars and is the last West Highland ship not to do so. She was built specifically for service between Mallaig and the Small Isles, entering service on 18th July 1979 and was a direct replacement for the *Loch Arkaig*. On the Small Isles service, the presence of only one steamer pier, at Canna, means that passengers and freight are still handled at Eigg, Muck and Rum by means of the island's small tender (usually a MacBrayne "red boat" or a local ferry boat) and by the crane of the *Lochmor*. Because of her year round service in what can be wild waters, the *Lochmor* has small but snug passenger lounges. Deck space, although limited, provides excellent all round views from the landing platform which is carried above her wheelhouse. This was a necessary addition to allow passengers to board at Mallaig at any state of the tide but it became a useful vantage point which allowed passengers to view the magnificent scenery in the Sound of Sleat and Kylerhea when the ship performed excursion sailings to Kyle of Lochalsh. Until the summer of 1985, the *Lochmor* extended her cruises to Portree but between 1986 and 1994, her excursion programme was reduced to twice weekly sailings from Kyle of Lochalsh to Eilean Donan Castle and the Crowlin Islands. However, between 1994 and 1997, her summer programme included only a once weekly return sailing from Mallaig to Kyle as there was apparently insufficient demand for the attractive cruises from Kyle of Lochalsh. In advance of the 1998 summer, even the weekly sailing from Mallaig to Kyle of Lochalsh via the dramatic Kylerhea narrows was quietly dropped from the timetable.

In 1996, Caledonian MacBrayne began to consider a replacement for the *Lochmor*, assessing a number of options, including the provision of slipways on the islands and at Inverie in Knoydart, which could also be served by a ship capable of carrying vehicles, when required. Implementation of the project was dependant upon securing European funding and slow progress meant that the *Lochmor* remained in service operating throughout the year, the last example of the type of cargo, passenger and mail service which was once common in MacBrayne territory. However, the necessary funding has now been secured for construction of her replacement ship and for the new terminals.

Events on the Clyde were equally encouraging for Caledonian MacBrayne. Between 1976 and 1984 the Ardrossan - Brodick summer service was in the hands of the 1964 built vessel *Clansman*, whilst winter generally saw the return of the former Arran ferry

*Caledonia*. With her drive through facilities and large carrying capacity, the *Clansman* proved to be a more useful vessel for the busy summer service than the somewhat restricted *Caledonia*. However, with traffic continuing to increase throughout the year, a larger and faster vessel was required by the early eighties, to fulfil the needs of this important lifeline and tourist route. What was needed was a purpose built vessel, capable of meeting the requirements of the Arran route all year round, and with sufficient flexibility to be used on other services when required. In 1982 plans for the construction of this impressive vessel were finalised.

### Isle of Arran

The attractive light grey hull with which she was launched soon gave way to the traditional black and 15th April 1984 saw the entry into service of the *Isle of Arran* on the Ardrossan - Brodick route. At 3200 gross tons she was Caledonian MacBrayne's largest Clyde vessel until that time. The new ship replaced the *Clansman* of 1964 as the mainstay of the Arran service but she also found relief work on other sectors such as the Ullapool - Stornoway service. A product of the Ferguson Ailsa yard at Port Glasgow, the *Isle of Arran* could carry 800 passengers and 80 cars on her Class III Certificate for the Summer Arran service and her two Mirrlees Blackstone engines drove her at a service speed of about 15 knots. She brought new standards of comfort to the Arran route and was the first in a long line of Caledonian MacBrayne "mini liners" which were to be built over the next fourteen years and which would transform passenger standards on the West Coast as well as increasing vehicle capacity. As built, her black hull paint was carried up to promenade deck level but her first overhaul saw this dropped a deck lower, revealing a handsome ship with, for a car ferry, somewhat elegant lines. Even following her introduction, traffic levels on the Arran route continued to grow and following nine successful years, the *Isle of Arran*

was herself relieved in 1993 by the even larger *Caledonian Isles*. Thus displaced, the *Isle of Arran* entered a new phase in her career. With effect from 26th August 1993, she transferred to the Kennacraig - Islay routes, replacing the *Claymore*. On this roster, she also visited Oban in Summer, sailing via Colonsay from Kennacraig and Port Askaig, and providing an interesting day trip from the Kintyre port. This link continues today, with a single weekly return sailing from Kennacraig via Islay and Colonsay to Oban in summer months. In winter, relief work took her to a wide variety of destinations and in her first year away from the Clyde, she visited almost all of the piers used by Caledonian MacBrayne in the West Highlands. During her overhaul in March 1998, her black hull paint was altered again, to incorporate a "step" spoiling somewhat, her nicely balanced profile. Nevertheless, the *Isle of Arran* continues to serve Islay and also provides winter relief sailings elsewhere in the West Highlands, as well as returning to serve on her original Arran route. But overall, the one time Arran boat has become a true West Highland ship.

The success of the bow loading "Island" class ferries in developing traffic on the shorter point to point services led to increased traffic demand being met by the placing into service of a quartette of identical ships (the first since the "Maids"), offering greater vehicle capacity and far better passenger facilities than those of the "Island" class vessels. Having started their careers in Clyde service, the ships of the first batch of "Loch" class ferries are now found on a variety of routes throughout the Firth of Clyde and in the West Highlands.

In 1986 these four double ended ferries were placed into service on the Largs - Cumbrae Slip, Colintraive - Rhubodach and Lochranza - Claonaig routes. Following the successful introduction of the Tarbert - Portavadie service in July 1994, the "Island" class vessel *Rhum* was soon replaced by one of the "Lochs" as traffic grew rapidly. Capable of carrying 12 cars in two lanes, the "Lochs" replaced several of the "Island" class ferries which were transferred to other duties. All four were built by Richard Dunston's yard at

*The **Isle of Arran** makes a fine sight as she approaches Ardrossan in early morning sunshine on 14th September 1993.* (Author)

The *Isle of Arran* shows off her lines to advantage as she speeds up the Sound of Islay towards Port Askaig on 27th May 1996. (Author)

As a West Highland ferry, the *Isle of Arran* powers towards Oban upon arrival from Colonsay and Port Askaig on 24th September 1997. (Author)

Hessle on the River Humber and have passenger accommodation in the form of full length seated lounges on both sides of the vessel, providing capacity for 203 passengers. On one side stands the wheelhouse, painted in Caledonian MacBrayne colours. With Volvo Penta diesel engines powering Voith Schneider propulsion units, the ships are capable of a service speed of 9.5 knots.

### Loch Striven

The first of the four "Lochs" to be delivered started her career on the Largs - Cumbrae Slip service, taking up the route on 4th July 1986. Although this remained her principal task, she has seen service on a number of services, including Fishnish - Lochaline, Iona - Fionnphort and she has also undertaken runs from Largs to Brodick, carrying road tankers and other dangerous cargoes, during Autumn and Winter of 1994/95. It was the *Loch Striven* which opened the new Winter service between Portavadie, Tarbert, Claonaig and Lochranza on 7th November 1996. On 28th July 1997, her home port changed as she moved north to take over the Raasay - Sconser service, replacing the Island class vessel *Raasay* which became the winter boat on the route in 1997/98, before becoming spare.

### Loch Linnhe

The *Loch Linnhe* began her life on the Fishnish - Lochaline service, entering service, like the *Loch Striven*, on 4th July 1986. A month later the *Loch Linnhe* became second ship on the Largs - Cumbrae Slip service, operating in consort with her sister. Between 1986 and 1998 she remained on the Cumbrae service for most of the year but she regularly took over at Fishnish for some of the winter months. Like the *Loch Striven*, she has also been in action on other services such as the Oban - Lismore and Iona - Fionnphort crossings, whilst she also undertook her share of sailings on the

*The **Loch Linnhe** is seen approaching Largs on 9th August 1986 during her first season in service.* (Author)

Portavadie - Tarbert - Claonaig - Lochranza service, during the winters of 1995/96 and 1996/97. But with further "Loch" class vessels arriving on the scene, the *Loch Linnhe* transferred to the Tarbert - Portavadie service, where she took up summer service on 29th March 1998, whilst 1999 sees her operate on the Tobermory - Kilchoan service.

### Loch Riddon

The launch of the *Loch Riddon* was unexpectedly delayed when, following her naming on 19th August 1986, she refused to budge from the slipway, finally making contact with the water on 4th September. The third of the original ships, she eventually took up service in the Kyles of Bute on 7th November 1986 as the regular

*It is a sunny day off Largs as the **Loch Striven** sets off for Cumbrae Slip on her regular service on 12th May 1994.*(Author)

*The **Loch Riddon** is seen amidst the magnificent scenery of the beautiful Kyles of Bute awaiting departure from Rhubodach on the five minute crossing to Colintraive on 14th May 1994. (Author)*

ship on the 5 minute crossing between Colintraive and Rhubodach. She served on the route for eleven years until she was replaced by a succession of vessels, with the *Isle of Cumbrae* becoming main vessel until the arrival of the former Skye ferry *Loch Dunvegan*. Having spent most of her life in the Kyles of Bute, the *Loch Riddon* moved to the Ayrshire coast to become a regular vessel on the Largs - Cumbrae Slip service in late 1997, sharing the job with the *Loch Alainn* from May 1998.

### Loch Ranza

The final route taken over by the original Loch class ships was the Lochranza - Claonaig service which was handed over to the *Loch Ranza* on 16th April 1987, replacing the *Rhum* on the seasonal route. This allowed the *Loch Ranza* to take up a number of other services on the Clyde and at Fishnish, during the winter months. But with the arrival of the *Loch Tarbert* in July 1992, the *Loch Ranza* moved round the Mull of Kintyre to operate the Tayinloan - Gigha service, with effect from 26th September of that year. She remains

the mainstay of the Gigha service.

Like the "Island" class ferries, the "Loch" class vessels are extremely flexible. Their design was emulated and improved upon for subsequent vessels including the *Loch Tarbert* and the *Loch Buie*. All four of the original "Loch" class ferries remain in service at the time of writing and, as the arrival of the further "Loch" class vessels has testified, their general design has proven to be successful. Meanwhile, traffic growth on major West Highland routes was substantial and warranted the construction of major new vessels to service the ever increasing demand.

### Hebridean Isles

At the launch of the *Isle of Arran* in December 1983, the Secretary of State for Scotland, Mr. George Younger, announced the construction of a new ferry to serve on the West Highland "Uig Triangle" services. The new ship would replace the faithful *Hebrides* which had performed extremely well in building up traffic since she was introduced in 1964. The introduction into service of the new

*Autumn sunshine illuminates the **Hebridean Isles** as she leaves Tarbert, Harris on 13th October 1992. (Author)*

*Transport links 1990's style. A Skyeways bus awaits passengers from the Hebridean Isles at Uig on 5th June 1992. (Author)*

vessel on 5th December 1985 witnessed several firsts for the Caledonian MacBrayne fleet. The *Hebridean Isles* was the first ship to be built in England specifically for the company, the first to be launched by a member of the Royal Family, namely HRH The Duchess of Kent, and the first to be launched sideways, into the River Ouse at her builders yard, Cochrane of Selby, on 4th July 1985. At the time, she was the largest vessel to be built at the yard. She ran her trials in the North Sea before taking up service on the Stornoway - Ullapool route, following which she relieved on the Oban - Craignure service until 2nd May 1986. However, the *Hebridean Isles* was built as the main component in a package which saw the upgrading of the terminals at Uig, where work was not completed until January 1987, Lochmaddy and Tarbert, to permit drive through operation. On 9th May 1986 the new vessel took over as the regular ship on the route, replacing the elderly *Hebrides* which had left the Caledonian MacBrayne fleet late in the previous year and whose crew transferred to the new ship. With excellent facilities for her 507 passengers coupled with her drive through capacity for 68 cars and her speed of 15 knots made possible by her Mirrlees Blackstone diesels, the *Hebridean Isles'* was an instant success. She dramatically speeded up turnarounds and improved timekeeping and passenger satisfaction, leading to an upward spiral in levels of usage of the routes from Uig. For most of her career to date, the *Hebridean Isles* has remained closely associated with the Uig Triangle services, rarely deviating from these routes, except to relieve the *Suilven* early in her career. She also undertook an annual charity cruise to the Shiant Islands and on 17th November 1991, took part in a Coastguard emergency exercise in the Sound of Mull.

In 1996, the Tarbert-Lochmaddy leg of her itinerary was dropped upon the introduction of the *Loch Bhrusda* on the new Otternish - Leverburgh service and as a result the *Hebridean Isles* provided a more frequent service from Skye to North Uist and Harris than had been possible in the past. With traffic remaining healthy, plans are afoot to replace her with a ship similar to the new *Clansman*, whilst debate rumbles on regarding the suitability of Uig Pier as an all weather terminal. It is likely that changes are imminent at the North Skye terminal and they will undoubtedly affect the future employment of the *Hebridean Isles*.

### Isle of Mull

With traffic continuing to develop rapidly on the Oban - Craignure crossing it was announced on 14th April 1986, that a £6 million ferry would be built to serve both Craignure and Colonsay, replacing the *Caledonia* on the summer sailings and the *Glen Sannox* in Winter. In effect, by taking over the sailings to Colonsay, where the pier received a new linkspan terminal, the new ship also partially replaced the *Columba* on a route which had been the preserve of the 1964 veteran during the summer months. Launched at the Appledore Ferguson shipyard, Port Glasgow on 8th December 1987 and fitted out by Govan Shipbuilders, the *Isle of Mull* took up sailings between Oban and Craignure on 11th April 1988, whilst serving Colonsay from 7th December 1988. As built, she shared similar dimensions with the *Isle of Arran* and the *Hebridean Isles*, being 279 feet in length with a draught of 10 feet. The association with Mirrlees Blackstone continued and her engines drove her at a service speed of 15 knots. Upon her arrival at Oban on 8th April 1988, the new ship towered over the older vessels in the Caledonian

*Taking shape on the slipway at the Port Glasgow shipyard on 26th June 1987, ship number 572 is destined to become the Isle of Mull. (Author)*

The *Hebridean Isles* sets off from her base at the North Skye terminal at Uig on 11th October 1998. (Author)

Late sunshine catches the *Isle of Mull* as she arrives at Oban on a magnificent summer day, 24th September 1997. (Author)

*Slow astern for the **Lord of the Isles** as she glides away from the pier on departure from Tobermory on 15th April 1995.* (Author)

MacBrayne fleet. Superseding the *Suilven* as the company's largest ship, she introduced new standards of passenger comfort to the routes out of Oban. Capable of carrying 1000 passengers and 80 cars, her size, at 4300 tonnes, meant that substantial reconstruction work was required at Colonsay and an extension was required at the ferry berth at Oban Railway Pier. With one ship taking on such a workload, the revised Colonsay schedule also meant that the island would have its link with Islay restored for the first time since 1973. From 1989, the service was provided by the Islay vessel, initially the *Claymore*, linking Kennacraig, Port Askaig, Colonsay and Oban.

The first year in service for the *Isle of Mull* was record breaking in terms of the traffic carried on the Mull route but a significant problem soon arose. In February 1988, Caledonian MacBrayne announced that the ship had been constructed with a weighty problem - she was found to be 114 tonnes too heavy. Measures were taken to lighten the ship but the situation was permanently rectified only by insertion of a seventeen foot long section in the hull which increased her length to 296 feet and her gross tonnage to 4719. The work was carried out at Tees Dock in Middlesborough and the essential alterations to the ship and to the piers at Craignure, Oban, Castlebay, Lochboisdale and Colonsay were funded by British Shipbuilders. With the necessary modifications completed, December 6th 1988 saw the *Isle of Mull* back at work. Since then, in addition to serving her own routes from Oban, she has also deputised for the *Suilven* and subsequently the *Isle of Lewis*, on the Stornoway station and has also visited Castlebay, Uig, Coll, Tiree, Lochmaddy and Lochboisdale on relief sailings. However, her main routes remain those from Oban to Craignure and Colonsay where she provides an indispensable, reliable and comfortable service.

## Lord of the Isles

Another new vessel appeared hot on the heels of the 1988 Mull giant. The new ship was launched on 7th March 1989, also from the yard of Appledore Ferguson at Port Glasgow and, as the *Lord of the Isles,* she entered service on 22nd May 1989 on a gruelling schedule which incorporated all sailings from Oban to Barra and South Uist as well as to Tiree and Coll. In this capacity she effectively replaced two ships, the *Columba* on the Tiree and Coll services and the *Claymore* on the Outer Hebrides routes. The new ship had capacity for 506 passengers, with overnight accommodation for 36, whilst she can carry 56 cars. With a gross tonnage of 3504, her Mirrlees Blackstone engines drove her at 17 knots on trial, making her the

*The **Lord of the Isles** makes a splash on her launch at Port Glasgow on 7th March 1989.* (Author)

fastest ship in the fleet, essential if she was to maintain her arduous schedule. On 29th April 1991 the *Lord of the Isles* was heading north in the Sound of Mull when she was "buzzed" by a Royal Navy Buccaneer jet which came within 50 feet of the ship before taking evasive action. Roll on - roll off facilities finally came to Coll and Tiree through installation of linkspan terminals which the *Lord of the Isles* opened on 5th June and 29th June 1992, respectively. Like the *Columba* before her, the *Lord of the Isles* continued to call at Tobermory on the Tiree and Coll sailings but following the opening of the linkspans at Coll and Tiree, the Tobermory calls were made to set down or uplift passengers only. This was to ensure that vehicles did not have to be manoeuvred on the car deck to allow the hoist to be utilised and allowed substantial speeding up of her roster, much to the appreciation of the Coll and Tiree folk, although the loss of the Tobermory vehicle link was not greatly appreciated on Mull. The *Lord of the Isles* suffered a serious breakdown whilst off Ardnamurchan on 1st September 1992 which saw her replaced for almost a month by the *Isle of Mull* and the *Pioneer*. She repeated this trick nearly a year later, on August 28th 1993 and required a further month off service. But in spite of these early setbacks, the *Lord of the Isles* had become a useful member of the fleet and her presence ensured that traffic on the Barra, South Uist, Tiree and Coll routes grew substantially over the years. Indeed, growth was so impressive that her replacement appeared in July 1998, in the shape of the new *Clansman* and on 9th April 1998, it fell to the *Lord of the Isles* to make the final call of the Tiree boat at Tobermory, her successor being too large to berth at the Mishnish Pier. From 5th July 1998, the *Lord of the Isles* transferred to Mallaig to operate the seasonal Skye crossings to Armadale, in addition to serving Castlebay and Lochboisdale twice weekly, introducing non landing overnight "B&B Cruises" to the Outer Hebrides in the high summer. On the Armadale crossing, her speed has ensured that life is far easier than on her previous strenuous schedule, whilst her superior accommodation gives her higher marks by comparison to her predecessor, the *Iona*.

# OVER THE SEA TO SKYE

In 1897 Kyle of Lochalsh became the railhead of the Highland Railway Company's line from Inverness and the railway company took over the operation of the Kyleakin Ferry. The first car ferry, the *Kyle,* was placed on the crossing in 1918. By the end of World War Two, the Caledonian Steam Packet Company had inherited the operation of the ferry from its parent company, the London, Midland and Scottish Railway, successors to the Highland and owners of the Skye ferry from the time of the railway grouping in 1923. In July 1957, matters were simplified when the CSP took over direct control of the route from British Railways. Here, in the heart of MacBrayne territory, the Skye Ferry continued to be an outpost of CSP operation throughout the late 1950's, 60's and early 70's. Upon the establishment of the STG in 1969, the crossing was in the hands of the small ferries *Lochalsh, Kyleakin, Portree, Broadford* and *Coruisk* but they soon found other employment upon the arrival of the double ended ferries *Lochalsh* and *Kyleakin*. The route came under the auspices of Caledonian MacBrayne in 1973 and car borne traffic increased steadily. The final 26 years of the history of the route saw a dramatic upsurge in traffic, forcing the Caledonian Steam Packet Co. and subsequently Caledonian MacBrayne to provide larger vessels and more frequent sailings, eventually on a 24 hour basis. This spectacular growth warranted the placing into service of two vessels, the *Loch Fyne* and *Loch Dunvegan*, which became the largest double ended ferries ever to sail on the West Coast. All of this ended with the opening of the long proposed Skye Bridge on 16th October 1995, and a distinguished history came to an end.

*The Skye ferry* **Lochalsh** *leaving Kyle of Lochalsh with white wheelhouse on 16th August 1983.* (Author)

### Lochalsh (III) and Kyleakin (III)

An early indication of the commitment of the STG to improving car ferry services to Skye was the building of these large double ended ferries by the Newport Shipbuilding & Engineering Company, Gwent, in 1969 for service on the Kyleakin - Kyle of Lochalsh Skye Ferry service. The *Kyleakin* took up service on 14th August 1970, followed by the *Lochalsh* on 31st March 1971. The two ferries boasted substantial capacity for 200 passengers and 28 cars and virtually eliminated traffic queues which sometimes extended for four hours at each side of the crossing. With a speed of 8 knots, both ships were powered by Gardner engines and Voith - Schneider propulsion units. Although deep in MacBrayne territory, the two ferries were originally CSP owned although they passed to Caledonian MacBrayne control in 1973. Built with white wheelhouses they were given Caledonian MacBrayne liveried wheelhouses during their overhauls early in 1987. Essentially identical twins, they were easily distinguishable as the *Lochalsh* sported large tetrapod masts at each end whilst the *Kyleakin* sprouted only a single navigational light support from her wheelhouse. Ever increasing traffic on the crossing led to the introduction of 24 hour operation on 28th April 1991 and the introduction of new ships. The *Lochalsh* was displaced on 27th May 1991 upon the arrival of the larger *Loch Dunvegan* whilst the *Kyleakin* was replaced by the new *Loch Fyne* on 12th September 1991. Both vessels were sold to Ireland for service on the Carrigaloe - Glenbrook service in County Cork, the *Lochalsh* being renamed *Glenbrook* and the *Kyleakin* becoming *Carrigaloe*, where they were eminently suited for this passage, the crossing time being 4 minutes - one minute shorter than the Skye ferry link.

*The mast arrangement of the* **Kyleakin** *was simpler than that of her sister. She is seen at Kyle of Lochalsh in August 1990 sporting her red wheelhouse.* (Author)

*The Loch Dunvegan is seen approaching Kyle of Lochalsh in October 1991 soon after her entry into service. The scenery beyond remained unsullied by the bridge which was then at the planning stage.* (Author)

### Loch Dunvegan and Loch Fyne

These two large double ended ferries entered service on 13th May 1991 and 2nd August 1991 respectively, having been built by Ferguson Shipbuilders of Port Glasgow for service on the Kyleakin - Kyle of Lochalsh Skye Ferry service. With a gross tonnage of 549 and powered by twin Volvo engines and Voith units, each ferry is capable of carrying 250 passengers and 36 cars in four lanes and has a service speed of 9 knots. Although they were the largest vessels ever to serve on the 5 minute crossing, their days at Kyle of Lochalsh were numbered from the outset as the construction of the long planned Skye Bridge was approved in November 1989, even before the ferries had been ordered in February 1990. Thus the vessels were built with alternative usage in mind but in reality they served only on the Skye route. However, they are now utilised on services elsewhere in the Caledonian MacBrayne empire. The opening of the Skye Bridge took place on 16th October 1995 and it was left to the *Loch Fyne* to have the honour of being the last Caledonian MacBrayne ferry ever to cross the narrows of the Kyle of Lochalsh. On arrival at Kyle, she disembarked four historic MacBrayne buses and, amidst much festivity, brought to an end the history of Caledonian MacBrayne and CSP operation on this long established ferry crossing. The two sisters retired to Greenock and were advertised for sale. Both vessels were thought to have been sold for further service overseas in August 1997 but the sales fell through and they remained at Greenock awaiting their fate. Their careers then took an interesting twist. The *Loch Dunvegan* saw further Caledonian MacBrayne service when she was revived from her slumbers and rushed to Fishnish to replace the stricken *Loch Alainn* in August 1997. On 27th September 1997, the *Loch Fyne* also made an unexpected return to service when she replaced the *Loch Dunvegan* which had herself been struck down by mechanical gremlins. It may have been fortuitous and coincidental, but the two sisters performed well in spite of being a little rusty and they were duly reprieved, the *Loch Fyne* remaining in the Caledonian MacBrayne fleet on the Fishnish - Lochaline service in place of the mechanically challenged *Loch Alainn* whilst the *Loch Dunvegan,* having helped out on the Mallaig - Armadale route in emergency, was used as a spare vessel in summer 1998. A useful pair of ships, the *Loch Dunvegan* even operated some passenger only sailings on the Wemyss Bay - Rothesay service in the absence of the *Pioneer* early in 1998 and she is now in service on the Colintraive crossing. Further north, with the closure of the Skye Ferry service, the slipway at Kyle of Lochalsh was converted to a car park, making it unlikely that any of the local proposals for continuation of the car ferry service would come to fruition.

## INTO THE NINETIES

*"CalMac boats today are large, fast and beautifully fitted. We of the west have been spoiled over the past decade with much improved service - even the food, these days, is wondrous". John Macleod, "The Herald" October 6th 1998.*

With the coming of the new decade, Caledonian MacBrayne faced its imminent divorce from the Scottish Transport Group in good heart. On January 27th 1988, the Secretary of State for Scotland, Malcolm Rifkind MP, QC, announced that the Scottish Bus Group was to be privatised, selling the STG subsidiary companies such as Lowland, Midland, Eastern Scottish Central Scottish and Highland Omnibuses into the private sector. Privatisation of Caledonian MacBrayne also came under consideration, but on 30th November 1988, Mr. Rifkind announced that most of the company would remain in public ownership, with a new Board which reflected islanders interests more strongly and which also included representatives from the commercial sector. Options for the Upper Clyde services were further examined but in June 1991, any change in the status of these routes was ruled out. On 2nd April 1990, the company came under the direct ownership of the Secretary of State and the link with the Scottish Transport Group was severed. By the time of the separation, much had been achieved through STG control over Clyde and West Highland shipping services. The wind of change had hushed but had left fundamental changes in its wake. The fleet of 1969 was comprised of 40 elderly passenger, cargo and steam powered excursion ships, whilst that of 1988 comprised 28 modern ferries of various specifications. Increases in fares had been held to levels below inflation whilst government subsidy had been reduced by about 30%. In 1969, 4.5 million passengers and 360,000 vehicles were carried. In 1989, 5.8 million passengers and 1.2 million vehicles used the services of Caledonian MacBrayne. Much had been achieved in twenty years. But in its new guise, the company entered an exciting phase of further development, building upon its successes by introducing its largest and finest vessels.

The late eighties and early nineties saw record years for Caledonian MacBrayne in terms of traffic growth. In 1991, the ships carried over six million passengers for the first time although the closure of the Skye ferry in 1995 reduced this figure to 4.9 million passengers in the year to March 1996. Thanks also to the ending of the Skye ferry service, the number of cars carried by the company had fallen to 909,000 in the year to March 1996. But by March 1997, passenger numbers had increased again, to beyond 5.1 million, and the number of cars carried increased to 943,500 in the same year. With an average annual increase of over 1.5% between 1991 and 1996, in spite of the loss of the Skye ferry, the company was clearly performing well. Indeed, the ten years between 1984 and 1994 witnessed a 30% growth in passenger traffic, whilst tourist journeys to Scotland actually fell by 30% overall in the same period.

But with the changes in ownership of 1990, the Conservative Government was again keen to investigate options for privatisation and undertook several studies into the possibility of this being achieved, the last reporting in mid 1994. Various private concerns had expressed interest in operating certain Caledonian MacBrayne services and the concerns of islanders, management and employees was thus aroused. In the early years of the nineties, the privatisation debate rumbled on with the island communities, trade unions, the Transport Users Consultative Committee and local authorities in the area rallying around Caledonian MacBrayne. Largely through the rising voice of opposition to privatisation, backed up by the government's own consultants' reports, the Secretary of State's conclusions were widely welcomed. It took until 28th October 1994 for him to announce that Caledonian MacBrayne was "the most cost effective and satisfactory way of providing support for lifeline services to the

*The **Loch Fyne** makes for Kyle with the partly completed Skye Bridge and the mountains of Skye as a backdrop on 27th May 1995.* (Author)

islands off the West coast of Scotland". Having expended much effort on ideological considerations, the Conservative government reluctantly acknowledged that there was little scope for privatisation of Caledonian MacBrayne. Everyone in the islands had known it for years, as the Islay experience of the early seventies had shown. The future for the company was secure and communities around the coast heaved a collective sigh of relief. It had been demonstrated that only an effective publicly owned ferry company could continue to serve the needs of the economically fragile island communities on the West Coast. With privatisation plans coming to nothing, the mid nineties saw the company begin to expand its sphere of operation to areas further afield.

Developments continued with the introduction of several new vessels. The early prospects for the last decade of the 20th Century envisaged two new large ferries being constructed to serve Arran and Lewis, with potential for further upgrading of several of the smaller routes and for the introduction of new ones such as those between Harris and North Uist, Tarbert and Portavadie and Barra and South

*The record breaking Clyde "steamer" **Caledonian Isles** ploughs familiar waters as she departs from Brodick in bright sunshine on 14th May 1994.* (Author)

Uist. The nineties also saw Caledonian MacBrayne spread their wings beyond Scotland as they expanded into Ireland in their own right. Initially on charter, one of their ships began operating the Ballycastle - Rathlin Island passenger and car ferry service in December 1996, with the *Canna* becoming the regular vessel on the route. In April 1997 the company was awarded a 5 year contract to operate the service on behalf of the Department of the Environment in Northern Ireland.

Growth of traffic on the Lochranza route meant that Arran's back door was opening ever wider, and so also was the front. Even with the *Isle of Arran* in service, it had become clear by 1990 that the continued upward growth in traffic on the main Ardrossan - Brodick route would require a still larger vessel. Construction of a new ship was approved by the Scottish Office on 3rd December 1991 and the resulting vessel, a further development of the *Isle of Mull*, was destined to smash all of the size records on the Clyde. On the company's northernmost route, traffic growth also demanded a new ship and the replacement for the *Suilven* on the Ullapool - Stornoway service was also to be a magnificent vessel.

### Caledonian Isles

Built by Richard's Shipyard of Lowestoft and launched by HRH The Princess Royal on May 25th 1993, the *Caledonian Isles* became the largest ship ever to operate on a Clyde passenger route when she took up service on the Ardrossan - Brodick route on 25th August of that year, her entry into service being delayed by a computer fault, such are the complexities of the modern fleet. At 308 feet in length she surpasses by 7 feet the famous Royal Mail Paddle Steamer *Columba* of 1878, previously the longest Clyde steamer of all time. However, even though she weighs in at 5221 gross tons, the *Caledonian Isles* is required to enter the narrow confines of Ardrossan Harbour in the course of her everyday employment and in her first two winters she frequently fell foul of bad weather and found herself having to divert to Gourock. An extremely well appointed vessel, the *Caledonian Isles* is the only Clyde ferry offering a full restaurant ser-

*The Caledonian Isles towers over her berth as she departs from Ardrossan on 10th April 1994.* (Author)

vice to her passengers and she is popular for non-landing Evening Dinner Cruises which are offered on the route. Her main beat is the crossing to Brodick but she has undertaken several charters and occasionally sails on Round Arran cruises when engaged on such activities. In addition, she has been popular with the Clyde River Steamer Club who have chartered her on several occasions for their Hogmanay cruise, usually to the north of Arran or round Holy Isle whilst on 2nd April 1996, she sailed round Cumbrae in connection with the launch of the new Ayrshire and Arran Tourist Board. A popular ship with the travelling public, she carries 1000 passengers and 110 cars and is driven by her twin Mirrlees Blackstone diesel engines at a service speed of 15 knots. With her ample open deck spaces and comfortable accommodation, she is an impressive vessel and it is likely that the *Caledonian Isles* will be the mainstay of the Arran service for several years to come.

### Isle of Lewis

The replacement for the faithful *Suilven* on the Ullapool - Stornoway route had been approved in July 1993 and the outcome was the magnificent *Isle of Lewis*. Built by Ferguson Shipbuilders of Port Glasgow at a cost of about £16 million, and launched on 18th April 1995 by HRH The Princess Alexandra, the *Isle of Lewis* entered service on the Ullapool - Stornoway service on 31st July of that year. She was the first UK flagged vessel to comply fully with SoLAS 95 regulations and at 6573 gross tonnes, she became the largest vessel to be operated to date by Caledonian MacBrayne, an honour which she inherited from the Clyde ferry *Caledonian Isles* which had held the title for a mere two years. Like her Hebridean predecessor, the new vessel has rarely deviated from the Stornoway service although she visited Lochmaddy and Tarbert on her delivery voyage and can berth comfortably at these piers. To accommodate her, a new passenger terminal and ferry berth was built at Stornoway and the *Isle of Lewis* began to use the facility on 28th April 1997. The new ship is much faster than the *Suilven*, having achieved almost 19 knots on trial and is capable of crossing the Minch in just over two and a

half hours, cutting almost an hour from the journey time taken by her predecessor. Internally, the *Isle of Lewis* is spacious and luxurious and can carry up to 968 passengers and 123 cars, which includes capacity for 30 cars on a hoistable mezzanine deck. She was unique in being the only vessel in the Caledonian MacBrayne fleet at that time to carry her name, *Eilean Leodhais* in Gaelic, on a plaque within the passenger accommodation and, like the *Suilven*, she does not operate sailings to Lewis on Sundays, thus recognising the Sabbatarian traditions of the islanders of Lewis and Harris. In her first year on the route, passenger carryings increased by 21% whilst cars and commercials increased by 16% and 11% respectively, demonstrating the beneficial effects of a new and improved ferry. Although she spends virtually all of her time on the Stornoway crossing, she visited Lochmaddy in April and again in June 1998 with army vehicles. It was the first of these sailings which led to the only major blemish on her service record to date when a breakdown

*The Isle of Lewis makes a fine sight as she sails up Loch Broom towards Ullapool on a placid morning on 29th August 1998.* (Author)

occurred due to failure of a propeller shaft bearing shortly after leaving Lochmaddy on 19th April 1998. This led to the absence of the *Isle of Lewis* until mid May whilst the temporary transfer of the *Isle of Mull* to Ullapool caused substantial problems for the company in finding a suitable replacement vessel at Oban, highlighting the need for additional spare capacity. But having now successfully maintained the Stornoway route for several years, the *Isle of Lewis* has become a popular and reliable ship, of modern but elegant appearance. A unique call took place on 28th November 1998 when the *Isle of Lewis* made a visit to Stromness in Orkney, on her return from overhaul on the Tyne. Her visit was an opportunity for her owners to show her off to local residents and business representatives and effectively signalled Caledonian MacBrayne's intentions to tender for services to the Northern Isles.

Meanwhile, continuing traffic growth on certain of the new short ferry routes led to the construction of new double ended "Loch" class vessels to take over from the remaining "Island" class ships. With their greater vehicle capacity and improved passenger facilities, these new ships would service demand on these routes for the foreseeable future. The new vessels were developments of the four original "Loch" class vessels and were built for the Lochranza - Claonaig, Fionnphort - Iona and the new Otternish - Leverburgh routes. At Largs, the *Loch Linnhe* and *Loch Striven* had become the mainstay of the Cumbrae Slip service but 1997 saw the *Loch Striven* depart to take over the Raasay - Sconser route, and events conspired to leave the way clear for a vessel designed primarily for West Highland service to take up residence at Largs. With further "Loch" class vessels joining the fleet, it fell to the new *Loch Alainn* to take over as the main vessel at Largs, in partnership with the *Loch Riddon*, from May 1998.

### Loch Buie

The *Loch Buie* was built by James M. Miller of St. Monans, Fife specifically to serve the island of Iona. Based on the original "Loch" class vessels she was nine feet shorter than the 1986 quadruplets and turned in a trial speed of 9 knots. She took up service at Iona on 8th June 1992 and although she is capable of carrying 10 cars and

*Ship number 608, destined to become the Isle of Lewis, takes shape on the stocks at Port Glasgow, on January 1st 1995. (Author)*

250 passengers, her car capacity is generally not required at Iona as only residents' vehicles are permitted on the island. She is powered by Voith-Schneider units and she rarely deviates from the Iona route although has relieved on the Largs - Cumbrae Slip service.

### Loch Tarbert

The *Loch Tarbert* was built in 1992, also by Millers of St. Monans and was a repeat of the hull design of the *Loch Buie*, although she carries 18 cars, six more than the original "Loch" class ferries and has passenger accommodation on the starboard side only. She undertook trials on the Forth, achieving 9.5 knots and, having sailed via the Caledonian Canal, she entered service on the

*The mighty Isle of Lewis seen here slipping away from Ullapool in her first full year in service, at Easter 1996. (Author)*

Lochranza - Claonaig route, on 25th July 1992. She replaced the *Loch Ranza* which migrated around the Kintyre peninsula to take up the Tayinloan - Gigha service, again providing greater capacity on a service which had been operated at first by an "Island" class vessel. Apart from relief sailings and occasional runs between Largs and Brodick to carry gas tankers, prior to this task being handled by the Ardrossan ferry *Caledonian Isles* from January 1995, the *Loch Tarbert* has made the Lochranza crossing her own, although the winter timetable often sees her in regular service on the Largs - Cumbrae Slip, Fishnish - Lochaline routes and elsewhere as required.

### Loch Bhrusda

Constructed by McTay Marine of Bromborough, the *Loch Bhrusda* took the "Island" class concept still further by being the first Caledonian MacBrayne vessel to be powered by Schottel Pump Jet propulsion, most suitable for the shallow waters of the new North Uist - Harris route for which she was designed. With a speed of 10 knots, a gross tonnage of 245 and capable of carrying 150 passengers and 18 cars, she opened this route on 8th June 1996 allowing the *Hebridean Isles* to abandon the Tarbert - Lochmaddy leg of her Uig Triangle roster. With the introduction of the Otternish - Leverburgh service, it was now possible to drive from South Uist to the Butt of Lewis, greatly enhancing communications in the Outer Hebrides. The *Loch Bhrusda* replaced the 38 passenger ferry *Endeavour*, which had been operated on the route by Mr. D. McAskill since 1981.

### Loch Alainn

A further development of the "Loch" class ferries, the *Loch Alainn* is a vessel similar in appearance to the *Loch Bhrusda*, but she is larger and has Cummins KT38M diesel engines driving Voith Schneider propulsion units. Intended for the Fishnish - Lochaline route, she was launched on 4th April 1997 at the Buckie Shipyard and was named *Loch Aline* on the 18th of that month. However, her name was changed to the Gaelic spelling, *Loch Alainn*, as the original name was belatedly found to be unavailable. Following ramp modifications, she took up service for a short time on the Colintraive - Rhubodach service, prior to opening her career on the Fishnish - Lochaline service on 19th July 1997, replacing the *Isle of Cumbrae* which transferred to the Clyde. But the *Loch Alainn* soon encountered major engine problems which necessitated her replacement at Fishnish by the reactivated *Loch Dunvegan* between 19th August and 25th September 1997. These problems continued and the *Loch Alainn* found herself out of action at Greenock until 25th February 1998 when she took up service at Colintraive before becoming the regular ferry on the Largs - Cumbrae Slip service on 14th May 1998. However, her technical problems continued to affect her. The *piece de resistance* occurred on 16th September 1998 when she lost power off Cumbrae Slip and the Largs lifeboat, a naval helicopter and the *Pioneer* stood by to assist. Her troubles continued on 13th January 1999 when she lost steering control and struck the pier at Largs. Capable of carrying 24 cars and 150 passengers, the *Loch Alainn* was intended to supersede her 1978 predecessor, the *Isle of Cumbrae*, at Lochaline, but this task fell instead to the former Skye Ferry *Loch Fyne*.

### Clansman (V)

In October 1996, the order for a new ferry to replace the *Lord of the Isles* on the long haul Barra, South Uist, Tiree and Coll services was announced. This impressive vessel was the first major new ship since 1984 to be given a name other than one bearing the "Isle" nomenclature and she revived a historic name in West Highland cir-

*Interested spectators brave a chilly day at St. Monans to witness the launch of the **Loch Buie** on 24th October 1991.* (Iain R. Murray)

cles. The first vessel to bear the name *Clansman* had been a passenger and cargo steamer built in 1855 whilst the most recent was the second of the 1964 car ferries which had been built at Aberdeen. The new, and fifth, *Clansman* was built at the Devon yard of AP Appledore, and was named by HRH The Princess Royal on 27th March 1998. The *Clansman* was floated out on 24th April and entered service, somewhat belatedly, on 4th July 1998, three months behind schedule. Constructed specifically for the revamped Oban - Castlebay - Lochboisdale and Oban - Tiree and Coll services, her entry into service allowed the *Lord of the Isles* to concentrate on serving Skye, Barra and South Uist, for which routes she was transferred to Mallaig in early July 1998 where she replaced the *Iona*.

Built at a cost of £15.5 million, the *Clansman* is powered by twin M.A.K. diesel engines, giving her a service speed of 16.5 knots. She is no faster than the *Lord of the Isles* although she is substantially larger. With a length of 99 metres and a gross tonnage of 5400, she is certified to carry 634 passengers and 90 cars, with a further 10 on her hoistable mezzanine deck and she is the first ship since the *Claymore* of 1955 to carry the MacBrayne "Highlander" emblem on her bow. The *Clansman* is too large to call at Tobermory and so it fell to the *Lord of the Isles* to make the final call there on 9th April 1998, thus ending the Mull "capital's" direct links with Tiree and Coll. This meant that Tobermory folk bound for these islands would now endure a long round trip to Craignure by road, followed by a ferry journey to Oban, there to board the *Clansman* bound for Tiree and Coll, on which ship, they would then sail past their own front doors several hours after leaving home. To make matters worse,

*The Sound of Harris ferry **Loch Bhrusda** makes a bright start from Leverburgh in September 1998.* (Brian Maxted)

*The Clansman powers her way out of Oban Bay as she heads for the Outer Isles on 19th September 1998.* (Author)

although the need to improve the entire length of the narrow Tobermory - Craignure road had been highlighted as long ago as 1973, it has received only partial upgrading and is still largely in single track condition between Salen and Tobermory. Nevertheless, the *Clansman* is a useful and welcome addition to the fleet and in 1999 she has also become a regular visitor to Colonsay.

In 1998, the introduction of the *Clansman*, together with the reactivation of the *Loch Fyne* and the *Loch Dunvegan,* allowed Caledonian MacBrayne to transfer various ships within their empire, leading to improvements in service on no less than seven different routes, such is the flexibility of the modern fleet. However, with the departure of the *Claymore* from the fleet and the sale of the *Iona* to Pentland Ferries in October 1997, Caledonian MacBrayne were short of suitable spare capacity to cover for breakdown or relief work, particularly at peak summer periods. The company approached the Scottish Office, now under Labour administration, in December 1997, with a view to securing approval for a new ship which would bring the fleet back to full strength and which would permit a vessel to be available to cover in the event of breakdown. But The Scottish Office encouraged the company to consider options other than a new build and to consider potential for private funding of any new ship. Meanwhile, Murphy's Law conspired to ensure that Caledonian MacBrayne were forced to go down the route of chartering a ship when the breakdown of the *Isle of Lewis* in April 1998, required the transfer of the *Isle of Mull* to replace her at Ullapool. The *Pioneer*, sent to cover at Oban, was replaced on her own Mallaig - Armadale service by the "Island" class ferry *Eigg,* which struggled to provide a limited car ferry service although the assistance of the *Loch Dunvegan* helped to alleviate the problem. Neither the Mull nor the Skye residents were impressed and Caledonian MacBrayne chartered their former vessel *Pentalina B* (ex *Iona*) to support the *Pioneer* at Oban whilst additional runs for commercial vehicles were provided by the Gardner vessel *Saint Oran*. The blame was laid at the door of the Scottish Office which had authorised the sale of the *Claymore* to Sea Containers, thus leaving the fleet short of spare capacity. Caledonian MacBrayne approached the Government again. This time the Scottish Office was more forthcoming. On 22nd July 1998, the new Transport Minister,

Henry McLeish MP, authorised the company to proceed with the construction, not only of a further major new ship, but also with the proposed new vessel to serve the Small Isles, the pair to be built at a total cost of £20 million.

# THE 21ST CENTURY IN SIGHT

The next new ships will not join the fleet until the 21st Century although construction is currently well underway. The new vessels will be interesting additions to the fleet.

*New Ship #1*

Access to European Union funding was essential to deliver the upgrading of the Small Isles service and on 18th December 1997, approval was secured from the Highlands and Islands Objective 1 European Programme, for the provision of slipways at Eigg, Muck

*The displaced Loch Alainn makes an approach to Largs Slipway on 31st August 1998.* (Author)

and Rum and for the provision of the new ship to replace the *Lochmor*. This was matched in July 1998 by the Scottish Office and on 1st February 1999, Caledonian MacBrayne announced that the Ailsa yard of Troon would build the ship, their first since the *Lochmor* herself. The new ship will be 50 metres in length and capable of carrying 200 passengers and 14 cars on her Class IIA Certificate. With a service speed of 13 knots she is due for delivery in the Spring of the year 2000. By all accounts, an interesting ship is planned, with the company opting for Azimuth thruster propulsion, whilst offering plenty of open deck space and a high standard of passenger facilities to meet the expected growing demand from the tourism industry in the Small Isles.

### New Ship #2

The latter and larger of the two new ships will be due for delivery in November 2000 and will be similar to the new *Clansman*. Intended to replace the *Hebridean Isles* on the services from Uig to the Outer Hebrides, she will be built by the Ferguson shipyard at Port Glasgow. Her arrival is likely to accompany the transfer of the 1985 ferry to the Mallaig - Armadale service where she will relieve the *Lord of the Isles*. With capacity for 90 cars, 18 of which will be carried on her hoistable vehicle platform, twin bow thrusters, twin M.A.K. diesel engines giving a speed of 16.5 knots and computerised navigational aids, the new ferry will be a fine vessel. With more open deck space than is to be found on the *Clansman,* she will be fitted solely with inflatable marine escape systems, dispensing with the need for lifeboats, which should allow for a more balanced appearance than her 1998 consort. Nevertheless, the new ship will be a far cry from the old *Hebrides* of 1964. The evolution of the Caledonian MacBrayne fleet continues.

## A PROUD HERITAGE LIVES ON

*"The man who has not taken ship by paddler to the enchantments of the Firth of Clyde is a man deprived and pitiable". Cliff Hanley, "The Scots" 1980.*

An outcome of the rapidly changing shipping scene was that 1974 became the first summer in 162 years in which the sound of paddle beats had not reverberated across the waters of the Firth of Clyde. But thanks to the dedication of a small group of enthusiasts, the Clydeside public suddenly woke up to the realisation that their long and proud paddle steamer heritage was in its final hours. The fact that it still exists many years later and perhaps more strongly than ever, is entirely due to the exploits of one very famous old paddle steamer. She has bridged the gap between the old and new generations of Clyde "steamer" and is hugely attractive to a new generation of the travelling public, for whom the heyday of the Clyde steamers would otherwise be nothing more than pages in the history books, were it not for this famous ship and her dedicated group of supporters

### Waverley

What ship could command more public affection than the magnificent paddle steamer *Waverley*? The famous steamer, completed by the shipyard of A&J Inglis of Pointhouse in 1947 for the London and North Eastern Railway excursion services to Loch Long and Loch Goil, has welcomed passengers across her decks at locations all around the British and Irish coastlines. She is the last in a long and proud line of Clyde Paddle Steamers which stretches back to 1812 and the *Comet,* Henry Bell's revolutionary little steamer. The *Waverley* made her first ever public sailing on 16th June 1947 on her regular service from Craigendoran to Arrochar and

Lochgoilhead, the last of the Clyde paddler steamers to enter service, but not the last sea going paddle steamer to be built. That honour went instead to the Bristol Channel steamer *Cardiff Queen*. But the honour of becoming a maritime legend was to fall to the *Waverley*. In 1948, following the nationalisation of Britain's railway companies, the 693 gross ton *Waverley* became part of the British Railways Clyde steamer fleet and her red white and black funnels gave way to yellow and black. She took up employment on Upper Firth routes and very seldom found herself undertaking anything more adventurous than a sailing Round Bute. She even saw service in the depths of winter, a task which ended with the arrival of the new car ferries in 1954. However, as the number of large steamers dwindled throughout the fifties and sixties, the *Waverley* found herself participating in excursion sailings to parts of the Firth well away from the haunts of her youth and she became a familiar sight at destinations as far apart as Inveraray and Stranraer. Her roster dovetailed with that of her former LNER fleetmate, the *Jeanie Deans* of 1931. But following "Jeanie's" withdrawal in 1964, the *Waverley* alternated with the paddler *Caledonia*, which transferred to the north bank as her new Craigendoran stable-mate. On 25th September 1972, with the *Caledonia* long gone, the former LNER Craigendoran base closed for ever and the *Waverley* found herself based at Gourock for the final year of her career in STG ownership. In 1973, the *Waverley* wore the colours of Caledonian MacBrayne for her first and only season and she was declared surplus at the end of that summer, too expensive to operate, poorly patronised and requiring major remedial work to her boiler to allow her to remain in service.

By now the last sea going paddle steamer in the world, her growing status had emotional ties but little economic value for Caledonian MacBrayne. At the end of the summer of 1973, her paddles fell silent following her last sailing, a Round Bute cruise, on 30th September 1973. Now irrelevant to the needs of the rapidly modernising Caledonian MacBrayne fleet, her future was in doubt and her owners had no further requirement for a passenger carrying paddle steamer in the new era of roll on - roll off diesel powered vessels. It seemed as if the era of the Clyde paddle steamers had come to an end. But in a magnificent gesture, the *Waverley* was sold by Caledonian MacBrayne for £1 to the Paddle Steamer Preservation Society and 22nd May 1975 saw the steamer make a triumphant return to service under their ownership, operated by a subsidiary the Waverley Steam Navigation Company Ltd. and wearing her restored LNER funnel colours. Since that time, she has weathered initial financial problems, overcome regulatory changes, has received a new boiler and new paddle wheels and on 15th July 1977, she survived a near fatal grounding on the Gantock Rocks near Dunoon. Yet she continues to churn the waters of her native river, a living reminder of the great days of the Clyde Steamers and with a fair

*A historic bridge opens for the **Waverley** as she passes through Tower Bridge, London, on 20th September 1986. (Author)*

*Bygone days are recalled as the **Waverley** shows a clean pair of heels whilst departing from Rothesay in May 1968 in Caledonian Steam Packet Co. livery. (Author's Collection)*

wind, she may sail well into the next century. The public, for their part, have responded magnificently and the *Waverley* has become a national institution. Although she still spends her main summer season on the waters of her native Firth of Clyde, the *Waverley* has, since 1977, spent substantial periods of time away from the Clyde in an effort to increase her potential operating revenue. This has meant that her travels around Britain have allowed many traditional "steamer" areas such as the Bristol Channel, the River Thames, the Solent and the West Highlands to hear again the beat of paddle wheels. Coupled with occasional forays into East Coast, Manx, Irish, Mersey and North Welsh waters she has visited places as far apart as Dundee and Deal, Stornoway and Sandown and Broadford and Bournemouth. Her magnificent Rankin and Blackmore triple expansion steam engines still drive her effortlessly at 16 knots and in 1997 she celebrated her 50th Anniversary, a miraculous feat which few thought would ever be possible. During the first fifty years of her career she has come a long way from her early days as a workhorse on the upper Firth of Clyde, to finding herself regarded as an object of national affection as she welcomes passengers aboard at piers and harbours throughout the British Isles. With detailed proposals now being finalised for a Heritage Lottery funded rebuild, which should ensure that she is restored virtually to her original condition, the future is bright for the continued service of the *Waverley*.

In 1986 the motorship *Balmoral* became her running mate and together, the ships continue to represent the last examples of the once numerous fleets of coastal passenger ships. No matter what the future holds for other projects, such as the proposed restoration of the *Maid of the Loch* and the Thames paddle steamer, *Medway Queen*, it is largely due to the *Waverley* and her continuation of the coastal cruising tradition that the nineties could contemplate such developments when, twenty years previously, they would have been laughed out of court.

*Prince Ivanhoe*

In late 1980, supporters of the *Waverley* purchased the redundant Portsmouth - Isle of Wight passenger ferry *Shanklin* with the intention of placing her on an excursion programme complementary to that of the paddle steamer. Having been built by Denny of Dumbarton in 1951, and a quasi - sister of the *Southsea* and the *Brading* of 1948, the *Shanklin* had been laid up by her operators, Sealink, in 1980. She arrived at Stobcross Quay, Glasgow, on 21st November 1980 following which her new owners, the Firth of Clyde Steam Packet Company, had her restored to top class condition. Bearing the name *Prince Ivanhoe*, she became very popular as a result of her brief appearances on the Clyde and in her role as the main excursion vessel on the Bristol Channel in 1981, her first summer season.

But 1981 was also to be her last season. On August 3rd of that

The **Waverley** arrives in Oban Bay on a fine day in May 1999. (Author)

*The full majesty of the paddle steamer is apparent as the **Waverley** approaches Whitstable on 20th September 1986.* (Author)

year, she struck a submerged object and was holed below the water-line off Worms Head in South Wales. With 450 passengers aboard, the *Prince Ivanhoe* was grounded on Port Eynon beach and all passengers were rescued. The vessel was declared a total loss and was broken up where she lay. Thus, a fine vessel came to a sad end, and with it, a potentially successful experiment which was not revived for a further four years with the purchase of another former Solent favourite.

### Balmoral

In 1985 the operators of the paddle steamer *Waverley* took a brave and ambitious step. In order to support the operations of the *Waverley* throughout Britain, they purchased the passenger motor vessel *Balmoral* which was lying in Craig Harbour, Dundee, at that time. Restored to active service by Clydedock Engineering at Govan,

*The motor excursion ship **Balmoral** approaches Largs on 27th September 1993 with an attractive colour scheme which reflected that of her former Red Funnel owners.* (Author)

the *Balmoral* was returned to service and once again took up her role as the regular Bristol Channel excursion vessel as she had done between 1969 and 1980. Built in 1949 by Thornycroft of Southampton for the Solent services of Red Funnel Steamers, the 688 gross ton *Balmoral* became surplus to their needs in 1968 and a long term charter arrangement saw her become a member of the Bristol Channel pleasure steamer fleet of P&A Campbell in 1969. Purchased outright by them in 1980, she was chartered to White Funnel Steamers and the Landmark Trust, owners of Lundy Island. But poor performance meant that, by October 1980, her twelve seasons in the Bristol Channel had come to an end and she was sold in 1982 to new owners, Craig Inns of Dundee. She spent several months as a floating pub in the city, before closing to the public. Following a period of redundancy, she was purchased by Helseam Ltd. and in March 1985 she sailed via the Pentland Firth to Glasgow before undergoing major restoration to return her to active service. A seaworthy vessel once again, she undertook her first public sailing, between Bristol and Ilfracombe on 13th April, 1986. Her history since then has been one of success in supporting the operations of the *Waverley* round the British Isles. Like the *Waverley*, the *Balmoral* has now become a well known and much travelled ship and she visits many areas beyond the Bristol Channel in the course of her summer season. In Scottish waters, she has been a frequent visitor to the Clyde, Forth and Tay estuaries and has also visited the ports of Inverness, the Moray Firth, the Solway Coast and East Coast harbours such as Peterhead, Anstruther, Montrose, Stonehaven and Eyemouth. Having undergone several livery alterations, the *Balmoral* is now to be seen in the restored White Funnel colours of her former owners, P&A Campbell, and indeed the Glasgow September Holiday weekend of 1997 saw a Campbell liveried vessel operate public sailings on the Clyde for the first time since 1888 when the brothers forsook the Clyde in favour of an illustrious future on the Bristol Channel.

*As a temporary East Coaster, the **Balmoral** approaches Stonehaven on 12th July 1997 wearing her restored P&A Campbell colours. (Author)*

*The **Southsea** prepares to leave Glasgow's Anderston Quay on 6th September 1987 on her first sailing during her short spell in northern waters. The crocked **Waverley** looks idly on. (Author)*

### Southsea

A Sealink ship which was ordered by Southern Railways for their Portsmouth-Ryde services on the Solent, and built by Denny of Dumbarton in 1948, the *Southsea* was essentially an older sister of the *Prince Ivanhoe*. Her main claim to fame relates to her relief sailings on the Clyde in September 1987, when she replaced the *Waverley* which had suffered severe boiler failure. Laid up at Newhaven since 1988, the *Southsea* was purchased from Sea Containers Ltd. in 1997 by Brasspatch Ltd with a view to eventual return to service. However, major problems with her propellers, first encountered in her later Sealink days, persisted. These problems led to financial difficulty and the ship was subsequently dry docked at Bristol and bought by Mr. Surinder Gill in March 1998, her fiftieth anniversary year. She is now laid up at Newport, Wales.

### Queen of Scots

This little passenger ship appeared on the Clyde in November 1974, having been bought by Sir Robert McAlpine & Sons for the purpose of ferrying workers from Rothesay to the oil platform construction site at Ardyne Point on the Cowal peninsula. She was built in 1935, as the *Coronia*, by Warrens of New Holland and operated excursion sailings from Scarborough before being taken over by the Admiralty during World War 2. In 1946 she returned to Scarborough, remaining there until 1967. From 1968 she found employment as the *Bournemouth Queen* under the ownership of J. Croson Ltd. and was employed on South Coast excursions from the resort of her name. From 1974 until 1977 she operated on the Clyde for McAlpine as the *Queen of Scots* and was little more than a workboat, ferrying construction workers to and from Ardyne Point. Her moment of glory came on 23rd July 1977 when she ventured forth from Glasgow bearing the colours of the paddle steamer *Waverley*. For over a month she endeavoured to maintain some kind of excursion programme whilst the paddler underwent repairs at Greenock following her disastrous grounding on the Gantock Rocks on 15th July 1977. The following two seasons saw the *Queen of Scots* continue on Clyde excursion work under the management of BB Shipping Ltd, a Dunoon based private concern, but the venture met with little success. She was laid up at Blairmore and in 1981 she was repossessed by the HIDB, major creditors of BB Shipping. She was sold to London owners and subsequently left the Clyde, finding her way back to England where she is currently serving as the *Rochester Queen* in a role as a restaurant ship, at Rochester on the River Medway.

## BY THE BONNY BANKS

*"I have never twice seen Loch Lomond under the same shifts of light and shade. But I have never seen it look more noble than once by midsummer moonlight."* Maurice Lindsay "The Lowlands of Scotland" 1953.

Quite apart from its storm ravaged or sun bathed coastline and its beautiful offshore islands, the West Coast of Scotland is well known for its freshwater inland lochs and it is still possible to view the beauties of the soaring mountains and the deep waters from the decks of some very attractive excursion vessels, both large and small, famous and obscure. Historically, the main inland loch sailings were located in areas close to the Central Belt of Scotland with its industrial masses seeking summer respite from their labours. As on the Firth of Clyde, such relief was provided by steamships of varying sizes and substantial steamer fleets developed on Loch Lomond, Loch Katrine and Loch Tay. The excursion steamer operations on these lochs were traditionally managed in association with the Clyde Steamer fleet and this situation prevailed well into the days of the STG, although the development of the motor car and its potential to offer excursionists opportunities to travel further afield on day or weekend trips had largely decimated the inland loch services by the end of the sixties. Nevertheless, careful marketing and promotion has meant that the future for the remaining ships can be viewed with some optimism.

*The much travelled **Queen of Scots** is seen in familiar colours during her short spell as a **Waverley** stand in during July and August of 1977. (Harold Sinclair, Author's Collection)*

Celebrated in song and story, Loch Lomond is undoubtedly the most famous of all Scottish lochs. At 23 miles in length between its northern and southern ends at Ardlui and Balloch respectively, it is the longest loch in Scotland and is flanked on its northern shores by steep mountains of which Ben Lomond at 3192 feet is the highest. At its southern end, the scenery is gentler but still beautiful and the base of the loch opens out into a six mile wide inland sea, studded with wooded islands and backed by rolling hills. It is this combination which has made the loch attractive for tourists, since William and Dorothy Wordsworth first extolled its virtues many generations ago. Today, a sail on the loch can still be experienced on a number of attractive craft, operating from Balloch, Inversnaid, Balmaha, Tarbet or other villages along the shores of the loch. But, much to the detriment of the local tourism industry, the queen amongst all of the Loch Lomond excursion vessels has not sailed for many years even though she is one of the most historic ships still to be found in any European country.

### Maid of the Loch

In 1953, A&J Inglis of Pointhouse constructed the new *Maid of the Loch*. *She* bore no resemblance to the other products which Inglis had turned out for British Railways Scottish steamer services that year, namely the diesel powered *Maid of Skelmorlie* and the *Maid of Argyll*. Instead the trusted combination of steam power and paddle wheels was chosen and the new "Maid", although a beautiful ship, was destined to become a permanent financial white elephant for her owners. However, the need to negotiate the shallow approaches to Luss Pier and to attract passengers back to the Loch Lomond sailings may have been the deciding factors for the Railway Executive. The last major paddle steamer to be built in Britain and the largest ever built for a Scottish freshwater loch, the *Maid of the Loch* was transported from the Glasgow shipyard to Balloch by rail where her prefabricated hull was reassembled on the loch shore and she was launched on 5th March 1953. The graceful paddler took up service on 25th May 1953, replacing the two old stagers *Prince Edward* and *Princess May* on Loch Lomond excursion services. Bearing the British Railways all white "lake liner" colour scheme, the new addition was certainly an attractive ship, with her yellow funnel and excellent passenger accommodation whilst her compound diagonal steam engines drove her at 14 knots. Between 1953 and 1969 she was in railway ownership, and like her Clyde consorts, she had operated under the pennant of the Caledonian Steam Packet Co. since 1957. But the newly established STG took an ever less favourable view of the Maid's continuing poor financial performance. In 1969, she was transferred to the ownership of Walter Alexander & Son (Midland) Ltd. which was also part of the Scottish Transport Group, although she was managed by the CSP and subsequently Caledonian MacBrayne on their behalf. She attracted Royal patronage when HM Queen Elizabeth, HRH The Duke of Edinburgh and HRH The Princess Anne sailed on board on 29th June 1971 as guests of the STG. By contrast, she disgraced herself on 9th June 1980 when she ran aground upon departure from the newly reopened pier at Luss, being refloated by small craft from around the loch. In spite of her undoubted attraction as a paddle steamer continued poor loadings forced Caledonian MacBrayne to withdraw the *Maid of the Loch* from service and she made her last sailing on 30th August 1981. It seemed that the long history of the Loch Lomond paddle steamers, which dated back to the *Marion* of 1817, had come to an end.

Between 1981 and 1993 the *Maid of the Loch* lay slowly rotting at Balloch Pier, a succession of private owners failing to fulfil promises, some of them highly fanciful, of a return to service in a variety of roles. In 1982, her first new owners, Alloa Breweries, replaced her with the *Countess Fiona* but even she was withdrawn

*Heady days recalled as the **Maid of the Loch** raises steam and prepares to depart from Balloch on 5th June 1977.*
(Author)

*The phoenix rises as the **Maid of the Loch** lies at Balloch in the early stages of restoration on 12th September 1993 with newly repainted red funnel and black hull. (Author)*

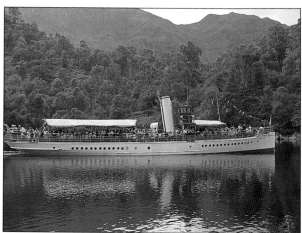

*The veteran **Sir Walter Scott**, now nearing her century, glides serenely away from Trossachs Pier on 29th July 1982. (Author)*

from service by the subsequent owners of the two ships, Sea Management Corporation of Queensland, in 1989, leaving Loch Lomond with no vessel which offered day sailings along the full length of the loch. In 1993, the two ships and the adjacent pier and slipway facilities were purchased by Dumbarton District Council and a trust was established with the intention of returning the *Maid of the Loch* to service. A successful public appeal has since seen ownership of the vessel transferred to the Trust and the wind now seems fairer for the "Maid" if the support of the Heritage Lottery Fund and other agencies can eventually be secured. In other countries where the value of tourism is seen as one of national image and prestige, rather than simply one of profit and loss, the *Maid of the Loch* would undoubtedly be resurrected and it would be a significant step forward for Loch Lomond and for Scotland if this fine ship was to see a return to service. We must hope that, in the 21st Century, the sound of the steam whistle will echo once again from the slopes of Ben Lomond.

Elsewhere on the loch, Cruise Loch Lomond operate a substantial fleet of small vessels from Tarbet, visiting Luss, Inveruglas, Inversnaid and Rowardennan. Their vessels range in age from the *Lomond Mist* of 1954 to the 146 passenger *Lomond Prince* of 1978. John Sweeney, a long established loch company, operates a fleet from Balloch Bridge including the sizeable 125 passenger *Silver Marlin*, and the Dunkirk veteran *Skylark IX*, which was built in 1934. Mullen's Cruises, also based on the River Leven at Balloch, operate a number of small cruisers, including the 47 passenger *Lomond Maid* and the larger *Lomond Duchess*. In addition, Britain's smallest mailboat, the *Marion* operates on her year round mail service to the islands of the loch, from MacFarlane's Boatyard at Balmaha. She shares this important duty and loch cruises with her larger consort the *Margaret*, built in 1955, continuing a family business which has now been in existence for over fifty years.

Not far from Inversnaid on the eastern shore of Loch Lomond, the equally beautiful Loch Katrine lies amidst fine mountainous scenery in the heart of the Trossachs, deep in Clan Gregor country, with its connections to Rob Roy MacGregor. The loch is 8 miles in length and 1 mile wide and its relative proximity to the Central Belt conurbation makes it an attractive day trip destination, in addition to being ever popular with tourists from further afield. The vision of Glasgow's Victorian city fathers had the impact that the loch was developed as the main water supply for the City of Glasgow and the flow was turned on in October 1859, assisting in the eradication of disease in the sprawling Victorian industrial city. Because of the need to maintain the purity of the water supply, only one ship is permitted to operate on the loch. For the steam enthusiast, she is one of the finest examples of her type still remaining in service.

*Sir Walter Scott*

Built in the year 1900 by Denny of Dumbarton, the graceful *Sir Walter Scott* has now plied the waters of Loch Katrine for almost a century. Named after the famous author who immortalised much of the Trossachs through his writings and brought the area to the attention of early Victorian tourists, the steamer is the last in a line of ships which have plied the loch since the *Gipsy* appeared in 1843. Powered by steam reciprocating machinery built by Paul & Co. of Dumbarton, the *Sir Walter Scott* was built for the Loch Katrine Steamboat Company of Callander but ownership passed to the Corporation of Glasgow in 1953, along with control of the tea-room and pier at Trossachs Pier. In 1969, ownership of the vessel passed to the Lower Clyde Water Board and to Strathclyde Regional Council in 1975 and the ship's funnel changed colour from yellow to white. With further local government reorganisation, the *Sir Walter Scott* came under the control of the West of Scotland Water Authority on 1st April 1996. She continues to provide morning and afternoon cruises on the loch with a daily return sailing from Trossachs Pier to Stronachlachar. This veteran, a relic of the Victorian era, has enjoyed a resurgence in her popularity in recent years and looks set to sail on for many years to come, a fine little monument to her famous Dumbarton builders.

In addition to Loch Lomond and Loch Katrine, several other freshwater Highland lochs have excursion vessels operating on their waters. On Loch Awe in Argyll, the tiny steamer *Lady Rowena*, built in 1926 and the more modern *Flower of Scotland*, dating from 1978, operate summer sailings from Lochawe Pier. Both are owned by the Lochawe Steam Packet Company.

Loch Ness, renowned world-wide as the home of the legendary but strangely elusive monster, is one of the chain of deepwater lochs which are strung together by the Caledonian Canal and which bisect the Highlands, linking the east and west coasts. On the loch there are a number of vessels operating short excursion sailings. The *Jacobite Queen* (the converted Tyne ferry, *Tyne Queen*, built in 1949) carrying 165 passengers and the *Jacobite Warrior* (1953) operate sailings from Inverness to Loch Ness and Urquhart Castle for "monster spotting" activities under the ownership of Rod Michie's Jacobite Cruises, whilst the 120 passenger vessel *Royal Scot* is based at Fort Augustus. On Loch Shiel, the *Sileas*, a 52 foot ex-admiralty launch built in 1940, offers cruises from Glenfinnan and Archaracle. Loch Tay in Perthshire, once had a sizeable fleet of small steamers but only the 30 passenger *Maid of the Tay*, operated by Croft na Caber is in service nowadays and she is based at Kenmore.

# FROM THE CLYDE TO THE FORTH

Unlike many European countries, Scotland does not boast a comprehensive canal network. However, there are two canals, the Forth & Clyde and the Union which once formed a coast to coast link across Central Scotland and also connected Scotland's two largest cities, Glasgow and Edinburgh. Although closed to through traffic in 1963, the Forth & Clyde and the Union have continued to support local excursion boats at a number of locations along their length. However, proposals to reopen the entire length of the canal system have been supported financially by the Millennium Commission and the canal may reopen to certain types of through traffic in the early years of the 21st Century.

Meanwhile, at The Stables Restaurant, Kirkintilloch, on the outskirts of Glasgow, three vessels are based. *The Ferry Queen* is a former Clyde Navigation Trust passenger ferry which is owned by the Forth & Clyde Canal Society and retains her original appearance. The *Caledonian* is also a former Clyde passenger ferry but has been substantially modernised as a restaurant boat and is not recognisable as the former Clyde Trust ferry. The *Lady Margaret*, in private ownership, is also based at Kirkintilloch. The Canal Society also operates the *Gipsy Princess* from Auchinstarry Basin. On the Union Canal, the *Pride of Belhaven*, the *Ratho Princess* and the *Pride of the Union* are operated from Ratho Bridge by the owners of the Bridge Inn.

# FERRIES GALORE

*"This ferry though boasted the best in Skye is detestable at least for carriages. But what can a ferry be for carriages, where ours is only the third that has passed this year". Lord Cockburn on the Kylerhea - Glenelg ferry, 1841.*

The indented nature of the Scottish coastline with its lochs, islands and peninsulas means that even today there are a number of small ferries and excursion vessels operating throughout the Highlands, many of which are employed on short crossings with little traffic at locations where there has been no change in the pattern of services for many years. Recent times have seen the replacement of many Highland ferries by road bridges, including those at Kylesku, Ballachulish, Kessock, and of course at Kyle of Lochalsh, where car and passenger traffic has built up to such a level where the ferry is unable to cope. But many ancient crossings have survived, especially where the traffic volume does not merit construction of a bridge. In addition, a number of small companies have operated regular passenger ferry services, particularly on the commuter routes on the Upper Firth of Clyde or on the Upper River. The history of some of these companies stretches back for many decades and they have often been family owned concerns. A number of these long established passenger and vehicle services continue to operate throughout the Clyde and West Highlands and some are associated with the services operated by Caledonian MacBrayne.

## Gourockian

Formerly the *Ashton*, this was a small passenger ferry built in 1938 by the CSP for excursion and ferry work. On 12th October 1962 she performed the last passenger sailing on the Forth & Clyde Canal, between Kirkintilloch and Bowling. In 1965 she was acquired by Walter Roy Ritchie for his service between Gourock, Kilcreggan and Helensburgh, in consort with the converted fishing boat *Granny Kempock*, and she was renamed *Gourockian* in 1968. A popular ship for charter sailings, she performed the last ever steamer call at Port Bannatyne on 9th August 1969. She was sold in 1972 upon the arrival of the *Countess of Kempock* into Ritchie's fleet and was renamed *Wyre Lady* under which name she saw further service at

Fleetwood and then on the Humber. Her former CSP sister ship, the *Leven*, can still be found operating excursion sailings from St. Helier as the *Pride of the Bay*.

Upon the death of Mr. Ritchie in 1978, his vessels were sold to Offshore Workboats Ltd. and his Clyde sailings were subsequently operated by Clyde Marine Motoring Ltd. of Greenock. The latter company dates from the 1940's and was set up by Mr. A. Dunlop Munro to offer tendering services to liners lying off Greenock.

## The Second Snark

This vessel was built in 1936 by Denny of Dumbarton for their own use as a shipyard tender. *The Second Snark* then operated cruises on the Firth of Forth between 1960 and 1964, before being used, during winter months, by Brown Brothers as a test vessel for marine stabilisers, being based at Cockenzie for this task. These trials ended in May 1969 and *The Second Snark* returned to the Clyde where she passed into the ownership of Clyde Marine Motoring and provided tendering, ferry services and summer excursions on the Upper Clyde, venturing from Greenock Princes Pier to destinations as far afield as Tighnabruaich, Carrick Castle and Millport. She is still employed on these activities and is a popular ship for charters by local groups and is occasionally used on the Kilcreggan and Helensburgh ferry services. Clyde Marine also own the *Rover*, which is used on relief passenger sailings and also undertakes some cruise work although she is more generally found operating on charter sailings.

## Kenilworth

Built in 1936 by Rowhedge Ironworks at Colchester as the *Hotspur II* for service on the Hythe - Southampton passenger service across Southampton Water, this little vessel was acquired by Clyde Marine Motoring Ltd. in 1979 for service on the passenger ferry routes from Gourock to Kilcreggan and Helensburgh. She is also well known for her short cruises around the Upper Firth visiting destinations such as the Gareloch and she generally undertakes the annual Paddle Steamer Preservation Society winter charter to Carrick Castle.

In bygone days there were many passenger only ferries which were operated free of charge to passengers under a charter of the Clyde Navigation Trust. They were located at a number of locations on the river, such as Whiteinch, Govan, Kelvinhaugh and Finnieston and in their heyday catered for the huge numbers of shipyard workers crossing the Clyde. Their decline mirrored the passing of the shipyards and the last of them, at Kelvinhaugh, was withdrawn in 1980. Some crossings were operated by double decked "Vehicular Ferryboats", the last of which was withdrawn from service in the early sixties. Only two vehicular crossings, at Erskine and at Renfrew

*The Second Snark, seen at speed in the Kyles of Bute on 26th September 1994, proves that small is beautiful.* (Author)

*The former Solent passenger ferry **Kenilworth** awaiting departure from Gourock for Kilcreggan on 1st September 1994.* (Author)

survived the sixties, and even the Erskine Ferry closed upon the opening of the road bridge in 1971.

### Renfrew Rose and Yoker Swan

The Renfrew Ferry is the last River Clyde crossing still in operation within the city and it dates back to the 15th Century. Since 1984 the crossing has been maintained by a pedestrian only ferry, utilising either the *Renfrew Rose* or the *Yoker Swan*. Both vessels were built by McCrindle's Shipyard of Ardrossan and are capable of carrying 50 passengers and an ambulance if required. The original ferries were operated by Renfrew Town Council who placed a steam driven chain ferry on the crossing in 1868. The route was taken over by the Clyde Navigation Trust in 1911 whose successors, the Clyde Port Authority were founded in 1966. They operated both the Renfrew Ferry and the Erskine Ferry until the closure of the latter in 1971. This left the Renfrew Ferry as the sole vehicular ferry on the upper river. With declining use being made by motor vehicles, due to the opening of the Clyde Tunnel, the 1952 built diesel electric chain ferry was replaced in 1984 by the new passenger vessels. The *Renfrew Rose* and the *Yoker Swan* were initially operated by Strathclyde Transport, but since local government reorganisation in 1996, they have been operated by Strathclyde Passenger Transport Authority. But the old chain ferry has been given a new lease of life as a floating entertainment venue. Catering for everything from jazz concerts to ceilidhs, she can still be found acting in this role on the Clyde in the heart of Glasgow.

### Minor Clyde Ferries

Two locally operated, passenger only, ferry services are still operated on the Firth of Clyde, both in outlying areas. The motor boat *Foxtrot* links Holy Isle to the Island of Arran at Lamlash, now serving the island's Buddhist monastery as well as the summer visitors to the island. On the fringes of the Firth, a motor boat links Campbeltown with Davaar Island at the mouth of Campbeltown Loch, which is accessible on foot at low tide, but which is cut off at high tide and can be reached only by boat.

### Spirit of Fife

Although regular car and passenger ferry services on the ancient Firth of Forth crossing between North and South Queensferry ended with the opening of the Forth Road Bridge in 1964, an attempt was made by a new company, Forth Ferries Ltd, to introduce a passenger catamaran service between Burntisland and Granton in 1991, combining commuter runs with short cruises. The *Spirit of Fife,* formerly the *Herm Trident IV* was the vessel employed. With a passenger

capacity of 250, the *Spirit of Fife* commenced her commuter services on 30th March 1991 and also offered a series of lunchtime and evening cruises on the Forth, carrying 90,000 passengers in her first year of operation. Regrettably the service was not a success and the *Spirit of Fife* offered only spasmodic sailings in 1993. She gave her last sailing on 13th June 1993 when she tendered to the *Queen Elizabeth 2* in the Forth. Following this work she was laid up at Port Edgar awaiting sale.

### Heather

Even with the opening of the Skye Bridge, the story of the Kyle of Lochalsh - Kyleakin Ferry was not quite over. This small launch, capable of carrying 50 passengers but no cars, was operated between Kyle of Lochalsh and Kyleakin by a local boat owner, Mr. Evander MacRae of Kyleakin in the summers following the opening of the Skye Bridge and withdrawal of the Caledonian MacBrayne service, becoming the last vessel ever to serve on the Kyle of Lochalsh - Kyleakin service.

### Eilean Bhearnaraigh

This vessel, built in 1983, was capable of carrying 4 cars and 35 passengers. One of the Western Isles blue hulled ferries, she maintained the link between North Uist and Berneray on behalf of Comhairle nan Eilean Siar (Western Isles Council) until 10th June 1996. On that date, the *Eilean Bhearnaraigh* passed into the operational control of Caledonian MacBrayne who ran her on charter, in consort with their new vessel, the *Loch Bhrusda*, making Otternish her base on North Uist. But with the construction of a £7 million causeway between North Uist and Berneray, which was completed on 17th December 1998, the *Eilean Bhearnaraigh* became redundant and she made her last crossing from Otternish on that date.

### Barra, Eriskay and South Uist Ferries

Comhairle nan Eilean Siar also operate the small ferry *Eilean na - h-Oige* which maintains the link between Eriskay and Ludaig (South Uist). Built in 1980 she carries 4 cars and 35 passengers on the 30 minute crossing. In July 1998, the *Allasdale Lass* was placed in service by Mr. J. Campbell, operating on behalf of Comhairle nan Eilean Siar, between Barra and South Uist and calling at Eriskay en route. Built at Rosneath, she is capable of carrying 69 passengers, but no cars, on her twice daily summer crossing.

*The last of the line of the Skye ferries is the **Heather**, seen arriving at the old slipway at Kyle in July 1996.* (Author)

*Now surplus to requirements, the Western Isles Council ferry **Eilean Bhearnaraigh** arrives at Otternish from Berneray. (Miles Cowsill)*

### Etive Shearwater

Built in 1954, this smart vessel continues to operate for Arisaig Marine on sailings from Arisaig to the Small Isles during the summer months. With capacity for 129 passengers, she has, on occasions, deputised for the *Loch Arkaig* and latterly the *Lochmor* on the Small Isles sailings during periods of overhaul. Her moment of fame arrived on 9th June 1997 when she conveyed a full complement of passengers to the Isle of Eigg to celebrate the ownership of the island passing into the hands of the local community, an event which gained her national TV and newspaper coverage.

### Western Isles

Owned by Bruce Watt, this converted fishing boat has been utilised, for many years on passenger services between Mallaig and Inverie on the Knoydart peninsula. Although Inverie is a mainland community, the rugged nature of the surrounding mountains means that there is no road to the village and the only way to reach it is by boat. Built in 1960, the *Western Isles* carries 81 passengers and also provides cruises to Loch Nevis, the Small Isles and Loch Coruisk. With a new vessel now being constructed as a replacement for the *Lochmor*, the opportunity exists to design the ship in such a way as to allow her to visit Inverie, if she is required to carry vehicles to the Knoydart peninsula.

### Eilean Dhiura

Ordered by Argyll & Bute Council in December 1997 for the Port Askaig - Feolin service, the *Eilean Dhiura* (translation *Isle of Jura*) was built at the McTay Marine shipyard at Bromborough and was designed by Stirling Ship Management. She can carry 50 passengers and 9 cars or one 44 tonne lorry. The *Eilean Dhiura* is the largest size of vessel capable of transiting the Crinan Canal and collectively, these characteristics gave her the builders designation

"Crinmax 44". The *Eilean Dhiura* is operated by Serco Denholm Ltd on behalf of the Council. Serco Denholm is a new name on the ferry scene but they are a long established concern well experienced in the operation of Royal Naval Auxiliary Service vessels. Named at Birkenhead on 24th June 1998, the *Eilean Dhiura* was built at a cost of £750,000 and replaced the *Sound of Gigha* on the 5 minute crossing on 15th July 1998, thus ending Western Ferries interest in the route and indeed, in the West Highlands, after almost three decades.

### Tobermory - Kilchoan - Morvern Ferry

Although a busy car and passenger service is provided by Caledonian MacBrayne in summer months, the lack of a winter service was proving to be a problem for the residents of the Ardnamurchan peninsula. In late 1997, the Kilchoan Ferry Action

*The Western Isles Council ferry **Eilean na h-Oige** arrives at the slipway at Ludaig, South Uist. (Brian Maxted)*

*Far from her old haunts, the Rosehaugh is seen setting off on the short Corran Ferry crossing at Easter 1996.* (Author)

*Argyll & Bute Council's new Sound of Islay ferry Eilean Dhiura at speed off Feolin in September 1998.* (Brian Maxted)

Group began a winter passenger service using the *Laurenca*, a 38 foot Aquastar launch with capacity for 12 passengers. Financial support is provided by the local authorities, local enterprise companies, the European Union and the National Lottery Charities Board and the *Laurenca* provides a frequent service between Kilchoan, Sunart, Drimnin and Tobermory between October and March.

### Corran Ferry

Located at the Corran Narrows, ten miles south of Fort William, this crossing is operated by the Highland Council and links Corran with Ardgour. The usual vessel on this route is the 16 car *Maid of Glencoul,* dating from 1975, which operated the Kylesku Ferry until 1984. However, she is occasionally replaced by the former Kessock Ferry, *Rosehaugh* which can carry 18 cars and was built in 1967.

### Loch Linnhe

Further up Loch Linnhe from the Corran Ferry, the *Cailin an Aiseag* was built at Buckie in 1980 and is the 26 passenger vessel which maintains the Highland Council passenger ferry service from Fort William across Loch Linnhe to Camusnagaul.

### Glenelg - Kylerhea

Formerly the point at which cattle drovers encouraged their beasts to swim between the Isle of Skye and the mainland, this was the oldest "Skye Ferry" in existence and it is now the only short crossing remaining, following the withdrawal of the Kyle of Lochalsh - Kyleakin service. Due to the 12 mile approach road via the steep Mam Ratachan pass, its inaccessibility means that it is a summer

only operation and is the last ferry in Scotland to be operated by a boat of the turntable type, once common at locations such as Ballachulish, Kyle of Lochalsh and Kessock. The regular ferry on the crossing is the *Glenachulish* which is operated by Roddy McLeod. She can carry 6 cars and was built in 1969, formerly operating at Ballachulish.

### Cromarty Ferry

The only remaining ferry on the East Coast of the Highlands, this long established service runs across the mouth of the Cromarty Firth, linking the beautiful Black Isle to Easter Ross between Cromarty and Nigg. Dating back 800 years, the route was used by King Robert the Bruce and King James IV in the 14th and 15th Centuries respectively. Today, the ferry is operated by Seaboard Marine, using the 2 car capacity *Cromarty Rose*, built in 1987 at Ardrossan. Although local government financial cutbacks led to the proposed closure of the three quarter mile link on 31st March 1997, finance was found to continue the service on a summer only basis, thanks to support from the Highland Council and the local oil rig construction companies. The crossing continues to operate, providing a magnificent alternative route for tourists wishing to avoid the rigours of the A9 trunk road.

### Kerrera Ferry

This passenger ferry is located some two miles south of Oban on the Gallanach road and is operated by Dunollie Estates utilising a twelve passenger motor launch to link the island of Kerrera to the mainland. A similar vessel is operated at *Ulva Ferry* on the Isle of Mull by Mrs. Howard, to convey passengers between the islands of Ulva and Mull.

### Easdale Ferry

A 12 passenger motorboat, built in 1993, is operated by Argyll and Bute Council on the short crossing between Easdale and Easdale Island, some 12 miles south of Oban.

### Cuan Ferry

Fifteen miles south of Oban, the *Belnahua* entered service in 1972, replacing the *Maid of Luing* and she maintains the link between the Isle of Seil and the Isle of Luing. Capable of carrying 5 cars, she is occasionally replaced by the *Grey Dog* during overhaul periods. In addition, a passenger only service is provided by the *Oronsay*, built in 1970, which is capable of carrying 21 passengers. Both routes are operated by Argyll and Bute Council.

*The reprieved Cromarty Rose arrives at Cromarty, filled to capacity, on 30th August 1998.* (Author)

### Lismore Ferry

North of Oban, *The Lismore* is a 24 passenger vessel which was built in 1988 and operates between Port Appin and Lismore, although the main vehicle ferry service is operated by Caledonian MacBrayne from Oban.

### Kyle of Durness

Finally, the most north westerly ferry on the Scottish mainland is the *Clo Mhor*, a twelve passenger vessel built in 1995, which is owned by John Morrison and crosses the Kyle of Durness in Sutherland. She is used by visitors intending to visit Cape Wrath.

## SUMMER BUTTERFLIES

In addition to excursion sailings operated on the Clyde by the main companies, a number of interesting vessels have appeared in recent years.

### *Sir William Wallace* and *Robert the Bruce*

Between April and September 1988, the Glasgow Garden Festival was in full swing on the former Princes Dock site on the south bank of the River Clyde. Two Amsterdam waterbus type vessels were placed in service by Clyde Marine Motoring Ltd. to operate from pontoon landing stages in Glasgow City Centre to those at the Glasgow Garden Festival Site two miles downstream. These two vessels, the *Sir William Wallace* and *Robert the Bruce* also offered evening candlelight cruises but following the end of the Festival in September 1988, there was little demand for a two ship service and *Robert the Bruce* left the Clyde by low loader bound for the Mersey on 29th May 1990 where she was renamed *Princess Katherine*. For the *Sir William Wallace*, the end came soon after. On 15th May 1991, she also left Glasgow on a low loader, her destination being Bowness on Windermere, where she entered service on the lake as *Miss Cumbria IV*.

### *St. Gerrans*

This interesting little ship arrived at Gourock in May 1988 and initially operated a programme of excursion sailings on Loch Fyne, based at Inveraray. She was not a success in this role and in July 1988 she reverted to charter sailings on the Clyde in addition to operating supplementary sailings on the Gourock - Kilcreggan route. On 9th September 1988 she ran aground in darkness on the Eileans in Millport Bay and her passengers were ferried ashore. Undaunted, she returned to service on 13th September 1988. But following thefts on board and having suffered the ignominy of being cast adrift by vandals at Gourock, the *St. Gerrans* made the last sailings of her short but eventful Clyde career on 29th March 1990, following which she was sold to Australian interests in April 1990.

A number of operators located in the various Highland coastal resorts still offer short cruises to nearby islands and places of interest in the Summer months. Still well patronised by the many tourists who visit the area, these little ships have become as familiar in the towns from which they operate as have the larger ferries and ships, with which they share the piers and harbours of the Scottish coastline.

In West Highland waters, the 100 passenger capacity *Soutars Lass,* built in 1948 as the *Weymouth Belle*, operates a cruise programme from the Crannog Restaurant at the former steamer pier at Fort William whilst a sizeable fleet of small pleasure cruisers, including the historic 77 passenger ship *Duchess*, operates from Oban to Grasspoint and Torosay on the Isle of Mull allowing visitor access to

*The ill fated **St. Gerrans** at Gourock with **Glen Sannox** beyond on 3rd September 1988.* (Author)

Torosay House, the Mull Railway and Duart Castle. Various charter hire companies operate on the Isle of Mull including Turus Mara, who operate the *Island Lass* and the *Hoy Lass*, and Craignure Charters. To the south of Oban, boat trips round the Garvellachs are operated by Mr. Lachlan MacLachlan of Luing.

On nearby Loch Etive, summer cruises to the Falls of Lora and towards the Glencoe peaks are operated by Donald Kennedy's *Anne of Etive* which is based at Taynuilt. The island of Iona is home to a number of excursion vessels - the *Iolaire of Iona*, owned by David Kirkpatrick, and the *Fingal of Staffa* and *Ossian of Staffa* which are operated by Gordon Grant. All of these vessels operate on Summer excursion trips between Iona and the Isle of Staffa where passengers can land to visit the famous basalt columns of Fingal's Cave.

Further North, on Loch Broom, Tanera Mor is the main island of the beautiful Summer Isles group. These islands are regularly visited by the small pleasure boats which operate from Ullapool, such as the *Summer Queen*, with capacity for 158 passengers, the *Islander,* carrying 93 passengers and the only boat which lands passengers at nearby Carn nan Sgeir, and Harry Macrae's wildlife excursion vessel *Guardwell*. Further along the Loch Broom coast, the *Hectoria*, takes visitors to the Summer Isles from Achiltibuie.

On the Firth of Forth, the present *Maid of the Forth* was built in 1988 and is the second ship to bear the name. Her predecessor of the same name originated on the Clyde where, as the *Maid of Bute*, she had appeared in 1937 and operated short cruises from Rothesay. She was sold to Fort William owners in 1973 and appeared at South Queensferry some years later, bearing the name *Maid of the Forth*. The present incumbent operates a programme of sailings on the Firth of Forth from South Queensferry to Inchcolm, where passengers can visit the historic 11th Century abbey. Although ordered by John Watson, she is now owned by Colin Aston and since the opening of the Deep Sea World aquarium at North Queensferry, the *Maid of the Forth* has reinstated the famous "Queensferry Passage" ferry service by operating between the two villages of the same name, restoring the ancient ferry crossing which closed to regular passenger traffic in 1964.

On the North Bank of the Firth of Forth, where it meets the North Sea, summer excursion sailings are provided from the East Neuk of Fife harbour at Anstruther to the remote bird sanctuary of the Isle of May on board Jim Raeper's modern *May Princess* which carries 100 passengers on her daily return sailing. In addition, the *May Princess* is also to be found providing upriver cruises on the River Tay, leaving from Dundee's Broughty Ferry Pier at weekends during summer months. On the opposite shore of the Forth, Mr. A. Marr operates the *Sula II,* built in 1971, from North Berwick to the dramatic Bass Rock.

An interesting event took place in 1995 when a "new" steamer

*The elegant days of the Victorian era are rediscovered as the steam yacht **Carola** makes a leisurely passage through the Kyles of Bute on 17th August 1996.* (Author)

appeared on the Firth of Clyde. The Steam Yacht *Carola* was originally a private yacht, which was built in 1898 by Scott's of Bowling for their own family use and remained in their ownership for many years. World War 2 saw her in use as a shipyard fire tender on the Clyde and she was sold to new owners at the end of the war. She fell into disrepair until purchased by South Coast owners who restored her to her former glory and in 1994 she was acquired by the Scottish Maritime Museum at Irvine. With a compound engine built in 1898 by Ross and Duncan, the *Carola* is available for charter and is frequently found throughout the estuary bringing the era of the steam yacht alive once again. In addition she has transited the Crinan Canal and is a regular visitor to her old haunts in the Kyles of Bute. Although she does not operate on a regular passenger schedule, her uniqueness merits her a place in the affections of Clyde steamer history.

A number of other small resorts and villages have local boat owners operating small vessels and they are still busily engaged in providing the ever popular fishing trips or wildlife trips to view seals, dolphins or even whales. On the West Coast, places where these cruises can be found include Plockton, Tobermory, Oban, Kylesku and Lochinver, whilst the resident dolphins attract much interest on the Moray Firth and Cromarty Firth. Sea fishing trips are popular in many other areas such as at Arbroath on the East Coast. Examples of these vessels include Moray Firth Cruises' *Miss Serenity*, built in 1980, which is based at Inverness and Dennis Beattie's *Girl Katherine II*, which is based at Arbroath and carries 72 passengers on fishing trips and excursions to the Bell Rock Lighthouse. Wherever there are islands to visit, historic places to explore or wildlife to see, these little ships are as busy as ever and long may they continue to sail.

The turntable ferry *Glenachulish* leaves Glenelg on a crossing to Kylerhea in May 1999. (Author)

The *Soutar's Lass* sets off for another cruise on Loch Linnhe at Easter 1996. (Author)

# Orkney & Shetland

*"There has long been a constant trade between Lerwick and Leith, which occupies two sloops, about seventy tons each". Arthur Edmonston, "Zetland Islands" 1809.*

## UP HELLY AA

Prior to the handing over of the Northern Isles to Scottish governance, Norse control remained supreme. Orkney and Shetland were as far from Scottish influence as they were from each other and it was only in the 15<sup>th</sup> Century that their connections with Scotland became tangible. Even today, whilst their inhabitants may reluctantly regard themselves as part of Scotland for administrative purposes, they are not Scots by origin and some may even suggest that the old Norwegian claim remains valid. Lowlanders would do well to remember this proud independence, celebrated in Shetland every January in the festival of Up Helly Aa. Trade in bygone days was more likely to be with North America or Bremen, Hamburg, Rotterdam or the Baltic ports and even in the mid nineteenth century mail bound from Scotland to Shetland arrived by chance, if it was lucky. Steam came late to the Northern Isles and before the advent of steamship services, there was little trade between the two groups of islands, even though they were in the same county, and although the first steamer appeared in 1829, sailing smacks continued to carry much of the trade.

In 1792, Arthur Anderson was born in a little house at Bod of Gremista, not far from the modern day Holmsgarth Ferry Terminal at Lerwick. He contributed much to the economy of Shetland through the establishment of the Anderson Educational Institute and the Widow's Homes in Lerwick, though there was a certain irony in his lack of direct connection with the shipping trade to the islands, until the 1970s. Instead, his efforts in shipping led, in 1834, to the creation of the giant Peninsular and Oriental Steam Navigation Company - the P&O Line - whose ships have graced waters worldwide and have carried famous names like *Arcadia*, *Oriana*, *Himalaya* and of course, *Canberra*. The task of pioneering steamship services to Orkney and Shetland fell instead to the North of Scotland, Orkney and Shetland Steam Navigation Company, and its successors, forever to be known simply as the "North Company". For over 130 years, they were to be responsible for linking the Northern Isles to the mainland of Scotland. The origins of the North Company went back to 1790 and the establishment of the Leith & Clyde Shipping Company, a forerunner organisation which became the North of Scotland and Orkney and Shetland Steam Navigation Company in 1873. In 1821, the first steamer, the *Velocity*, linked Leith with Aberdeen and steamer services expanded rapidly until, by 1838, a weekly steamer service was provided from Leith to Lerwick by the *Sovereign*, in support of the mail contract. The company subsequently adopted the names of Northern saints and warriors for most of their vessels. Hence a succession of ships bearing the names *St. Clair*, *St. Magnus*, *St. Ninian*, *St. Rognvald*, *St. Ola* and *Earl of Zetland* have steamed their courses across the history of the North Company, serving both Orkney and Shetland from the mainland ports of Leith, Aberdeen and, from 1882, Scrabster. For many years they also served the Caithness ports of Wick and Thurso, the Buchan fishing town of Fraserburgh and St. Margaret's Hope in Orkney, whilst maintaining a service to Loch Eriboll and running as far west as Stornoway in the latter years of the 19<sup>th</sup> Century. Thus it was possible for a keen traveller to journey all the way from Glasgow

*Wearing the blue funnel of P&O, the **St. Clair II** is seen riding out bad weather off Aberdeen in April 1977.* (Don Smith Collection)

*The handsome motorship **St. Ninian** departs from Matthews Quay, Aberdeen, in July 1967.* (Willie Mackay)

to Edinburgh by sea, taking ship from Glasgow to Stornoway by MacBrayne's steamer and changing at the Lewis capital for the North Company's Aberdeen bound ship and continuing on to Leith. This potential itinerary lasted for an all too brief period as the North Company subsequently concentrated their efforts on their Orkney and Shetland services, gradually withdrawing their interests in serving the North coast of Scotland altogether.

An Orcadian entrepreneur began the first regular steamer service to Orkney in 1856. John Stanger was a shipbuilder in Stromness who obtained the mail contract and placed a small paddle steamer, the *Royal Mail*, on the route from Stromness to Scrabster. In 1868, George Robertson, a much travelled Orcadian, operated a screw steamer named the *Express* between Scrabster and Stromness. Short lived railway competition appeared, replacing Robertson's steamer in 1877 by the *John o' Groat*, which remained in service until 1882 when the route became part of the expanding North Company empire. They placed the first *St. Ola* on the route in 1892, replacing their previous vessel, the *St. Olaf* which had operated, apparently with little success, between 1882 and 1890. But competition from air services during the 1930's and the spartan facilities offered by the *St. Ola* led to a decline in the popularity of the service which even the introduction of the second *St. Ola*, in 1951, could not reverse. However a familiar pattern was emerging as increasing car ownership was creating demand for new car ferry routes to permit tourists to enjoy the convenience of the family car whilst on holiday, whilst islanders also shared the desire to become car borne. The *St. Ola* began to carry cars using her derrick to embark and disembark vehicles, giving the Scrabster - Stromness route a new lease of life, and in January 1975, the third *St. Ola*, a purpose built, drive through car ferry took up service. But her arrival also heralded the end of the North Company's distinctive yellow funnel, the new ship introducing the standard blue of all P&O Ferries fleets soon after taking up service. Introduced by the new P&O regime, she sufficed until 1992 when, with car traffic continuing to increase, a larger, though older, vessel was introduced by P&O Scottish Ferries. With continuing increase in traffic, the fourth *St. Ola* now provides up to

three crossings daily, seven days per week in summer months, testifying to the faith put in the Scrabster - Stromness route by the North Company in the last century.

In 1956, with a continuing reduction in passenger numbers and the ongoing improvement of road links to the north of Scotland, the North Company services from Leith and Aberdeen to Caithness ceased whilst services between the Northern Isles and the mainland followed the inevitable pattern of replacement of traditional passenger and mail steamers by modern car ferries, reflecting the changing scene on the West Coast. In 1961 the North Company became a subsidiary of Coast Lines Ltd. which was itself absorbed into the P&O empire in 1971 although the North Company retained its separate identity. But there was a certain irony that the fleet had now come under the control of the company established by Arthur Anderson so long ago. Soon, hulls and funnels became blue, the renowned P&O flag appeared at mastheads and car ferries and roll on - roll off freighters became the norm as P&O introduced modern vessels bearing the historic names of their illustrious predecessors - *St. Magnus*, *St. Clair*, *St. Sunniva* and *St. Rognvald*.

George Robertson also began a steamer service from Kirkwall to the North Isles of Sanday, Stronsay and Eday in 1863, using a wooden steamer which he named *Orcadia*. In 1868 Robertson established a new company and built the second *Orcadia* which became the first ship to be owned by The Orkney Steam Navigation Company and which served the North Isles for over sixty years. After an eventful career she was broken up in 1934 and was replaced by two new ships, the *Earl Thorfinn* of 1928 and the *Earl Sigurd* of 1931, the last two steamers to serve Orkney. To replace them would have required substantial investment on the part of the Orkney Steam Navigation Company in the late fifties, money which the company did not have. And so, a new company, the Orkney Islands Shipping Company was established in 1960 under the terms of the Highlands and Islands Shipping Services Act and, backed by Government subsidy, they chartered from the Secretary of State for Scotland the new *Orcadia*, under similar terms as MacBraynes had chartered their 1964 car ferries. Perhaps surprisingly, the *Orcadia* was not a car ferry but a passenger/cargo motorship designed to operate passenger and freight services to the North Isles from Kirkwall. The *Earl Thorfinn* and *Earl Sigurd* were broken up in 1963 and 1969 respectively whilst the *Orcadia* and her new running mate, the cargo ship *Islander* of 1969 became the last vessels to undertake the leisurely round of the islands, before the advent of roll on - roll off services and the introduction of the new *Earl Thorfinn* and *Earl Sigurd* in 1990 and the *Varagen* in 1991. In 1995 the company changed its name to Orkney Ferries and adopted a new livery in which its vessels continue to sail. In Shetland, changes also occurred on routes within the islands, the general movement of trade leading to the development of short roll on - roll off ferry routes within Shetland and the eventual demise of the regular round of the local island communities provided by the much loved *Earl of Zetland*.

In 1990, the former North Company services from Leith terminated altogether and the island sailings were concentrated on Aberdeen and Scrabster whilst the company name was changed to "P&O Scottish Ferries" from the beginning of 1989. The 1990's also witnessed the arrival of competitors in the shape of Streamline Shipping and Orcargo. Newer ships, perpetuating the names *St. Clair*, *St. Ola*, *St. Sunniva* and *St. Rognvald* have appeared, although all of them are second hand or have been displaced from other P&O services. In the late nineties, following a review of the contracts awarded to operators on Northern Isles services, the islands could well see brand new vessels, and P&O have given a promise that if they continue to operate the services into the first decade of the new century, they will provide three new ships at a cost of approximately £100 million. Nevertheless, the current fleet is well placed to maintain the traditions established as an indirect result of the vision of Arthur Anderson all those years ago in establishing the mighty P&O Line.

# THE ONLY CHANGE YOU'LL NOTICE

As long ago as 1828, Robert Stevenson, the Inspector of Northern Lights, observed that transport between Orkney and Shetland was "perhaps as little as if the expanse of the Atlantic separated them". He proposed a mail service to Shetland which envisaged using Orkney as a stepping stone and he predicted, in some ways, the situation which prevails today, with the mainland ports of Scrabster and Aberdeen providing the jumping off points for short sea services to Stromness in Orkney and to Lerwick, the capital of Shetland. But at that time, Stevenson's views were regarded as somewhat eccentric. For many years, the main sea routes to the Northern Isles were long haul routes, often spanning days, and served by a fleet of fine ships operated by the North Company serving both archipelagos. But the picture changed with the arrival of the motor car and the introduction of roll on - roll off ferries throughout both groups of islands, providing frequent links between the islands and the mainland, and within the island groups themselves. Stevenson may have been a visionary before his time.

Unlike shipping services on the West Coast, the sea routes to the Northern Isles were not affected by the establishment of the Scottish Transport Group. Instead, their future direction was shaped by the acquisition of the North Company by Coast Lines in 1961. Ten years later, Coast Lines themselves became absorbed into the P&O Ferries Group, although the North Company identity continued in existence. But on 1st October 1975 the North Company name disappeared forever, to be replaced by the new title "P&O Ferries, Orkney and Shetland Services". To sweeten the pill, P&O played heavily on the Arthur Anderson connection, informing the public that "the change of name is the only change you'll notice". This was to prove to be something of an understatement. Yellow funnels quickly gave way to blue and the P&O flag appeared at mastheads but the scene was set to change beyond recognition as

*The cargo vessel **St. Clement** passes Hall Russell's shipyard as she gets underway from Aberdeen.* (Willie Mackay)

new car ferries entered service. Irony decreed that Arthur Anderson's great company should at last become the owners of the ships which served his home islands. Some fine vessels were inherited by the P&O Ferries group in 1971 but soon change was to come to the links between the mainland and the Northern Isles and to the services within the islands.

The period between 1961 and 1969 is the only one in which a tangible link has existed between Northern and Western Isles services, with Coast Lines having a shareholding in both the North Company and in David MacBrayne Ltd. Speculation leads us to consider a very different, and possibly much more closely related future for both areas, had Coast Lines seen fit to merge their interests during this period. Although current events may yet see the red funnel in the north, P&O Scottish Ferries will seek to ensure that they continue to provide the lifeline services between Scotland and the Northern Isles for the foreseeable future. But at the end of the nineteen sixties, the North Company remained supreme as the proud operator of a fine fleet of ships.

## St. Ninian

This handsome motorship was the first post war vessel to be built for the North Company, being constructed by the Robb Caledon shipyard at Dundee in 1950. At 2242 gross tons, she was the largest ship ever to sail in the North Company fleet until that time. A twin screw vessel, the second *St. Ninian* served mainly on the passenger and cargo "indirect" service from Leith to Aberdeen, Kirkwall and Lerwick, offering tourists a unique round trip by sea, leaving Leith on Mondays and returning from Lerwick on Saturdays. In addition, she acted as the relief vessel on the direct service between Aberdeen and Lerwick, from 1951 to 1960 and again between 1968 and 1971. She was a comfortable and speedy vessel, yet the changes introduced by the North Company also meant the end for the *St. Ninian* and indeed for all of the North Company services from Leith. She made her final North Company sailing on the Aberdeen - Lerwick direct route on 1st March 1971, returning to Aberdeen on the 3rd March and her departure from the fleet in 1971 meant the end for passenger services from the capital. Shortly after her final sailing, the *St. Ninian* was sold to Atlantique Cruise Lines for service between North Sydney, Nova Scotia, and St. Pierre et Miquelon. This venture fell through in 1972 and the ship was laid up for four years. In 1976 she was bought for further service between the Galapagos Islands and Ecuador, for which task she was renamed *Buccaneer*.

*A fine Orcadian evening as the **St. Ola** cruises into the pier at Stromness, with the hills of Hoy in the background.* (Charles Tait)

*The second St. Ola loads vehicles at Stromness using her derrick on 14th October 1972.* (Alasdair L. Munro)

*The North Company cargo ship St. Rognvald seen moving astern at Kirkwall.* (Willie Mackay)

### St. Clement

A cargo ship built by Hall, Russell of Aberdeen in 1946 with capacity for twelve passengers, she undertook the final North Company sailings to Wick and Thurso, following which the Caithness sailings were discontinued at the end of 1955. Between 1946 and 1966 the second *St. Clement* became a regular sight on the freight run from Leith to Kirkwall and Stromness, a service which she shared with the *St. Rognvald*, before making Kirkwall her regular and only Orkney port of call. But the movement of traffic to the new Pentland Firth roll on - roll off service offered by the car ferry *St. Ola* meant that demand for the services of the *St. Clement* was declining rapidly and she made her final sailing from Aberdeen to Kirkwall and Lerwick on 30th November 1976, returning to the Granite City on 5th December 1976. She was sold to E.G. Loukedes of Piraeus who renamed her *Gregorus* for further trading in the Mediterranean.

### St. Magnus (V)

The fifth vessel to bear the name *St. Magnus* was, like the *St. Rognvald*, a cargo vessel but she did not carry passengers. She was built in 1955 and was initially named the *City of Dublin*, being converted to provide refrigerated space and accommodation for livestock before she appeared in the North Company fleet in 1967. She operated between Leith, Aberdeen and Kirkwall, indirectly replacing the handsome passenger and cargo steamer which had previously borne the name and which had been the last true steamer to serve on the North Company routes. But the fifth *St. Magnus* was another casualty of the switch of traffic to the new roll on - roll off services offered by the car ferry *St. Ola* and, on 4th March 1971, it fell to her to operate the last North Company sailing from Leith, severing a link which dated back to 1790. Having operated between Aberdeen and Kirkwall since the ending of the Leith services, she was sold out of the fleet at the end of May 1977 and became the *Mitera*, being owned by Sunstar Lines of Cyprus.

### St. Rognvald (III)

The *St. Rognvald*, was built by Hall Russell of Aberdeen and entered service on 28th March 1955. The third vessel to bear the famous North Company name, she had been ordered in Summer 1952 as a passenger ship with capacity for 200 and was intended to serve Wick, Scrabster and Stromness from Aberdeen. But changing trade patterns dictated that she was completed as a cargo ship with capacity for only 12 passengers. She was the last ship to carry passengers from Aberdeen to Leith on 27th February 1971, following which all P&O / North Company passenger services to Shetland were concentrated at Aberdeen. In 1977 she transferred to the

Aberdeen - Kirkwall service in place of the withdrawn *St. Magnus*, although she saw service on a variety of routes. By this time, she was the last passenger / cargo vessel of the "traditional" type in the fleet and her departure was inevitable as P&O moved towards completion of their modernisation programme. Her last sailing was from Kirkwall to Aberdeen, arriving on 20th May 1978 and her arrival brought the curtain down on 23 years of her own sailings and on over a century of North Company cargo sailings to Kirkwall, which would not resume for a further 14 years. She was sold on 23rd May 1978 to Naviera Winst of Panama and, renamed *Winston*, she operated between the Sussex port of Shoreham and Gibraltar for a number of years. With her departure, the P&O Orkney and Shetland fleet had become comprised entirely of roll on - roll of ships.

### St. Clair (III)

Upon their acquisition of the former North Company fleet, P&O found themselves to be owners of this massive and beautiful ship which was, in 1971, the largest passenger ship employed on coastal or short sea routes anywhere within Scotland and indeed, she had seen service on North Channel services to Northern Ireland on relief duties. The *St. Clair* had been built at the Ailsa shipyard at Troon and was launched on 29th February 1960, entering service on the Aberdeen - Lerwick route later that year. With capacity for 500 passengers on her spacious four decks of accommodation, the *St. Clair* brought new comforts to the exposed Shetland services and, with a length of 297 feet and a gross tonnage of 3302, she was indeed a spectacular ship. For the carriage of freight, the *St. Clair* also broke new ground by being fitted with three large cargo holds,

*With her attractive hull lines revealing her intended passenger ship role, the St. Rognvald lies alongside Victoria Pier, Lerwick on 28th August 1974.* (Alasdair L. Munro)

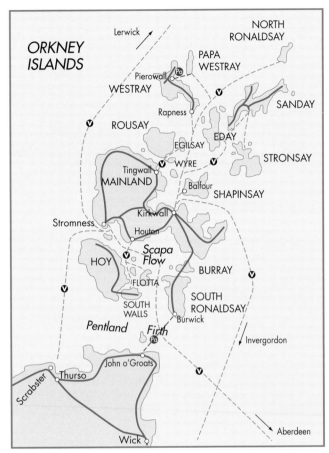

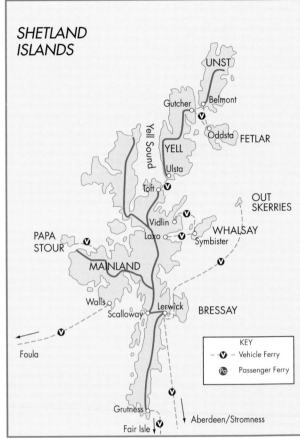

including chilled and refrigerated space and she was the first North Company ship to benefit from the fitting of anti roll stabilisers.

The first tangible signs of imminent change appeared on 16th February 1976 when the *St. Clair* returned to Aberdeen from annual overhaul with her funnel repainted in the new P&O light blue livery. Soon, the *St. Clair* herself, as well as the North Company colour scheme, would disappear from the Shetland route. Throughout her relatively short career the *St. Clair* gave sterling service to Shetland, normally sailing on the direct route from Aberdeen to Lerwick, until 2nd April 1977 when she sailed on what was intended to be her final homeward voyage from Lerwick. However, she was destined to make a rapid return to Shetland as the proposed introduction of her successor, the first car ferry to bear the name *St. Clair*, was delayed due to problems in completing the new roll on - roll off berth at Aberdeen. So the 1960 ship, with her name changed to *St Clair II*, saw further short spells of Shetland service, until 10th June 1977 when she left Lerwick on her last voyage to Aberdeen.

She spent a short time at Grangemouth before being sold to the Meat and Foodstuffs Co. of Kuwait and was renamed the *Al Khairat*. She sailed for the Arabian Gulf, bringing to an end the era of Shetland passenger and mail steamer services. Meanwhile, her replacement heralded the arrival of the car ferry era at Aberdeen.

### St. Ola (II)

The second ship to bear the name *St. Ola*, had been the mainstay of the Scrabster - Stromness route since her introduction into service in 1951. Built by Hall, Russell & Co. of Aberdeen, their first contract for the North Company, she replaced her ageing namesake on the Pentland Firth route where she provided substantially improved passenger facilities by comparison to her predecessor. The Scrabster - Stromness route is exposed and has potential to be wild at any time of the year and its attractiveness to passengers was questionable and so it was hardly surprising when the introduction of

passenger air services to Orkney rendered the service of only marginal significance. However, the arrival of the private car and the potential to develop shorter car ferry services was the salvation of the Pentland Firth route. The 750 gross ton *St. Ola* could carry up to 30 cars, loading and unloading by means of her derrick and the route became increasingly busy throughout the main tourist season, with 900 cars being carried in 1951, compared to 2200 in 1958. In addition, the *St. Ola* operated a programme of excursions to Hoy and Scapa Flow and in June 1954 she offered excursions round the Home Fleet which was anchored in Scapa Flow, the flagship being the battleship *HMS Vanguard*. Winters saw her relieve the *Earl of Zetland* on the North Isles of Shetland service, whilst the "Earl" frequently performed the reciprocal chore to cover for the overhaul period of the *St. Ola* on the Pentland Firth. Sunday services were introduced in 1959 and traffic grew to the extent that the company drafted in the *St. Clement* at peak periods from 1965 to assist the *St. Ola*. Even this tactic was not enough and the North company

*Early years in the P&O Orkney & Shetland fleet saw the* **St. Clair** *(ex Peter Pan) sail with a black hull.* (Don Smith Collection)

The big and beautiful *St. Clair* seen departing from Aberdeen whilst in North Company colours. (Don Smith Collection)

The new order arrives on the Pentland Firth as the third *St. Ola* is seen entering Stromness Harbour in her original P&O Ferries livery.
(Charles Tait)

realised that only the provision of a purpose built car ferry would adequately service the growing demand on the route, the number of cars being carried having risen again, from 4638 in 1961 to 9500 by 1975. A new passenger and car carrying vessel was built to replace her and the *St. Ola* made her final Scrabster - Stromness sailing in unusually calm and fine winter weather on 28th January 1975. On 31st January 1975, she was sold to Aquatronics International of Bermuda who named her *Aqua Star* for service on North Sea oil operations, close to her former haunts as a passenger ship.

### St. Ola (III)

Proposals for the provision of roll on - roll off services on the Pentland Firth were first revealed in September 1970. The first car ferry to be built specifically for services to the Northern Isles, the third ship to bear the name *St. Ola,* was ordered on 12th December 1972 from Hall, Russell & Co. of Aberdeen, to be built at a cost of £1.4 million. Although she joined the fleet on 29th October 1974, her entry into service was delayed by the late running of construction of the new pier and linkspan facilities at Scrabster and she entered service on the Scrabster - Stromness route in spring like weather on 29th January 1975. Capable of carrying 400 passengers and 90 cars at a speed of 15 knots, the new ship was a substantially larger vessel than her predecessor, having a gross tonnage of 1345. It was the new *St. Ola* which introduced P&O blue funnels to the north upon her return from her first overhaul on 19th November 1975, a livery change which did not play particularly well with the Orcadians.

Her impact was immediate. In 1974, prior to her introduction, 9500 vehicles had been carried to Orkney by the previous *St. Ola* but by 1976, the new vessel had developed the traffic to a throughput of 15,000 vehicles annually and had attracted significant trade away from the company's own cargo services. By 1991, the *St. Ola*

was carrying over 30,000 cars and over 6500 commercial vehicles annually, testifying to her success and to the revival of the Scrabster - Stromness as a major gateway to Orkney.

Near disaster struck when the *St. Ola* suffered a major engine room fire on 27th October 1982 whilst off Arran, en route to the Pentland Firth from overhaul on the Clyde. A lengthy absence required her replacement by a variety of vessels including the roll on - roll off freighter *St. Magnus,* the OISC vessel *Orcadia* and the Caledonian MacBrayne ferry *Clansman,* until the *St. Ola* returned to service on 7th February 1983. The new P&O Scottish Ferries dark blue livery was applied to the *St. Ola* in January 1989, the ship becoming the first vessel to receive the new colours. In November 1989 the *St. Ola* was fitted with side sponsons at the Appledore (formerly Hall Russell) yard at Aberdeen which increased her beam by 10 feet and further work to reduce rolling was undertaken at Lerwick in February 1990, leading to the first visit of the *St Ola* to Shetland.

Otherwise, her service on the route was steady and reliable. However, continually increasing traffic dictated that even the *St. Ola* became too small and she was replaced in 1992 by a larger though older vessel on the Orkney route. On 23rd March 1992, the *St. Ola,* having been renamed *St. Ola II* to allow transfer of the name to her successor, undertook her last sailing to Stromness following which she sailed to Leith where she was laid up for six months awaiting a buyer. On 15th October 1992, having been inspected at Aberdeen, she left the Granite City and took up service as the *Cecilia,* linking Grennaa (Denmark) with Helsingbørg (Sweden) and operating for Svenska Rederi AB Kattegat. However, she returned to Leith in January 1993, having proved uneconomic on her Scandinavian service and she was sold to Ventouris in April 1993 being renamed *Odigitria* in preparation for further service between Brindisi and the Greek port of Igoumenitsa. However, her travels have now taken her to China where she retains her name under the Chinese flag.

*The fourth **St. Ola** makes a fine sight as she powers her way out of Stromness Harbour into Scapa Flow shortly after entering P&O service on April 13th 1992. (Author)*

*The St. Ola inbound for Stromness seen against the cliffs of Hoy on a sunny evening.* (Willie MacKay)

*In her previous existence, the St. Ola is seen in Scandinavian waters as the Eckerö.* (Willie Mackay)

### St. Ola (IV)

The replacement for the *St. Ola* of 1974 was an impressive vessel which perpetuated the famous old North Company name but which was actually three years older, although substantially larger, than her predecessor. Built in 1971, at Papenburg, Germany, the fourth *St. Ola* was originally built as the *Svea Scarlett*, and operated on the "Skandinavisk Linjetrafik" ferry service between Copenhagen and Landskrona in Sweden. In 1980, she was sold to Scandinavian Ferry Lines and her Swedish terminal became Malmö. Following this, she operated on the Helsingør - Helsingborg service for a time but a further change of ownership occurred in 1982 when she came under ownership of the Eckerö Line of Finland. Renamed *Eckerö* she saw service between Grisslehamn (Sweden) and Eckerö in the Åland Islands. In 1991, her travels continued and she was purchased by P&O Scottish Ferries who intended that the ship would take up the Scrabster - Stromness service. She underwent modification for her new role at the Kotka shipyard in Finland, where she was renamed *St. Ola*, and she then sailed to Aberdeen, arriving there on 20th March 1992.

On her "show the flag" trip on 22nd March 1992, the new *St. Ola* called at Kirkwall, believed to have been the first visit there of any of the *St. Ola* ships, following which she entered service on 25th March, 1992, on the Scrabster - Stromness route. At 4833 gross tons and capable of carrying 120 cars and 500 passengers, the new vessel has brought enhanced standards of passenger comfort to the often stormy Scrabster - Stromness route and she has become a firm favourite with Orcadians and tourists alike. Like her predecessor, she rarely deviates from her route although she visited Lerwick in July 1993 when she replaced the *St. Sunniva* on the Stromness - Lerwick connection. The *St. Ola* continues in service but her future is now under review as, at nearly 30 years of age, her replacement will be considered in conjunction with the letting of the next contract for provision of services to the Northern Isles.

### Syllingar

The ending of the "indirect" cargo and passenger services from Aberdeen to Lerwick via Kirkwall had left the route between Orkney and Shetland without provision for passengers to be carried. The new *St. Magnus* functioned as a freight only vessel with passenger capacity limited to twelve. But the gap was temporarily filled in 1984 with the introduction of the *Syllingar* on a passenger service between Kirkwall and Scalloway. Formerly the second *Scillonian*, she had been built by Thornycroft of Southampton in 1955 for service between Penzance and the Isles of Scilly and had operated for P&A Campbell between 1977 and 1979, as the *Devonia*, on their Bristol Channel excursion sailings. Three further years with Torbay Seaways

as the *Devoniun* followed, then came a period in static use before she took up service in the Northern Isles under the name *Syllingar*. But her owners, Norse Atlantic Ferries, ceased trading on 19th August 1985 and the *St. Magnus*, with a temporary passenger certificate, was sent to Shetland to return large numbers of stranded passengers. However the relative success of the *Syllingar* encouraged P&O to revive inter island passenger services and in summer of 1986 they offered a weekend Kirkwall - Scalloway link using the chartered *Orcadia*, subsequently reinstating the indirect passenger service between Aberdeen, Stromness and Lerwick utilising the *St. Sunniva*.

## THE CAR FERRY ERA COMES TO SHETLAND

*"Fancy that, a cinema on board, as well as a shop and a music group - how the old-timers who used to sail pre-war on the north boats would have been amazed". George Mackay Brown, "Rockpools and Daffodils", 1992.*

In 1973 a contract was awarded to Hall, Russell & Co. of Aberdeen for the construction of a £3 million roll on - roll off car ferry for the Aberdeen - Lerwick service. However, the ship was never built, the shipyard withdrawing from the contract in September 1974 due to manpower shortages. Speculation soon arose that the *Lion,* the former Burns & Laird Ardrossan - Belfast ferry, was to be converted for the Shetland service. But by September 1975, the *Lion* had been earmarked for other work and P&O announced that the Southern Ferries vessel *Panther* would be coming north instead. In parallel with this development, major proposals were put in place to construct a new roll on - roll off terminal at Jamieson's Quay in Aberdeen and a new Shetland roll on - roll off terminal at Holmsgarth, over a mile from the former North Company berth in the centre of Lerwick, the intention being that the new car ferry service to Lerwick would begin

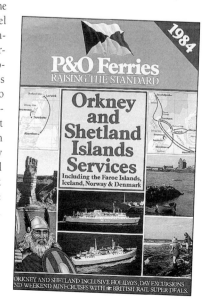

*The present **St. Clair** leaves Aberdeen on a fine summer evening in August 1998.* (Author)

in 1976. In the event, delays in constructing the new terminal at Aberdeen meant that the provision of roll on - roll off services to Lerwick were delayed until the arrival of the new *St. Clair* in 1977.

### St. Clair (IV)

This vessel heralded the dawning of the new age at Aberdeen as she brought with her the era of drive through passenger and vehicular ferries on the Aberdeen - Shetland route when she entered service on 4th April 1977. Her introduction into service brought with it a need to relocate the Aberdeen terminal from Matthews Quay to the new roll on - roll off berth at Jamieson's Quay, closer to the City Centre. Formerly the *sf Panther*, the *St. Clair* replaced the passenger vessel of the same name which became the *St. Clair II*. The elder ship assisted the new one for a short time, as the car ferry could not offer full drive through services immediately, due to delays in completing the new terminal at Aberdeen. At 402 feet in length, with a gross tonnage of 4468 tonnes and capable of carrying 700 passengers and 200 cars, the *St. Clair* became the largest ship to serve Shetland until that time. Indeed, the combined tonnage of the new *St. Clair* and the *St. Ola* was almost equivalent to the nine ships of the North Company fleet of 1914 and the bow thrust unit of the *St. Clair* alone had a power almost as great as the main engine of the *Earl of Zetland*. The new arrival had been built at Lübeck in 1964 as the *Peter Pan* for services between Oslo and Århus, but in 1973 she was transferred to the Southampton - San Sebastian route and was renamed *sf Panther*, being operated by Southern Ferries. During 1976, she again saw service between Oslo and Århus, being renamed *Terje Vigen* for this task which was undertaken on charter from the North Company, before the ship was introduced on the Shetland route. Her service on the Shetland crossing was reliable if

unspectacular, but she saw some interesting deviations in her employment, such as her annual charter to Noss for the RNLI and occasional visits to the Norwegian coast and fjords. In April 1985 she visited Harlingen, her passengers visiting the Dutch bulbfields, and in May 1987 she undertook a special sailing to Scheveningen. But probably the most significant deviation from her normal duties was the return voyage which she made to Gothenburg, leaving Aberdeen on 9th May 1983, when she sailed with Aberdeen Football Club supporters to witness their famous victory over Real Madrid in the European Cup Winners Cup Final.

The *St. Clair* undertook another unique duty on 7th October 1990 when she sailed to the Firth of Forth and was host to HRH Prince Edward as he switched on the floodlighting of the Forth

*A fine study of the **St. Clair** as she leaves Lerwick in April 1997.* (Author)

Bridge which had been installed in commemoration of the Centenary of the construction of the bridge in 1890. Prior to the introduction of the *St. Sunniva*, the *St. Clair* was relieved during overhaul periods by various ships, including the *Penn Ar Bed* and the Faroese ferry *Smyril*. On 5$^{th}$ March 1989, the *St. Clair* sailed to Bremerhaven for overhaul and when she returned to Aberdeen, she had acquired the darker blue P&O Scottish Ferries livery which she carried until her departure from the fleet. Renamed *St. Clair II* for a few days, her career with P&O Scottish Ferries ended on 27$^{th}$ February, 1992 and she left lay-up at Teesport on 26$^{th}$ June that year, bearing the name *Nusa Pejuang* and in the ownership of the Malaysian Government.

### St. Sunniva

In May 1986, P&O announced the purchase of a second passenger vessel to serve on the Aberdeen - Stromness - Lerwick route, effectively reviving the indirect passenger and freight route to Shetland. On 28$^{th}$ September 1986, the former Normandy Ferries vessel *nf Panther* arrived in Aberdeen under tow and underwent modification at the Hall Russell shipyard to provide overnight accommodation for 350 passengers. The complete upgrading of her passenger accommodation and replacement of her ageing engines were also undertaken, the total bill coming to about £6 million. The old North Company name *St. Sunniva* was bestowed upon her on 26$^{th}$ March 1987 and she entered regular service in the P&O Ferries fleet the following day, providing an alternative route from Aberdeen to Lerwick, via Stromness and reintroducing passenger traffic on the route for the first time in many years.

Built in 1971 at Helsingør, Denmark, *Djursland* had been the

*A midday departure from Aberdeen on 9th May 1998 sees the* **St. Sunniva** *outward bound for Stromness and Lerwick. (Author)*

newcomers' original name but in 1974 she was renamed *Lasse II* by her owners Jydsk Faergefart. Sold in 1979 to P&O Ferries, she was renamed *nf Panther*. She was sold to European Ferries in 1985 but retained her name until 1987 when she was returned to P&O for their Orkney and Shetland services and adopted her new name. The name *St. Sunniva* was regarded by some as an unlucky one, thanks to the sad end of the first ship of the name which stranded on Mousa in April 1930. The second *St. Sunniva* fared little better. Whilst employed on convoy duty during World War 2, she capsized on 22$^{nd}$ January 1943 whilst serving as a rescue ship with a transatlantic convoy. Although the reason for this was never clear it may have happened as a result of severe icing. The present *St. Sunniva*,

*The* **St. Sunniva** *makes a fine sight as she passes Erskine in the River Clyde on 6th May 1988. (Author).*

with a gross tonnage of 6350, and a speed of up to 18 knots, carries a total of 400 passengers and 180 cars or 25 x 12 metre trailers (12 trailers and 50 cars in summer) on the Aberdeen - Lerwick schedule on which she shares the direct sailings with the *St. Clair*. But the *St. Sunniva* also provides twice weekly sailings during the high season and once per week at other times on the "indirect" route on which she reaches Lerwick via Stromness. Her passage time of up to 20 hours on the "indirect" route allows a daily departure, excluding Sundays, from Aberdeen during summer months by either the *St. Sunniva* or the *St. Clair,* offering an excellent "mini cruise" opportunity. The potential popularity of this route, linking the two Northern Isles archipelagos, had been demonstrated by the *Syllingar* and upon her demise, P&O had been quick to spot the opportunity. In winter, in addition to her own duties, the *St. Sunniva* relieves the *St. Clair* during the overhaul period of the larger ship and also serves on the Scrabster - Stromness route to cover for the *St. Ola* during her overhaul period, whilst in March 1992, the *St. Sunniva* made her first calls at Kirkwall when engaged on livestock shipments in place of the freight ferry *St. Rognvald*. Her "unlucky" name has not proved to be unduly problematic although she was involved in something of a mishap on 29th June 1993 when she grounded at Stromness following an engine failure, later found to be sufficiently serious as to warrant her absence for 19 days whilst undergoing repairs.

A significant deviation from her regular service came in April 1988 when she took up a role as a temporary floating exhibition hall for Orkney and Shetland businesses. She sailed from Stromness for Glasgow via the Minch and the Mull of Kintyre and berthed alongside the city's Garden Festival for a short time, arriving in Glasgow on 28th April 1988. However, a seaman's strike whilst in port meant that her return northwards was delayed and she did not leave Glasgow until 6th May 1988, minus her passengers who had returned home by air. An unscheduled detour was made on 18th December 1997, when she called at Invergordon for the first time as a result of high winds closing her home port. The *St. Sunniva* remains a popular ship but, like the *St. Ola*, she is now almost thirty years of age and her replacement by a new vessel is likely to occur by the year 2002.

By 1988, P&O were considering a replacement for the *St. Clair* and proposals were advanced for a new vessel to be built at a likely cost of about £30 million. But with P&O Scottish Ferries being ineligible for European Union financial support, the construction of a completely new vessel was found to be impractical. When the next ship for the direct route appeared in 1992, it was another well seasoned traveller which arrived at Aberdeen and took on the famous old North Company name.

*St. Clair (V)*

In 1992 a new *St. Clair* took over the mantle of main Aberdeen - Lerwick vessel. At 8499 tons, the new vessel was substantially larger than her predecessor although her passenger and vehicle capacity is lower, being capable of carrying 160 cars and 600 passengers on the direct crossing to Shetland. The new ship brought with her a long and varied history, having been built at Bremerhaven in 1971 as the *Travemünde*. She operated between the town whose name she bore and Gedser in Denmark. Sold in 1981, she became the *Njegos* and saw service on routes from Italy to Greece and Yugoslavia. 1984 saw a move to the Ramsgate - Dunkirk service and a further change of name to *Tregastel* in 1985 when she operated for Brittany Ferries on their Plymouth - Roscoff service. Between 1989 and 1991 she was owned by Truckline Ferries and operated on their Poole - Cherbourg route before becoming part of the Northern Isles fleet as the *St. Clair*, for which task she underwent significant modernisation at her builders yard at Bremerhaven. Powered by M.A.N. Diesels driving twin screws, the *St. Clair* entered service between Aberdeen and

*An early morning arrival at Lerwick for the **St. Sunniva** in April 1997.* (Author)

Lerwick on 12th March 1992, becoming the largest ship ever to serve Shetland, although her bulbous bow means that she is unable to utilise her bow door, which was welded up in 1993.

Like her predecessors, the *St. Clair* has been the mainstay of the direct sailings between Aberdeen and Lerwick, on which route she sails overnight and is a very comfortable ship in all of the weathers which can be experienced on this most exposed of Scottish routes. On many occasions she has endured the worst of the North Sea weather and indeed, she became the first P&O vessel to visit Invergordon on 18th December 1997, having been diverted from Aberdeen due to heavy seas forcing her home port's closure. With a 14 hour journey time on the Lerwick service, comfort is essential and the *St. Clair* more than meets this need. She has occasionally deviated from her regular roster. Between 14th and 18th May 1992, she visited Stavanger where she took up a role as a floating exhibition centre, as part of the twinning celebrations between the Norwegian city and Aberdeen. From May 1993 to August 1997 she operated a summer weekend return sailing from Lerwick to Bergen, replacing the Smyril Line ferry *Norröna,* which had revived the ancient link between the Shetland Islands and their Norwegian neighbours. However from summer of 1998, this link was revived by the Smyril Line who brought the popular *Norröna* back to the service and the *St. Clair* ended her weekend jaunts to Norway. Although the *St. Clair* is a well appointed and popular ship, she is due for replacement by P&O Scottish Ferries as, like her fleetmates, she is now approaching her thirtieth year in service.

## P&O FREIGHT FERRIES

Although the cargo ships operated by the North Company had all but disappeared by the mid seventies, P&O introduced a number of freight ferries which utilised the roll on - roll off terminals at Aberdeen, Stromness and Lerwick and the company even witnessed a return to Leith for a time, to take advantage of the burgeoning demand for freight transport which was being generated as a result of the North Sea oil boom in Shetland.

*Rof Beaver*

In 1975, P&O acquired a freight vessel with the intention of serving the developing Shetland oil industry. The *Rof Beaver* was placed on a route from Leith, where she revived a link with Lerwick which had lapsed four years previously, becoming the first vessel to use the new Holmsgarth terminal on 18th June 1976. She also sailed to Sullom Voe although calls at the oil tanker terminal became less frequent after 1983. The *Rof Beaver* made a welcome return of P&O

*On a grey Orcadian winter day, the **St. Rognvald** attempts to berth at Stromness.* (Willie Mackay)

vessels to Kirkwall on 18th January 1984, the first "North Company" ship to visit the Orkney town since 1978. However, the return was caused by a diversion necessitated by damage to the linkspan at Stromness and was not to be a regular occurrence. Another unique sailing was made on 11th April 1985 when the *Rof Beaver* sailed from Granton to Ardersier and Lerwick, the first call at a Moray Firth pier by a "North Company" ship since about 1859. Formerly carrying various names, including *Bibiana*, *Irish Fame*, and later the *Helga One*, the *Rof Beaver* had been built at Elmshorn, Germany in 1971 and she made her final sailing for P&O on 3rd April 1987, from Leith to Lerwick, returning on the 7th April, following which the ship passed to the ownership of Torbay Seaways under the name *L.Taurus*. She is now operating in the Mediterranean as the *Cala Galdana*.

### St. Magnus (VI)

P&O Orkney and Shetland Services had first considered the provision of a roll on - roll off freight service to Orkney early in 1976. In 1977 the company announced that a freight carrier with capacity for twelve passengers would be placed on the service, but operating through Stromness instead of Kirkwall. In 1978, the 1120 gross ton roll on - roll off ferry *Dorset* took up service, initially on the Scrabster - Stromness route in place of the *St. Ola*, thanks to propeller problems on the latter ship. On 25th February 1978, the *Dorset* briefly took up service on the Aberdeen - Stromness - Lerwick freight run before sailing to Belfast for a major refit following which she was renamed the *St. Magnus* at Aberdeen, on 24th May 1978 and returned to her Northern Isles chores. In February 1979 she undertook some relief sailings between Dover and Boulogne whilst in late 1981 she handled the Sullom Voe sailings of the *Rof Beaver* for a time and also undertook occasional relief sailings on the Pentland Firth for which task she was granted a temporary certificate to carry 50 passengers instead of her usual twelve. In September 1986, she took part in the annual NATO "Northern Wedding" exercises and may have visited Anglesey, Norway and Esbjerg as part of a convoy. Obviously she was well suited for the

task as she repeated her involvement in November of the following year, taking part in exercise "Purple Warrior" in Loch Ryan. Repainted in the new P&O Scottish Ferries livery in August 1989, the *St. Magnus* took up Scandinavian sailings from Aberdeen to Stavanger and Hanstholm, being replaced on the Shetland services by the chartered *Marino Torre*. The Scandinavian services were not successful and the renaming of the *Marino Torre* and her arrival in the fleet on a permanent basis relegated the *St. Magnus* to become a spare vessel and she was laid up at Leith in April 1990. She subsequently sailed to Portsmouth where she took up service to Le Havre and Cherbourg before being laid up at Southampton Western Docks. Renamed *Parseta* in 1991, she is now owned by Conferries of Venezuela and bears the name *Donajuana*.

### St. Rognvald (IV)

This vessel, built in 1970, is a freight ferry of 5297 gross tons which is capable of carrying 41 lorries not exceeding 15 metres length, as well as 12 passengers on her regular freight run between Aberdeen, Kirkwall, Stromness and Lerwick. She was built at Lübeck, Germany and was originally to be named *Rhonetal* but she entered service as the *Norcape*, being renamed *Rhonetal* in 1974. Her name was conveniently shortened to *Rhone* in 1975, upon taking up services to Corsica for Meridional D'Armements of France. In 1987, she was bought by Conatir of Italy and renamed *Marino Torre*. In 1989 she was chartered for 6 months by P&O Scottish Ferries to operate alongside the freight ferry *St. Magnus*, retaining her name for the task. However the *St. Magnus* left the fleet in 1990 and the *Marino Torre* was bought outright by the company. She was renamed *St. Rognvald*, fourth of the name, and remains in service complementing the full passenger and vehicle service offered by the other three "saints" from Aberdeen and Scrabster. Her schedule sees her providing up to three round trips per week to Shetland, one operating via Orkney and she reintroduced calls at Kirkwall on 13th January 1992, after an absence of 14 years. On 5th March 1991 she was southbound for Aberdeen when heavy seas damaged the bridge and left her powerless and without communication. An emergency was declared and her crew stood by to evacuate the ship. However the emergency passed when partial power was recovered and the *St. Rognvald* managed to find shelter in Sinclair Bay, avoiding a potentially dangerous situation.

On 11th February 1990, the *St. Rognvald* had the dubious distinction of ending the regular P&O connection with Leith for the second time in the company history, although the last ever call was made by the *St. Clair* which operated a further freight run to Lerwick on 10th March 1990. In 1989 and 1990, the *St. Rognvald* sailed weekly from Aberdeen to Stavanger and Hanstholm, departing from her home port on Sundays, but the service was withdrawn after only ten months due to poor loadings. In 1993, the *St. Rognvald* saw service between Middlesborough and Gothenburg on charter to Ferrymasters, also a P&O Group member, whilst in July and August 1995 she operated between the Tyne and Bergen in support of the Color Line services operated by the *Venus*. Add to this her livestock sailings in partnership with vessels such as the chartered livestock carrier *Angus Express* and it can be seen that the *St. Rognvald* leads a varied life.

## SHETLAND ISLANDS FERRIES

Within Shetland, inter island steamer services had first been provided in 1868 by the Shetland Islands Steam Navigation Co. with the introduction of the 94 gross ton *Chieftains Bride*. She was replaced in 1877 by a new ship, the Paisley built *Earl of Zetland* which, after an illustrious Shetland career spanning nearly 70 years was replaced in 1946 by her diesel powered namesake. For many years, Shetland tradition meant that the cargo and passengers taken by the *Earl of Zetland* from Lerwick to the islands had been transferred from ship to shore using flit boats which had often been sixareens, traditional 30 foot long open fishing craft powered by six rowers or by a sail. But the geography of the Shetland Islands meant that serious competition was beginning to emerge from the overland route employing shorter sea crossings connecting with bus services. Ironically, the overland route was the longest established way to the furthest flung islands although over the years, it was the steamer service which had become the preferred route, on account of the crossings between islands being made in open sailing boats and the roads on land being poor. But from the nineteen thirties, motor ferry boats and improvements to island roads began to draw traffic away from the "Earls" and onto the overland route once again. Finally, in the nineteen seventies, a fleet of small roll on - roll off ferries was placed into service and, like so many of her consorts elsewhere, the *Earl of Zetland* became a casualty of the arrival of the car ferry.

In 1964, the Highlands and Islands Development Board and the former Zetland County Council produced a strategy for the development of a series of inter-island roll on - roll off ferry services. The suitability of such ferries was demonstrated by the Norwegian vessel *Rovdehorn* which visited Shetland for a short time in 1965 and toured the North Isles whilst sailing from a temporary linkspan at Lerwick. Her impact was to be long lasting. As improved roads snaked across Shetland, Government financial assistance meant that the *Earl of Zetland* was progressively replaced by the new small car and passenger ferries, operated initially by Zetland County Council, and now by Shetland Islands Council. These vessels introduced short sea crossings between the islands which allowed provision of much more frequent and reliable car and passenger ferry links than

*A period piece at Lerwick sees the **Earl of Zetland** loading for the isles in 1966. (Alistair Cormack)*

the old "Earl" could ever have maintained. The first batch of these ferries was placed into service in the period 1973 - 76 to maintain regular inter island services, developed largely along the style which had emerged in the Norwegian Fjords. Initially, five of the new ferries, similar in design to the *Rovdehorn*, were introduced and it soon became clear that the days of the coastal packet ship had come to an end in Shetland.

### Earl of Zetland

Built in 1939 by Hall, Russell of Aberdeen, the second *Earl of Zetland* operated on her intended route for a short time in 1939, but she served throughout World War 2 on the Scrabster - Stromness route as a military ferry and took up her civilian route, on a permanent basis, only in 1946. She earned her spurs by providing a regular and reliable coastal packet service between Lerwick and the Northern Isles of the Shetland archipelago : Yell, Skerries, Whalsay and Fetlar, terminating at Baltasound on Unst from where tourists could take a bus tour to view Muckle Flugga, the most northerly point in the British Isles. She continued on this service until replaced indirectly by the new car ferry services which began to link the islands, allowing more convenient and frequent crossings between the Mainland and the islands served by the *Earl of Zetland*.

Even when she entered service, the drift to the overland route was well underway and although she continued to be a great favourite with tourists, her usefulness for islanders was limited. Her leisurely roster - two departures per week to Baltasound and a shorter Wednesday round trip to Uyeasound - was proving to be inadequate for islanders' needs. As the new ferries were introduced on

*A fine view of the Earl of Zetland underway near Symbister.* (Tommy Watt, Shetland Museums)

routes such as the Bluemull Sound and Yellsound crossings and the overland route was provided with better and bigger buses, the *Earl of Zetland* was required to call at fewer communities, many of which had no suitable pier for her to use in any case. One by one, she bade farewell to communities where the new ferries were replacing her - to Yell and Unst in 1973 and to Fetlar and Skerries about a year later, until Symbister (Whalsay) and Skerries, remained the only communities still requiring her services. Her withdrawal was inevitable and she made a sad farewell to Shetland, undertaking her last journey to the islands on 21st February 1975.

However, her career was not over. Renamed *Celtic Surveyor*, she was sold to a St. Ives based company and took up employment in oil

*The Fylga is seen in calm waters as she sets off on a crossing of Yellsound.* (Miles Cowsill)

related activity on charter to Occidental before becoming a restaurant ship at Great Yarmouth and subsequently at Eastbourne, before being transferred to North Shields in February 1997 where she remains as part of the Royal Quays development.

### Fivla (I)

The first of the new small ferries to arrive in Shetland, the *Fivla* was built in the Faroe Islands and achieved ten knots on trial. Having been named at Toft on 17th May 1973, she opened the Ulsta (Yell) service from Toft, taking up service on 21st May 1973 and replacing the locally owned vessel *Shalder*. However, the *Fivla* moved south, opening the Bressay Sound service on 13th October 1975 and replacing the *Tystie* on the crossing. She remained on this route until the *Grima* replaced her in February 1976. With a gross tonnage of 174 and capacity for 12 cars and 93 passengers, she set the standard for all of the original five ferries. Upon the arrival of the *Hendra* in 1982, the *Fivla* was sold to the Newfoundland and Labrador Government and was renamed *Island Joiner*.

### Geira (I)

Like the *Fivla*, the first *Geira* was built in the Faroe Islands and entered service on the Bluemull Sound crossing between Gutcher (Yell) and Belmont (Unst) on 20th November 1973 replacing the locally owned launch, *Tystie* which transferred to the Bressay service. She remained the regular vessel on this crossing and also served Oddsta (Fetlar) from November 1974. She was sold to the Orkney Islands Shipping Company in April 1986, becoming the third *Hoy Head* before being sold to owners in Ramsgate for survey work under the name *Task One*.

### Grima

Built at Bideford, Devon, in 1974, the *Grima*, after entering service in the North Isles, was chartered in February 1975, by the former North Company to replace the *Earl of Zetland* on the route from Lerwick to Whalsay until a full roll on - roll off service came into operation on 2nd February 1976, under the control of Shetland

*It is a rainy day at Lerwick in July 1977 as the Grima loads for Bressay.* (Roy Pedersen)

Islands Council. The *Grima* then transferred to the Bressay service, replacing the *Fivla*, where she became the regular vessel until the introduction of the *Leirna* in 1992. She acted as Royal Yacht on 24th July 1986, carrying the Prince and Princess of Wales between Lerwick and Bressay. She is still in service.

### Fylga

Having also been built in the Faroe Islands, this vessel arrived in Lerwick on 19th January 1975 and took up her regular service on the Yellsound service between Toft and Ulsta, allowing the *Fivla* to transfer to the Bressay service later that year. However, with effect from the inauguration of roll on - roll off services on the route, she became the regular Whalsay vessel, until the arrival of the *Hendra* in 1982, saw her return to her former Yellsound haunts. Since 1993, she has been on the Bluemull Sound Fetlar crossing but now covers other services.

*The much travelled Spes Clara appears to be loading a horsebox, one of her many unconventional cargoes.* (Willie Mackay)

*An ongoing problem is solved at last as the Foula ferry **New Advance** approaches Lerwick.* (Willie Mackay)

### Thora

The *Thora* was the fifth of the original vessels and was also built in the Faroe Islands, arriving in Lerwick on 12th September 1975. Her regular service saw her become the second vessel on the Yellsound crossing, entering service on 5th April 1976. However, due to the requirement for winter relief vessels elsewhere, the double provision at Yellsound was only available in summer, until the arrival of the sixth ferry in 1980. A sister of the *Fylga* and the *Grima*, the *Thora* now services Symbister.

### Spes Clara

On 25th February 1975, Shetland Islands Council took over the operation of the Symbister - Skerries service from the North

Company. For the task, the Council's general purpose cargo vessel *Spes Clara* was utilised, operating initially from Symbister but sailing from Lerwick, with effect from 1976. She became spare in 1983 following the introduction of the *Filla* on the Skerries service. However, she continued to be deployed on a number of duties, visiting Foula and Papa Stour and she even made a sailing to Norway to collect a new propeller shaft for the *Hendra*. She is a useful general dogsbody of a ship and the *Spes Clara* remains in service today.

The original five roll on - roll off vessels were soon generating substantial traffic and they were quickly joined by other vessels. In 1978, a twenty car vessel was considered appropriate for the Yellsound route, although the sixth ferry eventually appeared with capacity for only twelve cars. In addition, 1980 saw the transfer of the operation of the Foula mail contract to the SIC for which they purchased the Foula mailboat *Westering Homewards*.

### Kjella

The sixth ferry in the SIC fleet was the *Kjella* which was acquired from the Norwegian operators A/S Torghatten Trafikselskap. She had been built in 1957 by Kaarbos MV A/S of Norway for service in Brønnøysund. After an extensive refit at Maaloy, the 163 gross ton vessel arrived at Lerwick on 10th July 1980 and became the regular vessel on the Whalsay service from Laxo, releasing the *Fylga* and permitting a two ship operation on the Yellsound crossings all year round. With capacity for 12 cars and 63 passengers, she retained her original name, *Kjella* when she took up service in Shetland. Despite being considered a stop gap vessel, until the arrival of new tonnage, she continued as the second Whalsay ship until April 1998 but, with her steelwork deteriorating after 41 years of service, she was sold to Babcock of Rosyth for scrapping in October 1998.

*The veteran Shetland ferry **Kjella** is seen reversing into the berth at Laxo in May 1997.* (Miles Cowsill)

*The **Leirna** departs from Lerwick on the 5 minute crossing to Bressay in May 1997. (Miles Cowsill)*

### Hendra

The new vessel for the Whalsay service was named *Hendra* and was built by McTay Marine of Bromborough in 1982. Her delivery voyage from the Mersey saw her stormbound at Stromness for five days but she eventually commenced service on 30th November 1982, releasing the *Fivla* which was sold, and the *Fylga* which transferred to Yellsound. With a car capacity of 18 and a gross tonnage of 225, the *Hendra*, was the largest vessel in the SIC fleet until the arrival of the *Leirna* in 1993. She is now a regular on the Whalsay service although Vidlin is used as the mainland terminal in preference to Laxo, under certain conditions.

### Filla

The new ferry for the Skerries service was built by the Iversen shipyard at Flekkefjörd, Norway and her inauguration took place on 28th November 1983. The *Filla* has capacity for 20 passengers in summer, 12 in winter, and she can carry 6 cars although she is used on freight services around Shetland when not engaged on her regu-

*The Thora is one of Shetland's first generation ferries, originally built for the Toft-Ulsta link. (Miles Cowsill)*

lar Skerries service from Vidlin or Lerwick. In appearance she resembles a small scale oil rig supply vessel, being of only 130 gross tons. She has a stern ramp, a hold and a strengthened deck with flush hatches to carry a lorry and she was fitted with a larger crane in 1998. On her introduction, in 1983, the *Spes Clara* became spare vessel.

### Fivla (II)

SIC went to the Clyde for the second ship to bear this name. The *Fivla* was built at the Ailsa Shipyard at Troon specifically for the Bluemull Sound service, serving Gutcher (Yell), Belmont (Unst) and occasionally, Oddsta (Fetlar). With capacity for 15 cars and 95 passengers and a gross tonnage of 230, she was larger than the previous ferries and she took up service on 22nd April 1985, being named on 29th April 1985 although she had already operated on the Whalsay service from 15th to 19th April 1985. She is still a regular vessel on the Bluemull Sound crossings.

### Geira (II)

A further large new ferry was built at Richard Dunstons yard at Hessle in 1988 and was allocated to the Ulsta (Yell) - Toft (Mainland) route on which she carries 15 cars and 95 passengers. She entered service on 22nd July 1988 and her arrival rendered the *Kjella* redundant although she remained in the SIC fleet. The *Geira* continues to partner the *Bigga* on the Yellsound crossing.

### Bigga

1991 saw the introduction of the *Bigga* on the Yellsound crossing. Having been built at the James Miller yard at St. Monans, Fife, she was named at Mid Yell on 19th April 1991. With capacity for 95 passengers and 17 cars, she continues to partner the *Geira* on the Toft (Mainland) - Ulsta (Yell) route although the *Bigga* is the main vessel. Between the two ships, up to 26 sailings per day can be operated on the busy crossing. She replaced the *Thora* which became spare vessel.

*Leirna*

At 420 gross tons the *Leirna* is the largest vessel in the SIC fleet. She was built at Ferguson Shipbuilders of Port Glasgow and was named on 14th November 1992 at Maryfield Terminal, Bressay. She took up service on the Lerwick - Bressay service on 2nd November 1992, replacing the *Grima* of 1974. The *Leirna*, powered by two Kelvin Diesels driving twin Voith - Schneider propulsion units, is capable of a service speed of 9.3 knots. With capacity for 19 cars and 96 passengers and with a gross tonnage of 420, she is the first and, so far, the only true double ended vessel in the SIC fleet. Since the introduction of roll on - roll off services on the Bressay route, the number of vehicles had increased from 14,800 in 1976 to 50,200 in 1992 whilst passenger numbers rose from 71,600 to 135,400 in the same period, testifying to the success of the new ferries.

## FALLING FOUL AT FOULA

The term "lifeline service" is commonly used in any discussion relating to Scottish island ferries. Nowhere is this term more applicable than in relation to the ferry services which operate to the remote islands of Foula and Fair Isle. Foula has a population of about 40, lying 27 miles west of Scalloway in Shetland, whilst Fair Isle, with a population of about 70, lies 25 miles south of Sumburgh Head, Shetland. Economically fragile communities with little contact with the outside world, these islands are more reliant than most for regular and reliable ferry links to sustain them. Tourism is a secondary consideration because the provision of a good ferry link means the difference between survival and extinction. Even within the SIC context, these services are regarded as unique routes with low frequencies of operation and low passenger usage, but with a need to employ sturdy ships capable of dealing with everything that the most exposed parts of the North Atlantic can throw at them. It was all the more frustrating therefore, for the residents of Foula, to find themselves caught up in one of the most farcical sequence of events in recent Scottish ferry history.

*Good Shepherd III, Good Shepherd IV, Westering Homewards, New Advance*

The *Good Shepherd III* was originally an inshore trawler which had been owned since 1972 by the islanders of Fair Isle and which had maintained the regular island service. In 1984, the SIC announced their intention to replace her with a new vessel and to transfer her to the Foula service, although she did, in fact end up serving Papa Stour. In February 1985, the new Fair Isle ship was ordered from James Miller & Son of St. Monans and she was named the *Good Shepherd IV*. Assembled at the Fife yard, but prefabricated by McTay Marine at Bromborough, she made her maiden voyage to Fair Isle on 24th May 1986. Capable of carrying only 1 car, which is craned on and off, and 12 passengers, this sturdy vessel is the main link between Fair Isle and Grutness, although Lerwick is occasionally used as her winter port on the Shetland Mainland and she also makes Lerwick calls in summer. The *Good Shepherd III* was subsequently renamed *Koada* and took up service between West Burrafirth and Papa Stour, but she became involved in the Foula saga which was about to unfold.

In 1989, a new ferry was ordered from Dingle Boats of Ireland to replace the *Westering Homewards*, a former RNLI lifeboat, on the Foula service. But this company were in financial difficulties and the construction of the new ship was transferred to the Jones Buckie shipyard on the Moray Firth. The new ship would also be called *Westering Homewards* and although only 45 feet long, her speed of 18 knots was to be impressive. All seemed well. But on trials the

*The **Good Shepherd IV** shares a busy Lerwick Harbour with the **Geira**, **Grima** and the **St. Sunniva**.* (Willie MacKay)

*Westering Homewards* managed a paltry 13 knots whilst other defects in the ship led to substantial delays to her delivery. Meanwhile the withdrawal and sale of the previous *Westering Homewards* had meant that Foula had only received one call per month on average, by the *Koada* or by the *Good Shepherd IV*. Clearly this was an unsatisfactory situation. The new *Westering Homewards* finally arrived in Shetland on 23rd July 1991, over a year late. However, SIC were unconvinced of her suitability and she was regarded only as a "fair weather water taxi" which was hardly suitable for one of the most exposed crossings in Europe. It was not that the *Westering Homewards* was a poor boat, simply that a combination of bureaucracy, inappropriate design and separation of the construction programmes for the Foula harbour improvements and for the ship herself had led to construction of a vessel which did nothing particularly well.

Alternative proposals for the Foula service were advanced, whilst efforts continued, to no avail, to find alternative employment for the *Westering Homewards*. In 1993, the *Koada* was based at Foula, crossing to Scalloway and Walls, giving Foula its first reliable service since 1990. However, such a service could only be operated in Summer when it was safe for the vessel to berth in the harbour at Foula, winter months requiring the ship to be taken out of the water to allow her to shelter from the weather and strong tides experienced at the exposed island terminal. Meanwhile the *Westering Homewards* lay in her cradle at Sella Ness, unused and neglected since her delivery in 1991. The situation was resolved in 1995 when the SIC acquired a vessel building at Penryn and construction was completed at Stromness before the new boat was named the *New Advance*. With a passenger capacity of 12 and being capable of carrying one sizeable vehicle, the *New Advance* entered service on the Foula route on 12th November 1996. Since then, she has provided the island with its long awaited home based ferry service, using Walls as the usual mainland terminal. For the *Westering Homewards*,

the end of this Norse saga came with her sale in August 1996 to the North Atlantic Fisheries College at Scalloway and she was renamed *Moder Dy*.

## CHANGE COMES TO ORKNEY

*"The north isles steamer maaks her roond, by Eday Pier an' Stronsay Soond; She lands the mails at Papey. The sooth boat wi' her mastheid lights glides doun the String on Friday nights. The Ola sails b' Scapey".* Extract from "Lament for the Legends" by Robert Rendall.

Steamer services to the outlying islands of Orkney had been provided by the long established Orkney Steam Navigation Company utilising the two old stalwarts *Earl Sigurd* (1931) and *Earl Thorfinn* (1928) successors to the original *Orcadia* of 1868. But by the early nineteen sixties these two vessels had become outdated and uneconomical, although they continued to run as sweetly as they had when built. The solution was to replace them with appropriate new tonnage but the Orkney Steam Navigation Company could not afford to provide the replacements, at a time when shipbuilding costs were spiralling upwards. But the 1960 Highlands and Islands Shipping Services Act allowed for Government subvention to be applied to the construction and operation of such essential lifeline services, legislation which had been of benefit to the West Coast through the construction of the first car ferries for MacBraynes. But in Orkney, neither the Orkney Steam Navigation Co. nor the North Company were willing to undertake the ongoing maintenance of the North Isles services and so the solution was to create a new company, government owned, which took over the assets of the Orkney Steam Navigation and placed the new ships into service. The new company was named the Orkney Islands Shipping Company (OISC) and their new vessel was to carry a famous name.

*A spring morning sees the Orcadia slip into the jetty at Pierowall, Westray.* (Alistair Cormack)

*The way it was before the advent of ro - ro as the* **Orcadia** *discharges cargo using her derrick on a wet day at Pierowall, Westray on 13th October 1972.* (Alasdair L. Munro)

### Orcadia

Built in 1961 by Hall Russell of Aberdeen, the new *Orcadia* arrived at Kirkwall on 30th June 1962 and immediately introduced a new level of passenger comfort to the North Isles of Orkney. With a gross tonnage of 896, she sailed on a regular mail, freight and passenger roster based on Kirkwall and her operation broadly mirrored those of MacBraynes mailboats on the West Coast and that of the *Earl of Zetland* in Shetland. She was partnered by the ageing steamer *Earl Sigurd,* until 1969 and subsequently by the *Islander.* Meanwhile, the *Orcadia* operated the main round of the islands for passengers, livestock and cargo and also undertook a programme of excursion sailings and charters. With capacity for 358 passengers, any vehicles conveyed by the *Orcadia* were loaded by her single derrick and it is perhaps surprising that no real consideration appears to have been made to providing a vehicular ferry at a time when many routes around the coast were seeing the introduction of such vessels. In addition to her regular round of the islands, the *Orcadia* undertook excursions from Kirkwall on public holidays and also visited Fair Isle during the 1960s and 1970s. A change to her routine occurred during the absence of the *St. Ola* in 1982, thanks to her flirtation with fire, and the *Orcadia* was chartered by P&O to cover on the Pentland Firth route between 2nd November and 27th November 1982 and again in January the following year although her sailings were from Kirkwall, with the mainland port often being Wick rather than Scrabster. The first rumblings regarding the introduction of roll on - roll off ferries to the North Isles arose around 1982 and it was clear that her days were numbered. But the *Orcadia* soldiered on. In 1986 she undertook an additional task, spending summer weekends linking Kirkwall and Scalloway on charter to P&O and developing traffic on the link which had been operated the previous year by the *Syllingar*. Traffic growth was sufficiently favourable to encourage P&O to acquire a dedicated vessel for the route, leading to the arrival of the *St. Sunniva*. However, by the end of the nineteen eighties, the *Orcadia* was proving to be outmoded for

the North Isles and the imminent arrival of new roll on - roll off ferries meant that her demise was at hand.

Upon the arrival of the new ferries, the *Earl Thorfinn* and the *Earl Sigurd,* the faithful *Orcadia,* the last of the "classic" inter island passenger and mailboats was withdrawn. On Sunday 5th August 1990, the *Orcadia* made a farewell cruise to the North Isles and made her last sailing of all on 24th August, visiting all of the North Isles except Eday where terminal reconstruction kept her out of the pier. The *Earl Thorfinn* duly arrived at Kirkwall and the displaced *Orcadia* sailed for Leith where she was laid up on 5th September 1990. In spite of a reported sale, she remained at Leith, eventually departing for Florida only in December 1994, having been sold to Admiralty Trading for inter island services in the Caribbean.

### Islander

The second vessel to be constructed for the new OISC inner and outer North Isles services was not a true passenger ship at all. The arrival of regular air travel to Orkney, in the shape of Loganair and British European Airways ensured that inter island travellers did not have to endure the often temperamental seas around the islands and consequently passenger numbers merited only one new passenger vessel. The *Islander* was therefore a cargo ship which carried only 12 passengers on her round of the North Isles and she complemented the full passenger service offered by the *Orcadia*. Built at the John Lewis & Sons shipyard in Aberdeen, the *Islander* was a ship of 250 gross tons and she entered service in July 1969. She struck the Muckle Green Holm whilst on passage between Westray and Shapinsay on 14th July 1975, necessitating her absence until 2nd October, during which period only the *Orcadia* and aircraft were available to cover for her. Similar trouble occurred on 2nd July 1976 when the *Islander* grounded on the Vasa Skerry near Shapinsay and she required repairs at Aberdeen. She continued her love affair with the Vasa Skerry by repeating the trick on 31st December 1987, seeing in the New Year high and dry before being refloated on 1st

January 1988. During her career, she undertook some unusual tasks including removing a farm from Egilsay to Peterhead on 11th May 1979 and visiting Fair Isle on numerous occasions to convey diesel fuel and other cargoes. She also visited the island in June 1980 to deliver a fire engine for the island's airstrip. The introduction of roll on - roll off services provided by the *Eynhallow* dispensed with the need for the *Islander* to serve Rousay, Wyre and Egilsay and she ceased to visit these islands as from 10th September 1987. The die was cast for the introduction of further new ferries and her calls at Shapinsay ended in May 1989. The *Islander* was finally rendered redundant on 23rd August 1991 upon the introduction of the new ferries for the North Isles. Duly laid up at Kirkwall, and at Stronsay for a time, the *Islander* remained in Orkney until 22nd January 1993, having been sold for further service to owners based in Casablanca. In appreciation of her service, she was escorted out of Kirkwall for the last time by the new *Earl Sigurd* and the *Varagen*.

### Clytus

This small ferry, with capacity for 31 passengers, was introduced by the OISC in July 1970 and provided the passenger service to Shapinsay from Kirkwall. She had previously been a Clyde pilot launch and was built in 1944 as the *Gantock*. However her OISC career ended with the introduction of the new roll on - roll off ferry *Shapinsay*. Surplus to the company requirements, the *Clytus* was withdrawn from service on 8th May 1989 and was sold for further use as a diving boat.

### Hoy Head (II)

This vessel, a passenger and cargo ship with capacity for 36 passengers and with a gross tonnage of 93, was built in 1955 and was

*A forlorn looking Orcadia awaits her fate at Leith in 1993.* (Willie Mackay)

the second ship to bear the name. She was the regular vessel on the South Isles services to Hoy and Flotta and was acquired by OISC on 1st April 1974 when her private owners, Bremner & Co merged with the OISC. Both the *Hoy Head* and her running mate the passenger ferry *Watchful*, a 1944 built converted MFV, maintained the South Isles services from Longhope but the *Watchful* was sold in

*The Orcadia makes one of her regular arrivals at the old pier at Stronsay.* (Alistair Cormack)

March 1976, to be replaced by the newly acquired vehicular ferry *Lyrawa Bay*. With the introduction of this vessel, the *Hoy Head* was relegated to spare vessel and she was sold out of the OISC fleet in 1987, to Viking Sea Taxis of Shetland, and subsequently to Arran owners in 1998.

### Lyrawa Bay

In January 1976, the OISC bought a small 4 car capacity ferry named *Sam* from the Faroe Islands and placed her on services to the South Islands serving Lyness, Longhope and Flotta in consort with the *Hoy Head*. Although she had been a roll on - roll off vessel when acquired, the absence of the necessary terminals meant that she was converted to provide conventional freight working. Protracted debate in Orkney surrounding the location for new roll on - roll off terminals to serve the South Isles meant that the introduction of such services did not occur until 1983 and the *Lyrawa Bay* was re-converted at Buckie in March 1983, to permit her to use these new facilities. The roll on - roll off services to the South Isles commenced from the new terminal at Houton on 25th April 1983 and became an instant success, with the *Lyrawa Bay* as the main ship and the passenger and cargo ship *Hoy Head* as spare vessel. Upon arrival of the *Geira,* soon to be the new roll on - roll off ferry *Hoy Head,* in April 1986, the *Lyrawa Bay* became spare ship and the arrival of another new ship, the *Thorsvoe* in 1991 saw the *Lyrawa Bay* become completely surplus to OISC requirements and she was sold in September 1991 to a fish farm owner.

## ORCADIAN EARLS

In 1983, the introduction of roll on - roll off services to the South Isles, using the *Lyrawa Bay,* had led to massive increases in usage of the new services, traffic increasing by an average of 179% over the first two years of operation. In 1986, the OISC revealed

*The Orcargo freighter **Contender** arriving at Kirkwall from Invergordon on 5th May 1993.* (Willie Mackay)

their plans to provide a new roll on - roll off service to the inner North Isles of Egilsay, Rousay, Wyre and Shapinsay. These islands would be provided by slipways which would be served by two landing craft type vessels which would be delivered in 1987 and 1989. These new ships duly arrived on the scene bearing the names *Eynhallow* and *Shapinsay*.

Consideration had been given to the conversion of services to the North Isles as long ago as 1981 when the OISC examined the provision of new ferry services based on a combination of stern and side loading vessels. However, protracted debate ensued, including a brief flirtation with the potential for introduction of "Storm Master" catamarans, and it was not until 1987 that approval for provision of two new roll on - roll off vessels was given. On 1st April 1987, the Orkney Islands Shipping Company was taken over by Orkney Islands Council and government approval was given to proceed with the conversion of steamer services to the North Isles of Westray, Sanday, Eday and Stronsay to roll on - roll off operation. With sub-

*The **Islander** laid up at Kirkwall at the end of her career on 15th April 1992.* (Author)

*A stormy day in April 1992 finds the **Eynhallow** at Tingwall as she backs away from the slipway en route to Egilsay.* (Author)

stantial government and European Community grants available for the project, and the seemingly endless debate eventually completed, progress was rapid on the construction of the new ships, although less spectacular on provision of the new terminals. Nevertheless, when the programme was completed, the North Isles of Orkney had witnessed a complete change of pace, from the rather laid back round of the islands provided by the *Orcadia* and the *Islander*, to a regular, frequent roll on - roll off ferry service to the islands, provided by a modern fleet, not of the proposed two vessels, but of three, the third appearing on the scene reluctantly and as a result of a somewhat disastrous experiment. The new terminals were eventually constructed at Rapness (Westray), Loth (Sanday), Stronsay and Eday with freight being crane loaded at North Ronaldsay and Papa Westray. The routes gradually opened up to full roll on - roll off operation by December 1992, whilst a regular passenger feeder service was introduced between Westray (Pierowall) and Papa Westray in Summer of 1994.

The new vessels for the North Isles, the *Earl Sigurd* and the *Earl Thorfinn*, arrived on the scene in 1990 and initially continued the "traditional" sailings of the *Orcadia*, gradually phasing in roll on - roll off operations, until such times as the new terminals became fully available for use. But even today, the roll on - roll off revolution has not reached North Ronaldsay or Papa Westray and these islands continue to be served once and twice weekly respectively by the "Earl" ships on a conventional basis, whilst Orkney Islands Council provides a subsidy to Loganair to operate a daily air service to serve additional passenger needs.

### Eynhallow

Built in 1987 at Bristol, the *Eynhallow* made a long delivery voyage from the Bristol Channel to Orkney, where she now maintains the Inner North Isles services to Egilsay, Wyre and Rousay from Tingwall. She is, in some respects, a larger version of the Caledonian MacBrayne "Island" class vessels and indeed she has occasionally been relieved by one of these ships during her overhaul period. The *Eynhallow* entered service on 24th August 1987, based at Wyre and quickly became a victim of her own success in generating traffic. To meet increased demand, she was lengthened in April 1991 to incorporate an additional 5 metre section providing additional car capacity. The work was undertaken at the Buckie Shipyard and the *Eynhallow* returned to service on 27th May 1991, with her capacity increased to permit her to carry up to 10 cars and 95 passengers.

### Shapinsay

The new roll on - roll off vessel to serve Shapinsay was built at the Jones Buckie Shipyard but with hull construction subcontracted to the Yorkshire Drydock Co. of Hull and the *Shapinsay* entered service on the Kirkwall - Shapinsay service on 30th July 1989, bringing a substantial improvement on the former passenger service offered by the *Clytus*. New slipways were constructed for use of the *Shapinsay* at Kirkwall and at Balfour on Shapinsay itself. With capacity for 91 passengers and 12 cars the *Shapinsay* has caused traffic to grow substantially on the 25 minute crossing. In addition to her regular service she has annually been employed on inner North Isles services on relief sailings during periods of overhaul for the regular vessel, the *Eynhallow*.

### *Earl Thorfinn* and *Earl Sigurd*

In late 1988, orders were placed for the two new vessels to operate the roll on - roll off services to the outer North Isles. Both vessels were to be 45 metres long with capacity for 27 cars and 144 passengers, although they can now carry 191 passengers. Both ships were built by McTay Marine of Bromborough although fitting out was undertaken by the Miller boatyard at St. Monans, Fife. The total cost of the two vessels eventually ran to £5.4 million. Happily, the arrival of the new vessels brought with it the resurrection of the old Orcadian "Earl" names which had been bestowed upon the two steamers of bygone days.

The first of the new ships to arrive in Orkney was the *Earl Thorfinn* which experienced rough weather on passage from the Mersey and arrived in Kirkwall on 19th August 1990 before taking up service on 27th August, serving the North Isles in a conventional role as the new terminals were not ready for use. She replaced the *Orcadia* almost directly and with the introduction of the *Earl Sigurd*, and the opening of the full roll on - roll off service, she now shares the Westray, Papa Westray, Sanday and North Ronaldsay duties with her twin although both utilise their 7 tonne cranes at North Ronaldsay and Papa Westray where no roll on - roll off facilities are available as yet. The *Earl Sigurd* entered service on 14th November 1990 and commenced her shared duties with her sister, continuing to do so until the introduction of the full roll on - roll off timetable. The two "Earl" ships rarely deviate from their joint roster and, apart from the inevitable mechanical glitches which affect all ships, they are generally reliable units of the Orkney Ferries fleet. An unscheduled visit to Aberdeen was made by the *Earl Thorfinn* on 29th November 1993 when gales forced her to seek shelter whilst she was en route to Leith for overhaul. On 25th April 1996 the *Earl Thorfinn* was again in the news when a breakdown near Eday meant that she required to be taken in tow, in good weather, by the *Earl Sigurd*, for which the crew of the *Earl Sigurd* received £3000 salvage between them. In 1995, the OISC changed its name to Orkney Ferries and a modified colour scheme was introduced which was applied to all ships, including the *Earl Thorfinn* and the *Earl Sigurd*, during the latter part of 1995. In 1998, the duo became excursion ships for a day

when, together with the *Varagen*, they operated public sailings to view the *Queen Elizabeth 2* which made her first ever visit to Orkney on the 1st August of that year.

### *Varagen*

In the mid sixties, fuelled by a visit to Kirkwall by Western Ferries *Sound of Jura* on her delivery voyage, Orkney interests began to consider the options for an alternative short sea crossing of the Pentland Firth to rival that of the Scrabster - Stromness route. The various investigations undertaken by the HIDB and Orkney County Council, encouraged the North Company to embark on the construction of their roll on - roll off ferry *St. Ola*, whilst local interests mused over the prospects for a shorter route linking South Ronaldsay to the Scottish mainland. In partial response, Captain William Banks operated a service in 1972 and 1973 using the converted launch *Pentalina*, between John o' Groats and St. Margaret's Hope. But although the venture was a short lived one, the issue remained live and in 1988 a new company, Orkney Ferries, was established by an Orcadian entrepreneur, with a view to operating a more cost effective service than that operated by rivals P&O Scottish Ferries. But the sites chosen for the terminals, at Gills Bay in Caithness and Burwick on South Ronaldsay, were regarded by those who knew these waters as a poor choice. Nevertheless, a new ferry was ordered for the proposed route at a cost of £2.5 million and construction work, funded by Orkney Islands Council, commenced on the new terminals. The new ferry was named *Varagen*, Norse for "our own" and was launched on 31st March 1989 at Cochrane Shipbuilders of Selby for the proposed service. With capacity for 33 cars and 150 passengers, it was intended that the crossing time of the *Varagen* would be thirty minutes and the service would operate every two hours from Burwick. This route would therefore have provided a short route to Orkney from the Scottish mainland and in spite of warnings from those who knew the Caithness coastline, Orkney Council proceeded to plough substantial amounts of money into the terminals, incurring an overspend of over £3 million on the budget of £1.8 million.

The *Varagen* began a service of sorts from Gills Bay on 15th

*The **Earl Thorfinn** seen at speed en route to Kirkwall.* (Willie Mackay)

*The **Earl Sigurd** rests at Kirkwall between sailings to the North Isles on 16th April 1992.* (Author)

August 1989, sailing to Houton rather than to Burwick, thanks to dredging problems, but the company's plans were soon in trouble. The *Varagen* was proving to be unsuitable for the task and the *coup de grace* occurred on 16th September 1989 when the Gills Bay terminal was severely damaged by heavy seas. The *Varagen* was laid up at Grangemouth and the Council approved further expenditure of £3.3 million on the terminals before realising that the entire project was in jeopardy, thanks to mounting problems with the terminals and the need to undertake substantial remedial work to the *Varagen* herself. Months of legal wrangles and disputes followed resulting in the ending of the ferry proposals whilst the *Varagen* found herself becoming a member of the fleet of the Orkney Islands Shipping Company on 15th March 1991. After 18 months laid up at Grangemouth, she returned northwards to operate in consort with the new *Earl Thorfinn* and *Earl Sigurd*, taking up service on the roll on - roll off services to the North Isles, based at Kirkwall. Meanwhile, £7 million, had been written off against the Gills Bay - Burwick project.

The *Varagen* returned to Orkney and, suitably modified, took up service on 30th August 1991 on services to the North Isles for which she appeared to be more suited. She has continued to operate in consort with the "Earls" leading a largely uneventful life by comparison with her stormy early days. In August 1995, the Orkney Islands Shipping Company was renamed and after much debate on the islands, the new name was established as Orkney Ferries. Thus, in a strange twist of fate, the *Varagen* found herself in the livery of a company which bore the same name as that for which she had been built and which had caused great financial and political embarrassment in Orkney.

## Hoy Head (III)

Development of traffic on the South Isles roll on - roll off services necessitated the introduction of the third vessel to bear the name *Hoy Head*. This ship was formerly the Shetland Island Council ferry *Geira* which was acquired by OISC and placed into service on the South Isles services in early April 1986, rendering the *Lyrawa Bay* spare. During overhaul at Scalloway in April 1987, her name became *Hoy Head* and she continued to serve the South Isles until April 1994 when she was replaced by a new vessel of the same name, However, teething problems with the new ship meant frequent calls to action for the displaced ship which remained at Scapa and available for emergency service. The *Hoy Head* was sold from the fleet in September 1994, for further service in Gabon but this sale fell through and she is now owned by Reid Marine and undertakes survey work on the English Channel.

## Thorsvoe

Built by the Campbeltown Shipyard and launched on 17th June 1991, the *Thorsvoe* was built with interchangeable bow doors to allow her to operate on either the South Isles or inner North Isles routes, where the terminals were either of linkspan construction or were slipway terminals respectively. The *Thorsvoe* entered service on the OISC South Isles services from Houton, her regular route, on September 2nd 1991, but she has also seen regular service on relief sailings on the Shapinsay crossing. The *Thorsvoe* carries 16 cars and 122 passengers on her regular South Isles roster, although she has now been superseded by the new *Hoy Head* on the Houton - Flotta and Lyness routes and deputises on other routes as required.

### Hoy Head (IV)

Further improvement and upgrading of the terminal at Houton, which necessitated the transfer of the South Isles operations to Stromness between 18th October 1993 and 21st February 1994, was accompanied by the introduction of the fourth, and largest, vessel to bear the name *Hoy Head*. The new vessel was built at the Bideford yard of Appledore Shipbuilders and is a roll on - roll off ferry capable of carrying 125 passengers and 18 cars at a service speed of about 9 knots. Her introduction into service was somewhat chequered and her first few months in service were dogged by various mechanical problems. However, she has now settled in to become the mainstay of services to the South Isles and in this capacity, she has relegated the *Thorsvoe* to the position of spare ship.

### Guide

The final route within Orkney to be taken over by OISC, now Orkney Ferries, was the South Isles service between Stromness, Graemsay and Hoy. Until 1995, the service was operated by the *Jessie Ellen* in the ownership of Mr. Steve Mowat but to maintain the service following her sale, the locally owned vessel *Guide* was chartered by Orkney Ferries until their new *Graemsay* appeared in 1996. Relieved from her ferry services, the *Guide* now offers unique opportunities to view the sunken German fleet in Scapa Flow through the use of remotely operated cameras, and is owned by Roving Eye Enterprises Ltd, being based at Houton.

### Graemsay

Built at the Ailsa - Perth shipyard at Troon, at a price of £590,000, but completed by the Cathelco Group who took over the yard in May 1996, the *Graemsay* is a tiny car ferry with a capacity for 8 tonnes of cargo, 73 passengers and 1 vehicle. She took up service on 21st June 1996, replacing the privately owned *Jessie Ellen* and the stop gap passenger ferry *Guide* and she operates between Stromness and the islands of Hoy and Graemsay. She is designed to provide a year round passenger and cargo service to the South Isles in support of the larger vessels operating from Houton.

### Golden Mariana

Built in 1973 at Bideford, this small ship carries 40 passengers but has no car capacity. At only 33 gross tons she was initially employed as a tourist boat at Ullapool before being purchased by Pentland Ferries of St. Margaret's Hope and offering cruises to Shapinsay and Balfour Castle. Prior to 1987 she was owned by Orkney Islands Council and was managed on their behalf by OISC, seeing service on the Houton - Flotta service amongst others. Since the introduction of the passenger shuttle service, she has been a regular on the Papa Westray - Westray (Pierowall) services in recent years but she generally operates only in summer, providing a feeder service into the roll on - roll off network by linking Pierowall with Rapness via a minibus connection.

With their new roll on - roll off ferry operations now largely in place, Orkney Ferries provide a regular and reliable range of services throughout the islands and have greatly facilitated improvements in transportation and communications throughout Orkney.

*In foul weather, the little **Graemsay** battles through a winter storm in Hoy Sound in November 1997.* (Willie Mackay)

*The fourth **Hoy Head** shows her mettle as she crosses Scapa Flow in bad weather.* (Willie MacKay)

## OTHER NORTH ISLES OPERATORS

P&O have not had it all their own way on operations between the mainland of Scotland and the Northern Isles. A number of other significant operations have been established over the years, mainly offering cargo services although passenger operators have also appeared on the scene. Foremost amongst the companies which have commenced operations and who have stayed the course are Orcargo, the Streamline Group and, on passenger sailings, John o' Groats Ferries.

### Pentland Venture

At 45 minutes duration, the shortest ferry crossing between the mainland of Scotland and Orkney is operated between the Caithness harbour of John O' Groats and Burwick, South Ronaldsay utilising the *Pentland Venture*, which was built in 1987 with capacity for 250 passengers. Both she and the smaller *Burray Lass*, with capacity for 48 passengers, are owned by John o' Groats Ferries and offer wildlife cruises in addition to the regular ferry crossings.

### Contender

With the failure of the Gills Bay - Burwick service, Orkney Islands Council assisted in the establishment of a new, Kirkwall based company named Orcargo which was established by two local businessmen. They acquired the freight ferry *Contender*, and now operate her on a six times weekly schedule from Invergordon to Kirkwall, attracting road traffic away from the long and difficult haul up the A9 to Scrabster. Built in 1973 at Le Havre, the maroon hulled *Contender* was formerly the *Indiana* and her services to Orkney commenced on 7th March 1992, offering space for 12 passengers as well as for freight and livestock. In spite of P&O winning the most recent round of tenders to receive subsidy for Northern Isles services in 1997, Orcargo continued to offer a regular service using the *Contender* on sailings to Orkney, leaving Invergordon six times weekly, with early morning departures, and arriving at Kirkwall in the afternoon with an overnight return sailing. The *Contender* carries 12 passengers in comfortable cabins whilst enjoying complimentary meals on board.

### Baltic Champ

In 1984, Streamline Shipping established a new containerised cargo service between Aberdeen and Lerwick, extending the operation to Kirkwall three years later. Today the company offers twice weekly departures to the Northern Isles using the container ship *Baltic Champ*. The introduction of the Streamline service introduced more competitive freight rates on services to the islands and may have contributed indirectly to the withdrawal of Government tariff rebate, there being a view that the free market could operate on freight services to the Shetland Islands without the need for subsidy on such lifeline cargo services.

### Pentalina B

The former Caledonian MacBrayne ferry *Iona* took up her new guise in October 1987 under the ownership of Pentland Ferries who intended to revive the much vaunted Burwick - Gills Bay service during 1998. However, problems in developing suitable terminals in Orkney, coupled with the need to invest in new facilities at Gills Bay, meant that, apart from her period on charter to her former owners, the *Pentalina B* has remained laid up at St. Margaret's Hope.

*The handy little **Golden Mariana** seen on passage in calm seas off Westray.* (Willie MacKay)

*The Shetland ferry **Leirna** gets underway from Lerwick on one of her many daily crossings to Bressay.* (Miles Cowsill)

# The Future

## TOWARDS THE NEW MILLENNIUM

We stand at the doorstep, not only of the new Century but also of the new Millennium. In the last thousand years, the onward march of history has turned the waters of Scotland from trade routes to routes of war and back to trade routes in a process which has seen technological advances which would have been unimaginable to our ancestors. Journeys which would once have been perilous and of many days duration can now be accomplished comfortably in a few hours or less. The advent of steam power and subsequently the diesel engine, has changed Scottish ferry routes beyond imagination and passengers now know that, whether in fair weather or foul, their journey will be comfortable and safe. No doubt the 21st Century will witness many changes which it is not possible to anticipate from this distance and although the powers of the Brahan Seer are beyond this author, it does no harm to speculate as to what events might transpire in the near future.

On the Firth of Clyde, there seems little doubt that the principal services will continue to be provided by Caledonian MacBrayne in the near future. With years of experience and their long established connections with the local communities, it is unlikely that any major change of operator will occur in the foreseeable future. Current concerns must address the future of the Gourock - Dunoon route, the only one on which serious competition, from Western Ferries, exists. In a final act before its election defeat in May 1997, the outgoing Conservative government commissioned a further review of the Cowal routes and final recommendations are awaited with interest. It is clear that the three "streaker" ferries, *Jupiter*, *Juno* and *Saturn*, are relatively close to the end of their useful lives, whilst earlier local concerns, regarding the suitability of Western Ferries to be the sole operator, appear to remain strong. With Dunoon Pier recently suffering storm damage and requiring substantial repairs, it will be intriguing to observe what kind of ships replace the trusty "streakers".

At Arran, it is difficult to imagine a vessel much larger than the *Caledonian Isles* even though passenger traffic continues to increase throughout the year, particularly at peak periods. Does it seem feasible that this route could be the first in the Caledonian MacBrayne empire to witness the arrival of some type of fast craft to complement the car ferry, in the not too distant future?

Meanwhile, the private sector innovators, Western Ferries, have succeeded in developing their McInroy's Point - Hunter's Quay service. A product of the era of the motor car, they owe their existence entirely to the need for short sea crossings, with basic facilities and a regular frequency of service. The point which they first sought to make in 1968 has been well illustrated and it is not surprising that many of the principles of their Norwegian style operation have been adopted by their larger competitor. For the future, they may introduce a car ferry service between Ardmaleish on Bute and Ardyne on the Cowal peninsula.

In the West Highlands, the last new Caledonian MacBrayne ship of the 20th Century was the Devon built *Clansman*, reviving a long established MacBrayne name and underlining the importance of the company within the remote and dispersed communities of the West Coast. The immediate future requirements will see further development of the services to the Small Isles with the *Lochmor* being replaced by a vessel capable of carrying a limited number of vehicles. The new ship will be the first new vessel of the 21st Century

*The new Barra ferry **Clansman** is seen making a call at Castlebay with Castle Kismuil, stronghold of the Clan MacNeil, beyond.*(Brian Maxted)

and should be delivered in spring of the year 2000, meaning that the days of the *Lochmor* are numbered.

Another large vessel is also due to be delivered in the early years of the new century. Destined to be a virtual repeat of the *Clansman* of 1998, it would be a historic touch if another former MacBrayne name was to be applied to the vessel. The *Clansman* was the last new ship of the second millennium and it would be most appropriate if the venerable old name of *Columba* was to be bestowed on the first large vessel of the third millennium, especially given the importance of the Celtic saint in spreading the Christian doctrine in these parts, over fourteen hundred years ago.

The development of shorter sea crossings may yet revive the potential for an overland route linking Coll, Tiree and the Outer Isles with Mull using a purpose built terminal at the north end of the island, together with an upgraded road from Craignure. Channelling the Hebridean traffic over Mull would undoubtedly require further upgrading of the Oban - Craignure service to cater for increased traffic and may also solve the problem of the bypassing of Tobermory, although it is unlikely that the residents of Coll, Tiree, South Uist and Barra would necessarily favour this option. It is likely that the last link will be provided in the Western Isles by provision of a Barra - South Uist link using another new "Loch" Class vessel similar to the *Loch Bhrusda*, permitting easy and frequent driving from Vatersay to the Butt of Lewis and linking the components of the "Long Island" in a way which has never been possible before.

The debate over the proposed overland route to Islay continues, but is unlikely to proceed to action given the need to upgrade the full length of the mainland road and also the single track road on Jura whilst providing a massively upgraded Sound of Islay ferry crossing. There is little doubt that any such developments would destroy much of the character of this peaceful island whilst major upgrading of the terminals at Feolin and Port Askaig, together with the provision of larger vessels, would make the costs of such an option extremely high.

With Government policy now favouring more environmentally friendly forms of transport, leading to the gradual return of freight to rail, even on lines in the Highlands which were regarded for many years as no-go areas for rail freight development, opportunities may also open up for the increased carriage of freight by sea. Previous Governments have encouraged the free market to determine the nature of the movement of goods and in the Highlands, much of the maturing forestry plantations have been removed by huge lorries grinding their way over single track roads, often from locations where access by sea is easier than by road. This is hardly an environmentally friendly proposition. It would indeed be ironic if the argument put forward by the Glenlight Shipping Company at the time of their demise, was seen by the new Scottish Parliament as a desirable policy. Successor to the puffer companies, Glenlight lobbied Government in favour of the movement of bulk cargoes, such as timber, by sea, but thanks to the ending of their Scottish Office subsidy, they could not continue to operate such services beyond 1994. Although MacBrayne's cargo services came to a close with the passing of the *Loch Carron*, recent events may be the prelude to the appearance of a new generation of dedicated freight ferries. In October 1998, Highland Haulage began a containerised freight service between Kyle of Lochalsh and Stornoway, utilising a dedicated vessel, the *Highland Carrier*, whilst in November 1998 proposals were advanced by Streamline Shipping for the operation of a trailer ferry service between Ullapool and Stornoway, utilising a 1500 tonne, 71 metre vessel. The West Highlands could be witnessing the return of dedicated freight services, but it remains to be seen whether such services can be operated on a long term commercial basis, without public subsidy.

Discounting the summer excursion sailings of the *Highland Seabird*, there has never been any attempt to introduce fast ferries to the West Highlands. Given the need to cater for light passenger traffic at off peak times of the year, together with large numbers of agricultural and commercial vehicles in all weathers, high speed operations are not yet likely to be commercially viable. Nevertheless some form of fast ferry operation could eventually become appropriate for services to the islands of the Western seaboard of Scotland, as they have become in other parts of the world. Busier routes, such as those to Brodick, Dunoon, Craignure and Stornoway would seem to be prime candidates for fast ferry operation given their relatively high levels of traffic throughout the year, in comparison to many other routes on the West Coast.

Fixed links are also in vogue. With a bridge and causeways now linking Scalpay, Vatersay and Berneray to their larger island neighbours of Harris, Barra and North Uist respectively, and proposals for a causeway between Eriskay and South Uist now in the planning stages, some of the shorter inter - island crossings could disappear entirely. Whilst the economic benefits for these communities are likely to be substantial, the ending of the ferry service can also create direct job losses and, in some cases, reduce the appeal of an island as a tourist destination.

This would certainly be the case if any future fixed link was constructed across the Sound of Iona, where the ambience of the island of Iona, once referred to by Lord George MacLeod of Fuinary as a "thin place, where only a tissue paper separates the material from the spiritual" has attracted tourists and pilgrims from all over the world. Generations of visitors have experienced the peace of Iona, with its Benedictine Abbey. It would indeed be a sad day if the experience of this unique island was destroyed through the construction of a fixed link giving the internal combustion engine free reign on the otherwise traffic free island. Paradoxically, the economy of the island is dependant on visitors seeking the Iona experience and there is a need to balance the economic well being and future transport needs of the community with the preservation of this beautiful island. Surely there is no greater test for the concept of sustainable tourism. Meanwhile, the dedicated ferry service provided by the *Loch Buie* continues to provide the lifeline for the island's permanent residents.

Central to all of these issues is the possibility of the establishment of a single Highland transport authority which would have a major impact on future developments. Whilst the new Scottish Parliament will legislate on such a body, it is clear that Government would look favourably upon its establishment, setting up an agency whose powers could be fundamental to Highlands and Islands ferry

*The mighty **Isle of Mull** presents an imposing sight as she cuts through the glass like waters of Oban Bay on 17th October 1993.* (Author)

services and their connections, within an overall Scottish transport strategy.

The future seems brighter for the Paddle Steamer *Waverley* than has been the case for many years. With her Millennium rebuild expected to be completed in time for the Summer of the year 2000, her owners have the onerous responsibility for ensuring that this national treasure continues to provide the unique experience of the sea going paddle steamer for future generations. Were it not for the *Waverley*, these generations would have knowledge only of the modern ferries, and for them, the *Waverley* is a tangible link with a more spacious era and an altogether less frenetic form of transport. Not for the *Waverley* is the prospect of static preservation in a dry dock or as a floating pub or restaurant. Instead, her future is to function as a piece of living history, bringing pleasure for many more thousands of passengers throughout the British Isles.

But there is now the distant prospect of her being joined by a newly restored *Maid of the Loch* on Loch Lomond. If the necessary funding is eventually secured, Scotland could be uniquely blessed by the presence of two of the worlds finest paddle steamers, one sea going, the other a magnificent inland loch steamer and the last of her type built in Britain. There could be no finer testimony to the proud heritage of the famous Clyde Steamers which has given rise to the modern ferry services of the last thirty years.

# THE RACE FOR THE NORTH

Much has changed in the Northern Isles in the last thirty years. The future is no more certain given the ongoing need to modernise the P&O Scottish Ferries fleet and the potential for the arrival of other operators on the scene, than it was during the times of greatest change. Yet in many ways, the pace of change has continued in the Northern Isles at a rate which it has not done on the West Coast and future developments remain the subject of speculation and some degree of uncertainty.

The Shetland Islands Council fleet may see the withdrawal of the oldest vessels in service whilst the debate rumbles on regarding the potential to provide a bridge to Bressay. The future plans of the SIC envisage a reduction in fleet size by withdrawing three ships and providing fewer, larger vessels on the Yellsound, Whalsay and Skerries routes in a "Super Ferry" plan which has not been well received by islanders. Otherwise, the islands continue to benefit from the steady, unspectacular but sometimes controversial activities of this diverse and interesting fleet.

With the failure of the attempt by Orkney Ferries to establish the Gills Bay - Burwick service in 1990 and the introduction of new freight services to Orkney by Orcargo and the Streamline group, it became apparent that overcapacity was reducing the viability of these lifeline services and that rationalisation was inevitable. In addition, a discrepancy existed between the way in which support for essential lifeline services was provided to the Western Isles by comparison with those in the Northern Isles. As a result, the Government undertook a review of all subsidised shipping services in Scotland with the study being commissioned in September 1993. This was the study which finally dispensed with any notion of privatising Caledonian MacBrayne services but a further recommendation was believed to be that the operations to the Northern Isles should be transferred to the public sector to allow replacement of the P&O ships with new tonnage. This was unpalatable to the then Conservative government. Most contentious of all was the Government decision to replace the Tariff Rebate Subsidy scheme with a block grant system from 1st May 1995, the new system benefiting a single carrier on a competitive tender basis, whereas TRS had been divided amongst all of the operators. Only livestock sailings would continue to receive subsidy on the TRS basis. In the summer of 1995, the Scottish Office invited companies to tender for the new

The *Isle of Lewis* at Stromness on her courtesy call of 28th November 1998. (Willie MacKay)

contract to serve the Northern Isles but there was to be no level playing field as Caledonian MacBrayne, being a public company, were excluded from the tendering process. Politics intervened and the General Election and change of Government in May 1997 led to delays in completing the tender process. But on 24th July 1997, the new Secretary of State, Donald Dewar MP confirmed that P&O Scottish Ferries had won the contract in the face of stiff competition and would operate the lifeline services for a further five years.

The twist in the tail was that a new tendering process would begin almost immediately. This time around, Government evaluation of the requirements for services to the Northern Isles appeared to open the door to Caledonian MacBrayne if they wished to submit a tender for the operation of the services from 2002. What is certain is that there is a need for new and more modern vessels to replace the current ageing fleet of P&O Scottish Ferries and to meet the provisions of the Stockholm Agreement, put in place following the *Estonia* disaster in the Baltic. Indeed P&O Scottish Ferries indicated in their submission that they would provide these vessels if they won the contract, especially since funding rules may now permit European Union money to be made available for such an operation. Other political changes, such as the establishment of the new Scottish Parliament may also bear on the terms of the next tender and only time will tell how the Northern Isles shipping services will fare amongst these wider issues, especially if the proposed Highland transport authority becomes a reality.

Meanwhile, P&O Scottish Ferries soldier on with the trusty stalwarts, the *St. Ola*, the *St. Clair* and the *St. Sunniva* providing passenger and vehicle services, supported by the freight only vessel *St. Rognvald*. If the company secure the next contract for serving the Northern Isles, then all of these ships are likely to disappear within the next three years, to be replaced by the next generation of ships to carry forward the traditions and the names, of the old "North Company".

But on Saturday 28th November 1998, the P&O Scottish Ferries vessel *St. Ola* departed from Stromness on her usual morning crossing of the Pentland Firth. As she headed into Hoy Sound, an unfamiliar ship with a much more modern profile emerged from the misty shroud of Scapa Flow and slipped into the vacated pier at Stromness. The mystery visitor was the Caledonian MacBrayne ferry *Isle of Lewis*, making a courtesy call on her return from overhaul on the Tyne. Her arrival in Orkney made her owners' intentions very clear. During her two day visit she was thrown open to the public and the modern facilities of the *Isle of Lewis* impressed Orcadian residents, councillors and business people alike. The gloves were off and the race for the North was only just beginning.

*The **Iona** is seen here leaving the Skye terminal during her last season on Mallaig - Armadale route.* (Miles Cowsill)

## APPENDIX 1 - FURTHER READING

There is a vast range of books dealing with various aspects of the history of Scottish coastal shipping, and Scottish history in general. The following works have been consulted in the production of this book      :

*Balmoral* (1986) Holyoak J.
*British Nationalised Shipping* (1969), Clegg W. P. and Styring J.S.
*Caledonian MacBrayne - The Fleet* (1994), Cowsill M, Hendy J, and MacDuff L. J.
*Clyde Piers* (1982) McCrorie I.C. and Monteith J.
*Clyde Pleasure Steamers* (1986) McCrorie I.C.
*Clyde River and Other Steamers* (1972) 3rd Ed. Duckworth C.L.D.D. and Langmuir G.E. and (1982) 3rd Ed. Supplement.
*Collins Encyclopaedia of Scotland* (1994) Keay J. and Keay J.
*European Ferry Fleets* (1976) Clegg W.P.
*Ferries of the British Isles* (Various Editions) Widdows N.
*Ferries of the British Isles & Northern Europe* (1998) Widdows N.
*Hebridean and Clyde Ferries* (1985) McCrorie I.C.
*Highlanders* (1996) McLeod J.
*Light in the Glens* (1996) Paterson L.
*Northwards by Sea* (1978) Donaldson G.
*Scottish Coastal Steamers 1918-1975* (1996), Patton B.
*Scottish Islands* (1986) Grimble I.
*Shanklin - Ill Fated Prince* (1985) Brown A.
*Ships of the Fleet - Caledonian MacBrayne* (1980) 1st & 2nd and Eds. McCrorie I.
*Solent Passages and their Steamers* (1982) Davies K.
*Speed Bonny Boat* Whittle J.(1990)
*Steamers of the Clyde and Western Isles* (1965) McCarthur I, McCrorie I., MacHaffie F.G.
*Steamers of the Forth* (1976) Brodie I.
*Steamers of the Highlands and Islands* (1987) McCrorie I.C.
*Swifts & Queens - Passenger Transport on the Forth & Clyde Canal* (1984) Bowman A.I.
*The Caledonian Steam Packet Company* (1971). McCarthur I.C.
*The Orkney Story* (1985) Schei L.K. and Moberg G
*The Sea Routes to Arran* (1993) McCrorie I.
*The Second St. Ola* (1977) McRobb A.W.
*The Sound of Silence* (1976) Wilson A.
*The Scottish Lochs* (1980) Weir T.
*Waverley* (1984) McGowan D.
*Waverley - the Golden Jubilee* (1997) Waverley Excursions Ltd.
*West Highland Steamers* (1987) 4th Ed. Duckworth C.L.D.D. and Langmuir G.E.
*Wightlink, Isle of Wight Ferries* (1993) Hendy J.

In addition, the following newspapers, periodicals & other publications have been of invaluable assistance      :

*Clyde River Steamer Club Annual Review*
*Clyde Steamers*
*European Ferry Scene*
*Greenock Telegraph*
*OAG Cruise and Ferry Guide*

*A breezy day in April 1996 sees the **Raasay** prepare to leave the island whose name she bears, with the Red Cuillin of Skye beyond.* (Author)

*Paddle Wheels*
*Scotland on Sunday*
*Sea Lines*
*Shetland Times*
*Ships Monthly*
*Stornoway Gazette*
*The Herald*
*The Motor Ship*
*The Oban Times*
*The Orcadian*
*The Scotsman*
*The Scots Magazine*
*Timetables & Publications from various companies*
*West Highland  Steamer Club Newsletters*
*West Highland Free Press*

In the information technology era, the Internet is a valuable source of further information concerning the various Scottish ferry fleets and the following websites will be of interest to readers wishing to find further detailed information about the various companies, their current timetables, services and recent company news.

| | |
|---|---|
| *www.calmac.co.uk* | *Caledonian MacBrayne Ltd* |
| *www.orkneyislands.com/travel/orkfer* | *Orkney Ferries* |
| *www.jogferry.co.uk* | *John o' Groats Ferries* |
| *www.poscottishferries.co.uk* | *P&O Scottish Ferries* |
| *www.orkneyislands.com/orcargo* | *Orcargo* |

# APPENDIX 2 - MAJOR VESSELS AND THEIR ROUTES

*The White Funnel returns to the Clyde as the* **Balmoral** *shows off her P&A Campbell colours at Tighnabruaich on 29th September 1997. (Author)*

| COMPANY | SHIP NAME | REGULAR SERVICE* |
|---|---|---|
| Caledonian MacBrayne | Bruernish | Spare |
| | Caledonian Isles | Ardrossan - Brodick |
| | Canna | Ballycastle - Rathlin |
| | Clansman | Oban - Tiree, Coll, Barra & South Uist |
| | Eigg | Spare |
| | Hebridean Isles | Uig - Tarbert & Lochmaddy |
| | Isle of Arran | Kennacraig - Port Askaig & Port Ellen |
| | Isle of Cumbrae | Tarbert - Portavadie - |
| | Isle of Lewis | Ullapool - Stornoway |
| | Isle of Mull | Oban - Craignure & Colonsay |
| | Juno | Upper Clyde ferry & Excursions |
| | Jupiter | Upper Clyde ferry & Excursions |
| | Loch Alainn | Largs - Cumbrae Slip |
| | Loch Bhrusda | Otternish - Leverburgh |
| | Loch Buie | Fionnphort - Iona |
| | Loch Dunvegan | Colintrave - Rhubodach |
| | Loch Fyne | Fishnish - Lochaline |
| | Loch Linnhe | Tobermory - Kilchoan |
| | Loch Ranza | Tayinloan - Gigha |
| | Loch Riddon | Largs - Cumbrae Slip |
| | Loch Striven | Sconser - Raasay |
| | Loch Tarbert | Lochranza - Claonaig |
| | Lochmor | Mallaig - Small Isles |
| | Lord of the Isles | Mallaig - Armadale, Barra & South Uist |
| | Pioneer | Upper Clyde ferry |
| | Raasay | Oban - Lismore |
| | Saturn | Upper Clyde ferry & Excursions |
| | Ulva | Tender to Lochmor at Eigg |
| Waverley Excursions | Balmoral | Clyde & East Coast Excur. |
| | Waverley | Clyde Excursions |
| Western Ferries | Sound of Sanda | McInroy's Point - Hunter's Quay |
| | Sound of Scalpay | McInroy's Point - Hunter's Quay |
| | Sound of Scarba | Spare vessel |
| | Sound of Shuna | McInroy's Point - Hunter's Quay |
| | Sound of Sleat | McInroy's Point - Hunter's Quay |
| P&O Scottish Ferries | St. Clair | Aberdeen - Lerwick |
| | St. Ola | Scrabster - Stromness |
| | St. Rognvald | Freight services to Kirkwall & Lerwick |
| | St. Sunniva | Aberdeen - Stromness - Lerwick |
| Orkney Ferries | Earl Sigurd | Kirkwall - Outer North Isles |
| | Earl Thorfinn | Kirkwall - Outer North Isles |
| | Eynhallow | Tingwall - Rousay, Egilsay & Wyre |
| | Golden Mariana | Westray - Papa Westray |
| | Graemsay | Stromness - Hoy & Graemsay |
| | Hoy Head | Houton - Flotta, Lyness, |

| COMPANY | SHIP NAME | REGULAR SERVICE* |
|---|---|---|
| Orkney Ferries | Shapinsay | Kirkwall - Shapinsay |
| | Thorsvoe | Spare |
| | Varagen | Kirkwall - Outer North Isles |
| Shetland Islands Council | Bigga | Toft - Yell |
| | Filla | Lerwick/Vidlin - Skerries |
| | Fivla | Gutcher - Unst |
| | Fylga | Relief |
| | Geira | Toft - Yell |
| | Good Shepherd IV | Grutness - Fair Isle |
| | Grima | Relief |
| | Hendra | Laxo - Whalsay |
| | Koada | West Burrafirth - Papa Stour |
| | Leirna | Lerwick - Bressay |
| | New Advance | Walls/Scalloway - Foula |
| | Spes Clara | General work |
| | Thora | Whalsay |
| Clyde Marine Motoring | Kenilworth | Gourock - Kilcreggan - Helensburgh |
| | The Second Snark | Clyde Excursions |
| John o' Groats Ferries | Pentland Venture | John o' Groats - Burwick |
| Comhairle nan Eilean | E. Bhearnaraigh | Otternish - Berneray |
| | Eilean na h-Oige | Barra - Eriskay - South Uist |
| West of Scotland Water | Sir Walter Scott | Loch Katrine Excursions |
| Hebridean Island Cruises | Hebridean Princess | Luxury cruises from Oban |
| Argyll & Antrim S.P. Co. | Claymore | Campbeltown - Ballycastle |
| Orcargo | Contender | Invergordon - Kirkwall |

*as at Summer 1999